THE
FUR TRADE
IN
COLONIAL
NEW YORK
1686–1776

THE
FUR TRADE
IN
COLONIAL
NEW YORK
1686-1776

Thomas Elliot Norton

THE UNIVERSITY OF WISCONSIN PRESS

Publication of this book has been made possible
through a grant from the Ford Foundation

Published 1974
The University of Wisconsin Press
Box 1379, Madison, Wisconsin 53701

The University of Wisconsin Press, Ltd.
70 Great Russell Street, London

First printing

Printed in the United States of America

For LC CIP information see the colophon

ISBN 0–299–06420–4

For
Jackie

CONTENTS

PREFACE

FUR TRADERS, frontiersmen, and Indians have long been topics of interest to historians as well as to a wide variety of other writers. Usually limiting themselves to particular geographical areas, historians have written about the fur trade in most of the localities where it was of importance. Frederick Jackson Turner, for example, published his doctoral dissertation under the title of *The Character and Influence of the Indian Trade in Wisconsin* (Baltimore, 1891).

Considering the fur trade's popularity as a subject of historical research, it is surprising that no one has previously written a full account of this commerce in colonial New York, where it played a crucial role in the struggle for empire between France and Great Britain. My research into the subject soon began to show that the trade involved complex economic, political, and social relationships between New York, Canada, and the Iroquois Confederacy. It also became clear that many of the traditional historical concepts about the fur trade and especially about the commercial center of Albany are misleading. In the following pages I hope to unravel some of the complexities as well as to correct the misconceptions.

To whatever extent success has been achieved in these goals, much of the credit belongs to the many people who have helped with this project. Professor Milton M. Klein provided both indispensable assistance and constant inspiration. A number of improvements in the manuscript were suggested by Professors Galen Broeker and John Finger. From time to time in the course of my research and writing it was necessary to correspond with various experts, and I greatly appreciate the thoughtful responses received from William L. Davisson, Wilbur R. Jacobs, Jacob Judd, Sung Bok Kim, Lawrence H. Leder, Jacob M. Price, William I. Roberts III, and Allen W. Trelease. Special acknowledgment must be given to Lawrence A. Harper and David A. Armour, who loaned me microfilm or photostats in their personal possession. A large number of librarians provided more services than can be enumerated, but I am particularly grateful to the staffs of the New York State

Library, the New-York Historical Society, and the New York Public Library. Much of my research was made possible by a Ford Foundation grant for ethnic studies.

A few comments are necessary on my use of manuscripts. Old Style dates have not been converted to New Style, but the first day of each year has been designated as January 1. Spelling and capitalization remain the same as in the original except that archaic abbreviations have been modernized.

THOMAS ELLIOT NORTON

West Tisbury, Massachusetts
June 1974

THE
FUR TRADE
IN
COLONIAL
NEW YORK
1686–1776

1

INTRODUCTION

ON THE HOT AFTERNOON of September 19, 1609, the *Half Moon* rode at anchor on the great river that was soon to bear the name of its captain—Henry Hudson. Having followed the floodtide to its northernmost reaches, the small ship had arrived in the vicinity of what is now Albany, New York. One of the *Half Moon*'s officers had been keeping a personal account of the voyage, and on this day he noted, "The people of the Countrie came flocking aboord, and brought us Grapes and Pompions, which wee bought for trifles. And many brought us Bevers skinnes, and Otters skinnes, which wee bought for Beades, Knives, and Hatchets."[1] Thus began a fur trade that was to become the economic mainstay of New Netherland and was later to play a major role in the struggle between France and Great Britain for control of North America.

When the merchants of the Netherlands learned of Hudson's discoveries, they wasted no time in attempting to exploit the new trade. In the summer of 1610 they sent a vessel with trading goods to North America, and for several years afterwards such captains as Adriaen Block and Cornelius May continued to explore the region.[2] In 1614 the various mercantile groups interested in these explorations established the New Netherland Company with a charter from the States-General of the Netherlands, subject to renewal within four years. Except for constructing a small trading post on an island a few miles south of where the Mohawk River enters the Hudson, the New Netherland Company accomplished very little and expired upon the termination of its charter. After a short period of free trade, many of the company's most powerful merchants united in 1621 to form the Dutch West India Company. In addition to providing these entrepreneurs with great power in the Dutch

1. Robert Juet, "The Third Voyage of Master Henry Hudson," in *Narratives of New Netherland, 1609–1664*, ed. J. Franklin Jameson (New York, 1909), p. 22.
2. Van Cleaf Bachman, *Peltries or Plantations: The Economic Policies of the Dutch West India Company in New Netherland, 1623–1639* (Baltimore, 1969), pp. 4–9; Thomas A. Janvier, *The Dutch Founding of New York* (New York, 1903), p. 8.

commercial world, the States-General granted them full control over colonization in North America.[3]

In 1624 the West India Company sent its first colonists to the New World aboard the ship *New Netherland*. A few of the newcomers established a settlement on Governor's Island, just to the south of Manhattan, but the main body of colonists went 150 miles upriver, where they built Fort Orange on the site of present-day Albany. Two years later, Peter Minuet, the first director-general of the colony, made his famous purchase of Manhattan Island from the Indians, and with continuing strong support from the West India Company, New Netherland seemed to be on the road to success. By the end of the decade, however, many members of the company had begun to lose interest in their colonial enterprise, having found that they could make greater profits by exploiting opportunities in world commerce than by attempting to nurture a weak colony with an uncertain future.[4]

The original enthusiasm of the Dutch merchants had arisen from their belief that the colony could be turned into a profitable agricultural enterprise, which would produce a valuable export crop while sustaining the nonagricultural activities. When this expectation failed to materialize, the company decided to reduce its investments in the colony. Not even the fur trade was successful enough to keep the merchants interested. Apparently the profits resulting from the trade were insufficient to justify the expense of protecting the monopoly from every resident of the colony. Consequently, in 1629 the company's charter was altered to allow wealthy Dutch entrepreneurs the privilege of carving out quasifeudal domains or patroonships for themselves in New Netherland.[5]

Although he never visited America himself, Kiliaen Van Rensselaer, a powerful Amsterdam merchant, acquired the colony's most important patroonship, covering an area of approximately 700,000 acres. Rensselaerswyck encompassed Fort Orange, which had already become New Netherland's major source of furs. Ostensibly, the patroonships were established as agricultural enterprises, but all of the new patroons hoped to profit from the fur trade. Under the charter of 1629 they received

3. John Romeyn Brodhead, *History of the State of New York*, 2 vols. (New York, 1859–71), 1: 135–36; Thomas J. Condon, *New York Beginnings: The Commercial Origins of New Netherland* (New York, 1968), pp. 21–24, 32–36; Edmund B. O'Callaghan, *History of New Netherland; or, New York Under the Dutch*, 2 vols. (New York, 1846–48; reprinted, Spartanburg S.C., 1966), 1: 81–87.

4. Bachman, *Peltries or Plantations*, pp. 81–83, 89–94; Brodhead, *History of New York*, 1: 151–52; Condon, *New York Beginnings*, pp. 102–5.

5. Bachman, *Peltries or Plantations*, pp. 95–97, 107–8. For a full account of the patroonship system, see S. G. Nissenson, *The Patroon's Domain* (New York, 1937).

certain fur trading concessions, and throughout the 1630s Van Rensselaer and others constantly attempted to make further inroads into the
company's monopoly. At the end of the decade, the fur trade was opened
to anyone who would pay a small duty on imports and exports to the
West India Company. When the company discontinued the operation of
its trading house at Fort Orange in 1644, the traffic in furs fell completely into the hands of private traders.[6] At first, however, the commerce was
not totally unrestricted, because the Van Rensselaer interests attempted
to monopolize it for themselves. They even claimed that Fort Orange
and the surrounding village of Beverwyck belonged to the patroonship.
Rather than allow the trade to fall into the hands of a single family,
Peter Stuyvesant, the director-general, personally intervened on the
side of those traders who were trying to compete with the Van Rensselaers; and in 1652 he established Fort Orange and Beverwyck as a
separate township with political autonomy.[7]

In the meantime, while the people of northern New Netherland were
vying for control of the fur trade, the colonists around New Amsterdam
were in the process of destroying or subjugating the local Indian tribes.
During Governor Kieft's War from 1641 to 1645, as many as a thousand
Indians lost their lives. In the following years many more native inhabitants were pushed off their lands as the population of the southern areas
of the colony gradually increased.[8] Conversely, the people of Rensselaerswyck and Beverwyck avoided any serious disputes with the Indians. As Professor Allen W. Trelease has pointed out, the Indians and
the Dutch of northern New Netherland were economically dependent
on one another, and although relations between the two groups were
sometimes strained, warfare never broke out between them.[9] As the
years passed, relations actually improved as the two sides worked out
procedures for settling their differences. Indian conferences in the Dutch
village became frequent occurrences, and in the last decades of the
seventeenth century a special board evolved for conducting negotiations
with the Indians, especially with the Iroquois Confederacy or, as it was
also known, the Five Nations.

From the English conquest of the colony in 1664 until the 1680s relations between the fur traders and the Indians remained almost un-

---

6. Condon, *New York Beginnings*, pp. 124–41; O'Callaghan, *History of New
Netherland*, 1: 124–27; Allen W. Trelease, *Indian Affairs in Colonial New York:
The Seventeenth Century* (Ithaca, N.Y., 1960), pp. 49–51, 112–13.

7. Trelease, *Indian Affairs*, pp. 113–15; O'Callaghan, *History of New Netherland*,
2: 177–83.

8. Trelease, *Indian Affairs*, p. 83.

9. Ibid., p. 115.

changed, but in the meantime France and England had entered upon a collision course in North America. Throughout the seventeenth century the French had been establishing footholds in the interior of the continent by following the St. Lawrence River to its source on the eastern end of Lake Ontario and then traveling westward. The Dutch had not shown much desire or capacity for going farther than Albany, but expeditions sponsored by the English in the 1680s pushed westward against the current of the Mohawk River and then turned north over an easy passage of portages and waterways. These New York explorers and traders entered Lake Ontario at the mouth of the Oswego River, not far from the origin of the St. Lawrence. As the French and English pushed forward in search of peltry, competition became inevitable. Once the economic rivalry evolved into a struggle for political control of the continent, the two sides competed vigorously for the allegiance of the various Indian tribes. Before there was any hope of concluding an alliance with a particular tribe, however, it was first necessary for the Europeans to establish commercial connections. Political friendship with the Indians depended upon good economic relations arising from the fur trade.

With their ability to acquire inexpensive merchandise and West Indian rum, New York traders had a considerable commercial advantage over the Canadians. On the other hand, the latter built forts deep in the interior and were often able to persuade the western Indians to trade with them. Although New Yorkers hoped to win some of these western tribes away from the French, their first concern was to maintain friendly relations with the Iroquois.

Like the British and the French, the five (and later six) tribes making up the Iroquois Confederacy also had a vested interest in the trade routes surrounding Lake Ontario, and they possessed enough power to exert considerable control over the use of these commercial channels. To maintain military security and economic prosperity, the Iroquois in the eighteenth century played a game of diplomacy designed to give themselves the balance of power between the American colonies and French Canada. Although the Canadians could not realistically hope to ally themselves with their traditional Iroquois enemies, they wanted at least to keep them neutral and thus reduce the chances of a successful British invasion over the Lake Champlain route to Montreal. The Iroquois took full advantage of the situation by demanding from the French the right to hunt in areas controlled by Canada's Indian allies and by requiring the British to supply them with inexpensive goods, presents, and other economic privileges. To understand the fur trade as it affected both imperial diplomacy and political disputes within the British colonies, the influence of the Iroquois Confederacy cannot be overlooked.

Albany was ideally situated not only for acquiring peltry but also for negotiating with the Iroquois. Thus, for most of the years from 1664 until the mid-eighteenth century, and especially after it acquired a charter granting it a monopoly of the fur trade in 1686, Albany controlled the New York side of a complex diplomatic and economic relationship between the various Indian tribes and the two European powers. Although not particularly interested in helping to create a British empire, the Albany Dutch were deeply concerned with Indian relations for reasons of economic prosperity and military security. In the eighteenth century the fur trade became proportionately less important to them, but at the same time the need for military security became much greater as France and Great Britain advanced toward a violent confrontation over supremacy in North America. Despite the services performed by the Albany Dutch in maintaining the allegiance of the Iroquois Confederacy, history has afforded them few accolades. In fact, historians have generally been critical of them.

The reasons for the criticisms of colonial Albany are not difficult to understand. After the first decade of the eighteenth century, New York politics were often dominated by a close-knit group of politicians who favored policies designed to bring about the expulsion of the French from Canada. Usually allied with the New York governors, these men advocated aggressive anti-French policies even when their own province was woefully unprepared to initiate military action. Their frequent insistence on attacking the French placed them among the most energetic imperialists in the colonies or in Great Britain. Often proposing bold policies without careful deliberations, this faction encountered opposition from the cautious citizens of Albany, who advocated the building of a strong defensive establishment before proceeding with more ambitious plans. According to their critics, Albany residents disloyally interfered with all efforts to chastise the French and alienated the Indians through their shortsighted exploitation of the fur trade. In addition to portraying themselves as farsighted realists, the imperialists implied that they were the true friends of the Indians. The proposals of both factions, however, were often frustrated by assemblymen from southern New York, who had little concern with frontier defenses or imperial adventures. Unfortunately for the image of the Albany Dutch in history, their imperial-minded opponents were extremely prolific writers, and their literary polemics were far more numerous than those of their adversaries.

In light of all this written evidence and the generally poor reputation of fur traders, it is little wonder that the motives of the Albany Dutch were often misunderstood. While modern historians have not accepted the contention of Cadwallader Colden that the residents of northern New York were an evil people, they have generally agreed that Albany policy represented short-range economic goals, involving the protection of the trade with Canada. An acceptance of these conclusions, however, results in a distorted picture of the Albany Dutch, the Iroquois, and the role of the fur trade in the conflict between Great Britain and France. Thus, this volume will re-evaluate the economic and diplomatic activities of the Dutch in northern New York, concentrating on the period following the establishment of Albany's monopoly of the fur trade in 1686.

In actuality, as the following chapters will point out, the diplomatic policies of the Albany Dutch were beneficial to British interests, and, after the devastation of King William's War (1689–97), their main concern was not selfishly to protect the fur trade but rather to provide for the military security of New York. In the first three-quarters of the eighteenth century, the amount of peltry acquired by New Yorkers did not vary a great deal from year to year; but, after Albany began to profit from the trade in foodstuffs to the West Indies, the fur trade became proportionally less important as an economic factor. On the other hand, as the years passed, the increasing danger of all-out war with France caused great anxiety among the frontier inhabitants. In Queen Anne's War (1702–13) and especially in King George's War (1744–48), the desire of Albany to remain neutral was based primarily on its recognition that the inadequate defenses of New York were extremely vulnerable to attacks from Canada. The Albany Dutch and the Iroquois found themselves bound together by mutual self-interest involving their economies and their concern for military security, and they worked out a policy of peaceful coexistence which resulted in protection from French Canada during a period when neither of them could expect help from anyone else. Once Great Britain and other colonists were ready to accept the responsibility of meeting the French challenge, Albany citizens could justly declare that for more than a century they had used the fur trade to maintain the friendship of the powerful Iroquois Confederacy, and had thus contributed to the security and survival of the province of New York.

2

IROQUOIS WARFARE AND

DIPLOMACY

In 1642 life seemed as good to the Hurons as it had been for decades. Possibly the ravages of smallpox and the annual Iroquois raids had been more troublesome than usual, but the people of Huronia, numbering as many as thirty thousand, rested content in the knowledge that none of their neighbors—European or Indian—could match their wealth and power. Within a decade they were gone. Wolves prowled through deserted villages, and a small remnant of the tribe, driven hundreds of miles from their homeland between Georgian Bay and Lake Simcoe, settled under French protection near the city of Quebec.[1]

The Hurons had fallen victim to a new Iroquois policy of unrelenting warfare, launched against them in the summer of 1642 and culminating in terrible bloodshed in 1649; they dispersed and fled into the wilderness, where their destruction was completed by starvation and disease.[2] Although warfare between these two Indian confederacies had persisted for half a century, no one in earlier years would have predicted that either side faced the danger of annihilation. Until the 1640s their annual conflicts consisted of ritualistic affairs involving matters of religion, personal vengeance, and the attainment of manhood, but now something much more compelling drove the Iroquois to military ventures on a far greater scale than previously seen in North America.[3]

An understanding of the reasons for this new aggressiveness is needed in order to comprehend the development of Iroquois diplomacy in the eighteenth century. The immediate cause of the sudden change, however, is not clear, and a scarcity of evidence will probably continue to prevent anyone from completely solving the riddle. The most widely

1. Bruce G. Trigger, *The Huron: Farmers of the North* (New York, 1969), pp. 1–2, 9–13.
2. George T. Hunt, *The Wars of the Iroquois: A Study in Intertribal Trade Relations* (Madison, Wis., 1940), pp. 74–75, 92–94.
3. Trigger, *The Huron*, p. 52.

accepted theory maintains that the Iroquois were motivated by economic necessity.[4] As beaver became increasingly scarce in Iroquois country sometime after 1640, the theory postulates, they launched a series of assaults against the Hurons in an effort to supplant them as middlemen between the Europeans and the Indians of the Canadian interior.[5] Although this theory clearly has validity and is not completely rejected even by its strongest disputant, there remains a real possibility that other factors precipitated the greatly increased military activities of the Iroquois Confederacy.[6]

The evidence suggesting that the New York Indians by 1640 had destroyed their indigenous beaver population is far from conclusive. The Dutch and the Iroquois had not initiated commercial contacts until 1626.[7] It is unlikely that the relatively small Iroquois population would have been able to kill off all the beaver in such a vast area during such a short period of time, especially in light of their conservation policies, which prohibited the destruction of entire beaver colonies and protected the females.[8] The trade relations with the Dutch had not only given the Iroquois additional incentive to conquer the Hurons but also the firearms to enable them to do so. It may not have been coincidental that the Iroquois initiated their militant attacks at exactly the same time the Dutch fur traders began to sell them guns. The acquisition of firearms may also have coincided with an intensification of ancient animosities between the Iroquois and their neighbors, resulting from the inevitable accumulation of family feuds. Such a combination could easily have led to full-scale war.[9]

Although the motives of the Iroquois in 1642 remain partly obscure, their expansion in later years became increasingly influenced by economic necessity. Within five years after destroying the Hurons in 1649,

4. Peter Wraxall, *An Abridgment of the Indian Affairs Contained in Four Folio Volumes, Transacted in the Colony of New York, from the Year 1678 to the Year 1751*, ed. Charles H. McIlwain (Cambridge, Mass., 1915), pp. xliii–xliv.

5. Hunt, *Wars of the Iroquois*, pp. 33–37. In his introduction to Wraxall's abridgment of the New York Indian records, Charles H. McIlwain does not set the date of the extinction of beaver in New York until about 1671; see Wraxall, *Abridgment*, ed. McIlwain, p. xliii.

6. Allen W. Trelease, "The Iroquois and the Western Fur Trade: A Problem in Interpretation," *Mississippi Valley Historical Review* 49 (1962): 51.

7. Hunt, *Wars of the Iroquois*, pp. 25–35.

8. Louis Armand Lahontan, *New Voyages to North America*, ed. Reuben G. Thwaites, 2 vols. (Chicago, 1905), 1: 82, 2: 481–84; Lewis H. Morgan, *League of the Ho-Dé-No-Sau-Nee or Iroquois* (New York, 1904), p. 335.

9. Harold A. Innis, *The Fur Trade in Canada*, rev. ed. (New Haven, 1962), pp. 35–36; Trigger, *The Huron*, p. 2; Hunt, *Wars of the Iroquois*, pp. 167–68; Anthony F. C. Wallace, *The Death and Rebirth of the Seneca* (New York, 1970), p. 102.

they drove three more tribes of the Niagara region—the Petuns, the Neutrals, and the Eries—into oblivion. An intensification of old blood-feuds cannot explain all these conflicts. Personal animosities had not previously existed between the Iroquois and the Neutrals, but the latter did occupy the Niagara portage, an extremely vital location for the successful control of the fur trade.[10] By 1670 the Iroquois had almost certainly exhausted their supply of beaver, and now their very survival depended on their ability to obtain new sources of peltry.[11]

In spite of their many victories, the Iroquois were unable to accomplish their objective of becoming middlemen between the Dutch and the western Indians, because the commercial position of the Hurons was taken over almost immediately by the Ottawas, who for many years had enjoyed friendly relations with the Hurons and had shared part of the fur trade with them.[12] The Ottawas, living far to the northwest near Michilimackinac and receiving effective support from the French, remained the successful rivals of the Iroquois until the signing of a peace treaty between them in 1701.

Reacting to the arrival of Ottawa peltry fleets at Montreal in 1654 and 1656, the Iroquois directed a major offensive against their new competitors in the winter of 1656–57, but they were unable to achieve success. By the end of the decade they had given up their attacks in preference to the old, but not entirely effective, procedure of employing raiding parties to blockade the Ottawa River, the best route between Michilimackinac and Montreal. Even this tactic was scaled down when in 1663 the Iroquois became embroiled in a war with the Susquehannahs, who had begun to push into Iroquois territory from the South in search of peltry. By the time the Iroquois defeated this new enemy twelve years later, the Ottawas had consolidated their position.[13]

Unable to conquer their rivals to the north, the Five Nations turned to diplomacy in the fall of 1670, sending several ambassadors to winter among the Ottawas in an effort to negotiate a commercial treaty. Although no firm agreements were reached, the Iroquois diplomats suc-

10. Hunt, *Wars of the Iroquois*, pp. 95–102; Trigger, *The Huron*, p. 18; Arthur C. Parker, "The Iroquois," *History of the State of New York*, ed. Alexander C. Flick, 10 vols. (New York, 1933–37; reprinted, Port Washington, N.Y., 1962), 1: 94–96.

11. Rémy de Courcelles, "An Account of what occurred during the Voyage of Monsieur de Courcelles, Governor of New France, to Lake Ontario, 1671," in *Documents Relative to the Colonial History of the State of New York*, ed. Edmund B. O'Callaghan and Berthold Fernow, 15 vols. (Albany, 1856–87), 9: 80, hereafter cited as *NYCD*; Memorandum by a missionary, 1671, in *Royal Fort Frontenac*, ed. A. Richard Preston and Leopold Lamontagne (Toronto, 1958), p. 103.

12. Hunt, *Wars of the Iroquois*, pp. 47–48.

13. Ibid., pp. 102–3, 138–42.

ceeded in convincing the Ottawas that the English sold quality goods at far lower prices than the French.[14] This ability of the English to undersell the Canadians was a key factor in both the fur trade and in the struggle to control the continent of North America. As long as they had a supply of inexpensive goods, the traders of Albany could rest assured that the Indians would bring their furs to New York despite aggressive French policies that included the building of forts on the strategic passes at Niagara and Detroit. In addition to high transportation costs, the French faced considerable difficulties in obtaining the two most important items in the fur trade—a type of woolen cloth known as strouds, which was manufactured in England, and West Indian rum, which the Canadians had little success in securing because they produced few products needed in the Caribbean.[15]

Naturally, neither the French nor the English could expect to form alliances with particular Indian tribes unless they maintained commercial relations with them. "The Indians," one Englishman observed, "frequently repeat that Trade was the foundation of their Alliance or Connexions with us and that it is the chief Cement which binds us together. And this should undoubtedly be the first Principle of our whole System of Indian Politics."[16] Not only did the French recognize the need to keep the friendship of the neighboring tribes as protection against Iroquois attack, but they also knew that the loss of the fur trade would mean disaster.

Under the circumstances, the Canadians in the 1670s could not have helped feeling uneasy when they observed the overtures of Iroquois diplomats toward the Ottawas. Indeed, they were particularly disturbed by the knowledge that the Five Nations had proposed the establishment of a trading center "on the shores of Lake Ontario," where they would provide the Ottawas with English merchandise in exchange for peltry.[17] Although such a commercial arrangement was not developed, French fears increased when they discovered that a party of young Ottawas was trading among the Iroquois in the spring of 1671. French missionaries labored to defeat the Iroquois designs, and Frontenac, who became governor of Canada in 1672, vowed to intervene, because an Iroquois-Ottawa treaty "was of too great" an importance to "the trade of the country not to oblige him to prevent its ratification." In building Fort

14. Courcelles, "An Account," in *NYCD*, 9: 84.

15. Cadwallader Colden, Memoir on the fur trade, November 10, 1724, ibid., 5: 728–29.

16. Wraxall, *Abridgment*, ed. McIlwain, p. 153n.

17. Frontenac to Colbert, November 13, 1673, in *Royal Fort Frontenac*, ed. Preston and Lamontagne, p. 109.

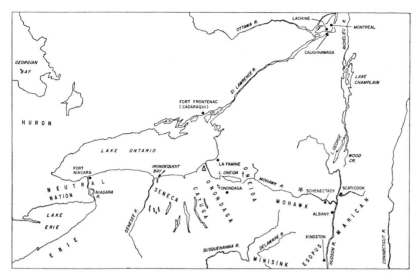

Figure 1. The Iroquois Country. From Allen W. Trelease, *Indian Affairs in Colonial New York: The Seventeenth Century* (Ithaca, N.Y., 1960). Reproduced by permission of Cornell University Press, Ithaca, New York. Additions to the original: △ Oswego; † Great Carrying-Place; * Fort Johnson.

Frontenac near the source of the St. Lawrence on Lake Ontario, he hoped to cut a main avenue of communication between the Iroquois and the Canadian Indians.[18]

As a result of French intrigues and Ottawa reluctance, the Five Nations were unable to arrange any kind of commercial relationship with that tribe, and in the late 1670s they turned their attentions toward other western tribes in an effort to obtain peltry. Even at this time, thirty years after having instituted their aggressive policies, their exact intentions are not apparent. Obviously they wanted to obtain furs from distant lands, but were they attempting to become middlemen between the western tribes and the Europeans or were they simply hoping to acquire hunting rights in areas used by other Indians? If they did aspire to the middleman position, to what extent did they hope to control the trade?[19] An answer to these questions would unlock some of the mysteries of Iroquois economic and diplomatic policy in both the seventeenth and eighteenth centuries.

18. Courcelles, "An Account"; Journal of Frontenac's voyage to Lake Ontario in 1673, in *NYCD*, 9: 85, 95–96.

19. For discussions of the historical interpretations concerning Iroquois commercial policies, see Trelease, "The Iroquois and the Western Fur Trade," and the bibliographical note to this book.

Although the Iroquois ambassadors either in 1670 or shortly there-after had offered to act as middlemen between the English and the Ottawas, such a status would certainly have fallen far short of giving them a controlling position between the hunting tribes and the two European powers. If they had ever contemplated such a grand scheme, they had probably recognized by this time the near impossibility of achieving it. Nevertheless, the low cost of English goods continued to present the chance of attracting the Ottawa furs into their own country, and this had been one of their objectives in opening negotiations in 1670. At the beginning of diplomatic conferences, negotiators often present demands representing their greatest aspirations, knowing that they will settle for less. The Iroquois, skilled in the arts of diplomacy and capable of managing "their Interest with the most learned, most polite, and artificial Nation in Europe," understood this tactic perfectly well and probably employed it in making their proposals to the Ottawas.[20] Al-though hoping to open up a trade with them, the Iroquois may have been prepared to accept a treaty giving them the right to hunt in terri-tory controlled by their competitors.

Undoubtedly, the Iroquois in 1670 wanted to hunt on lands belonging to Canadian tribes, and were, in fact, actually doing so. Intendant Jean Talon complained to Louis XIV that the Iroquois intended to "ruin the trade of the French; hunt for Beavers in the country of the Indians who have placed themselves under the King's protection, perpetuate robber-ies on them and despoil them of their peltries."[21] In a letter to Louis XIV's adviser, Colbert, Governor Frontenac confirmed the intendant's observations: steps must be taken "to prevent the Iroquois from carrying to the Dutch the skins which they get from the Ottawa territories and compel them as it is just, to bring them to us, since they come to hunt in our lands."[22] When war once again broke out among the Indians, the Iroquois maintained that a hostile course of action had become neces-sary "on account of Our beaver Hunting being Very much disturbed."[23]

Obviously the Iroquois Confederacy would not accept any political

20. Cadwallader Colden, *The History of the Five Indian Nations of Canada, Which are Dependent on the Province of New York in America, And Are a Barrier Between the English and French in That Part of the World*, 2 vols. (New York, 1902), 1: 191. The earliest edition was published in 1727, but later Colden added a great deal of supplementary material.

21. Talon to Louis XIV, November 10, 1670, in *NYCD*, 9: 64.

22. Frontenac to Colbert, November 2, 1672, in *Royal Fort Frontenac*, ed. Pres-ton and Lamontagne, pp. 105–6.

23. Minutes of a conference between the Cayuga sachems and the magistrates of Albany, June 27, 1687, in Cadwallader Colden Papers, New-York Historical So-ciety, New York City.

situation that prevented them from exploiting the beaver hunting grounds in Canada. They believed themselves completely justified in crossing the Great Lakes, since these lands constituted the spoils of war taken from the Hurons and other Indians.[24] Stretching for eight hundred miles, this territory included most of present-day Michigan and the great triangle of land between Lakes Huron and Erie and, according to the Iroquois, had been used by them for many years to "hunt beavers . . . it being the only chief place for hunting in this parte of the world that ever wee heard of . . . ."[25] The protection of their interests in this area became the cornerstone of Iroquois foreign policy.

The Ottawas, who did relatively little hunting themselves, and usually traded with remote tribes, probably were willing to accept the presence of hunters in the disputed territory.[26] Certainly they preferred to have the Iroquois engaged in peaceful pursuits rather than expending their energies in raids against Ottawa canoes on the way to Montreal with full cargoes of peltry. The French, on the other hand, displayed great annoyance at the Iroquois habit of hunting in Canada while trading at Albany, and they suspected the English of encouraging them in their actions.[27] These suspicions were well-founded. As relations became increasingly strained between the Five Nations and Canada after 1680, the Albany magistrates told the Iroquois not to be intimidated and to hunt beaver as usual. The new English governor, Thomas Dongan, who arrived in the fall of 1683, immediately made known his plans to enlarge New York's share of the fur trade.[28]

In 1684 Governor La Barre of Canada led a force of 1200 men to Fort Frontenac with intentions of bringing Iroquois competition to an end, but ironically he ended up providing them with an opportunity to make certain that everyone understood their policies. Weakened by hunger and disease, the French army quickly became incapable of crossing the St. Lawrence. Undaunted by this setback, the bold but foolhardy La

24. Indian Conference, July 21, 1701, in *NYCD*, 4: 907.

25. Deed from the Five Nations to the King, July 19, 1701, ibid., p. 908.

26. Jacques Duchesneau, Memoir on the Indian nations, November 13, 1681, ibid., 9: 160–61.

27. Report on an Assembly of Officials at Quebec, October 10, 1682, in *Jesuit Relations and Allied Documents: Travels and Explorations of the Jesuit Missionaries in New France, 1619–1791*, ed. Reuben G. Thwaites, 73 vols. (Cleveland, 1896–1901), 62: 157; Extracts of an addition to the memoir of Talon to Louis XIV, November 10, 1670, in *NYCD*, 9: 65; Frontenac to Colbert, November 2, 1672, in *Royal Fort Frontenac*, ed. Preston and Lamontagne, pp. 105–6.

28. Lawrence H. Leder, ed., *The Livingston Indian Records, 1666–1723* (Gettysburg, Pa., 1956), p. 77; Allen W. Trelease, *Indian Affairs in Colonial New York: The Seventeenth Century* (Ithaca, N.Y., 1960), pp. 261–62.

Barre proceeded with his healthier soldiers to La Famine on the southeast shore of Lake Ontario, where he had arranged a conference with the Iroquois in hopes of bluffing them into making concessions. On September 5 La Barre began the meeting with an impassioned speech, probably directing his remarks to the Onondaga orator who would speak for the Five Nations. La Grand Gueule, the Iroquois spokesman, fixed his gaze on the end of the long pipe that he puffed from time to time and listened impassively as the French governor made one threat after another. When the long harangue reached its conclusion, La Grand Gueule, having a sense for the dramatic, walked around the ring of French and Indians for several minutes in deep thought before proceeding to ridicule La Barre for having come before them with such an obvious bluff.[29] Having assured himself of wide publicity by treating the governor so outrageously, the Onondaga sachem then made his point: "We are born Freemen, and have no dependence either upon the *Onnontio* [the French] or the Corlar [the English]. We have a power to go where we please, to conduct who we will to the places we resort to and to buy and sell where we think fit."[30]

Not only did this statement affirm Iroquois intentions of traveling wherever they desired, but it also implied by using the words "buy and sell" that they had not abandoned their hopes of achieving some sort of position as middlemen. Certainly their activities in these years indicate the existence of such a desire. Having defeated the Susquehannahs to the south in 1675, they began in 1677 to attack the Illinois, who had been funneling the furs of the Mississippi Valley to the French.[31] Clearly the Iroquois enjoyed taking the plunder that such a war offered, but their motives were more complex, probably involving an effort to impose themselves as middlemen between the Indians of the Ohio Valley and the English. All of the French observers believed this. Jacques Duchesneau, the intendant, complained that the Iroquois were attempting "to force the Illinois to bring their beaver to them, so that they may go and trade it afterwards with the English; also, to intimidate the other nations and constrain them to do the same thing."[32] Accusing the Iroquois of attempting to "absolutely intersect the path to the South," La Barre argued that the outcome of the war with the Five Nations would "determine who will be master of the Beaver trade to the south and southwest; and that the Iroquois, who alone supply the English with

29. Lahontan, *New Voyages to North America,* ed. Thwaites, 1: 74–80.
30. Ibid., p. 82.
31. Hunt, *Wars of the Iroquois,* p. 149.
32. Duchesneau, Memoir on the Indian nations, November 13, 1681, in *NYCD,* 9: 163.

considerable beaver, have a deep interest in despoiling us of that advantage by applying it to their own benefit. . . ."[33] The explorer La Salle, a perceptive observer of the Indians, maintained that the Iroquois threatened war against the French allies "unless they would carry the Beaver to them by Lake Ontario and afterwards to New-York."[34]

It therefore seems clear that Iroquois diplomatic policy was twofold: first, to insist on the right to hunt north of the Great Lakes, and second, when the possibility presented itself, to act as middlemen between the New Yorkers and tribes to the north or west. If necessary, they would relinquish the latter, but the former constituted an inviolable principle. By the beginning of the eighteenth century, they began to realize that in order to achieve more basic objectives they would have to give up their hopes of becoming middlemen.

The Five Nations wanted to remain as independent as possible, but the French attitude toward Iroquois competition forced them into closer relations with the English. Although their fears may have been eased by La Grand Gueule's triumph, the aggressive stance taken by La Barre had greatly disturbed them. A month before the conference at La Famine in 1684, Onondaga and Cayuga sachems had told Governor Dongan, "You are a Mighty Sachem and we but a Small People. . . . you must Protect us from the French, which if you dont we shall loose all our Hunting and Bevers: The French want all the Bevers and are Angry that we bring any to the English."[35] In the spring of the next year they again heard reports of French military preparations, and this time even the distant Senecas came to Albany with requests for assistance.[36]

The Iroquois fears were well justified, for the French suspected that with English encouragement the Five Nations had developed a scheme designed to do far more than simply seize the trade of Canada: "That undertaking is, to destroy, one after the other, all the nations allied to us . . . in order that, after they have taken from us all the trade in peltries, which they wish to carry on alone with the English and Dutch . . . they may attack us alone."[37] Governor Denonville, who succeeded La Barre in 1685, reopened the hostilities against the Five Nations with a successful attack on the Senecas in 1687, but his actions aroused the Confederacy, which then dealt him several setbacks including the

33. La Barre to Seignelay, November 4, 1683, ibid., 9: 201–2.

34. Gustave Lanctot, *A History of Canada*, 3 vols. (Cambridge, Mass., 1964), 2: 81–84; La Salle, Memoir concerning Fort Frontenac, 1684, in *NYCD*, 9: 213.

35. Wraxall, *Abridgment*, ed. McIlwain, August 2, 1684, p. 11.

36. Leder, ed., *Livingston Indian Records*, pp. 76–77.

37. Report on an assembly of officials at Quebec, October 10, 1682, in *Jesuit Relations*, ed. Thwaites, 62: 157.

famous Lachine massacre in 1689. Thus, when war broke out between England and France in that year, the Iroquois must have felt confident, as they now had expectations of English protection for their villages.[38]

King William's War, however, was a disaster for the Five Nations. Under the leadership of Frontenac, who had returned from France to replace Denonville, the Canadians and their Indian allies made repeated forays into New York, inflicting severe casualties on the Iroquois. As early as 1693 the Five Nations asked for negotiations to end the war, but Frontenac was determined that when peace came it would be on French terms. Realizing the inadequacy of English support, the Five Nations renewed their old policy of attempting to make peace with the Ottawas, but the French, aided by violence between Iroquois and Ottawas who had been hunting together during a truce, succeeded in preventing any possibility of a treaty. As the war began to taper off between New Yorkers and Canadians, the latter continued to apply pressure against the enemy Indians. The Peace of Ryswick in 1697 actually hurt the Iroquois, since they were not included in its terms and now found themselves facing the French entirely alone. Although they immediately began to sue for peace, Frontenac continued the war against them. During the following year the Five Nations lost as many as one hundred warriors, and the death of the Onondaga sachem Black Kettle added to the long list of important military leaders killed during the war. Preliminary negotiations finally began when Frontenac offered them peace in the fall of 1698.[39]

The Five Nations faced an extremely precarious future. As they themselves had demonstrated on several occasions, Indian tribes could be broken up and dispersed as a result of far lesser calamities than the Iroquois had suffered in the 1690s. They would not have come to Frontenac early in the war with "words of submission and respect" unless, as the French explorer Cadillac noted, they had not experienced considerable losses and viewed themselves "on the brink of total ruin."[40]

38. Lanctot, *History of Canada*, 2: 106–11; William Kingsford, *The History of Canada*, 10 vols. (London, 1887–98; reprinted, New York, 1969), 2: 101–7.

39. Lanctot, *History of Canada*, 2: 123–31, 141; W. J. Eccles, *The Canadian Frontier, 1534–1760* (New York, 1969), pp. 122–24; William M. Beauchamp, *A History of the Iroquois: Now Commonly Called the Six Nations* (New York, 1905; reprinted, Port Washington, N.Y., 1968), p. 125; Minutes of a general meeting of the Albany magistrates [February 3, 1690?], in Cadwallader Colden Papers; Royal memorial to Frontenac and Champigny, May 26, 1696, in *Supplement to Dr. Brymner's Report on Canadian Archives, 1899*, ed. Edouard Richard (Ottawa, 1901), pp. 316–17; Wraxall, *Abridgment*, ed. McIlwain, July 22, 1698, p. 29.

40. Cadillac, Memoir on the negotiations in Canada with the Iroquois, 1694, in *NYCD*, 9: 585.

At least half of their warriors had been killed by the end of 1698, and Governor Bellomont of New York believed that without relief they would be entirely destroyed within a few years.[41] After a visit to the Onondagas in the spring of 1700, Robert Livingston wrote, "The Indians are much dejected and in a staggering condition, though they are so proud and will not own it, they are daily made so uneasy by the French that I despair of a good issue . . . ."[42]

The Canadians found themselves in an extremely good bargaining position, and probably many of them felt the same way as the Jesuit Étienne de Carheil, who recommended that the Iroquois be "completely tamed and reduced to subjection."[43] The French, however, had difficulties of their own, which called for a less drastic policy than an attempt to conquer the Iroquois—an action that would have required the invasion of New York. Governor Callières of Canada suspected that a renewal of hostilities with England could not long be avoided, and he recognized the value of Iroquois neutrality in such a conflict. An overland attack on Montreal could hardly succeed without Iroquois participation.[44] In addition, the Ottawas, probably the most important allies of the French, began once again in 1700 to seek peace with the Five Nations by asking some Iroquois hunters to arrange a conference for that summer.[45]

The Iroquois diplomats were faced with problems that involved the very existence of their people. They needed furs, which before the war they had been securing largely by plunder. Now they would have to acquire the means of economic survival through peaceful measures. Although the loss of their hunting grounds in Canada would have caused serious economic problems for the Iroquois, the French and their Indian allies knew that to deny the Iroquois a share in the fur trade would be shortsighted. With effective assistance from the English, the Five Nations might prove to be the key element in the destruction of New France in a future war.

---

41. Population statistics of New York, in *Documentary History of the State of New York*, ed. Edmund B. O'Callaghan, 4 vols. (Albany, 1850–51), 1: 468; Bellomont to the Board of Trade, May 18, 1698, in *NYCD*, 4: 305; Bellomont to Francis Nicholson, November 12, 1698, in *Calendar of State Papers, Colonial Series, America and West Indies*, ed. W. N. Sainsbury et al., 43 vols. to date (London 1860–), 17: 140, hereafter cited as *Calendar of State Papers*.

42. Robert Livingston to Bellomont, May 3, 1700, in *Calendar of State Papers*, 18: 270.

43. Étienne de Carheil to Governor Callières, August 30, 1703, in *Jesuit Relations*, ed. Thwaites, 65: 223.

44. Lanctot, *History of Canada*, 2: 150.

45. Memorial of Johannes Groenendyck and Abraham Provoost, June 16, 1700, in *Calendar of State Papers*, 18: 435–36.

On the English side, Governor Bellomont also understood the importance of these western hunting grounds to the Iroquois: "The only good
Beaver hunting lyes in that part of the country where the Dowaganhas
and those other Nations live, and thither our 5 Nations are forced to goe
a beaver-hunting, which is one reason of that perpetual war between
those Nations and ours . . . ."[46] Peace depended on the settlement of
this issue.

The opportunity to solve the problem occurred when Ottawa ambassadors came to the central council fires at Onondaga in June 1700.
The five Ottawas represented three nations, composed of sixteen villages
and probably between three and four thousand people, who wanted to
move closer to Lake Ontario in order to be in a better position to trade
for the inexpensive English merchandise.[47] "We make a firm league with
the Five Nations and Corlaer," they proclaimed, "and desire to be
united in the Covenant Chain; our hunting places to be one . . . and
because the path to Corlaer's house [Albany] may be open and clear,
doe give a drest elke skin to cover the path to walk upon." The Iroquois
sachems answered, "We are glad to see you in our country, and do accept of you to be our friends and allies, and do give you a Belt of Wampum as a token thereof, that there may be a perpetual peace and friendship between us and our young Indians to hunt together in all love and
amity." Having stated their own terms, the Iroquois then agreed to the
Ottawa proposals: "Let this peace be firm and lasting, then shall we
grow old and grey-headed together, else the war will devour us both.
Brethren, we open a path for you to go quite to Corlaer's house, where
you shall have equal liberty of egress and regress to trade as we ourselves."[48] Although this treaty does not seem to have been officially rati-
fied in 1700, the terms were probably those agreed upon at the great
Indian conference in Montreal during the following summer.[49]

The Ottawas, a people more inclined toward business than warfare,
must have been delighted by the arrangement. They could now trade
with the side offering the highest prices and no longer had to fear the
loss of trading fleets to Iroquois raiding parties.[50] The Five Nations, in
turn, had received recognition of their long-standing claim to hunting
rights in Canada. Technically, they did not completely win their point
since they had always claimed complete ownership of this territory, and

46. Bellomont to the Board of Trade, November 28, 1700, in *NYCD*, 4: 796.
47. Indian Conference, June 30, 1700, in *Calendar of State Papers*, 18: 438–39.
48. Ibid., p. 439.
49. Indian Conference, August 31, 1701, in *NYCD*, 4: 741.
50. Hunt, *Wars of the Iroquois*, pp. 48–49.

the treaty implied a joint ownership, but for all practical purposes they had no complaints. By allowing the Ottawas the right to travel through their territory, a privilege probably never before granted to a major rival, the Iroquois made it clear that they no longer intended to strive for the role of middlemen between the Ottawas and Albany.[51] This did not mean, however, that they had entirely forsaken the concept of themselves as traders.

The English naturally found these terms to their liking, and Bellomont told the Iroquois that it would be a "prudent and good Policy in you to try all possible Means to fix a Trade and Correspondance with all those Nations . . . and then you might at all times go a hunting into their Country without any sort of hazard which I understand is much the best for Bever hunting."[52] Although Bellomont considered the agreement to be a "mighty blow to the French," the Canadians did not seem greatly disturbed.[53] They also wanted peace among the Indians and expected that their influence with the Ottawas and several planned forts would prevent the development of an extensive trade from north of Lake Ontario to Albany. Furthermore, an oversupply of furs, accompanied by a considerable decrease in the demand for beaver in Europe, had reduced their fear of losing a few pelts to the Albany traders.[54]

Having cleared the first hurdle on the road to peace, the Iroquois now had to deal with their European neighbors. Later in the summer of 1700 Iroquois diplomats traveled to Montreal, where they succeeded in terminating hostilities with the French. For the Iroquois sachems, the English presented the greatest problem by a constant interference that threatened to upset the delicate negotiations. Although they desired peace between the Five Nations and the French Indians in order to expand the trade of Albany, the New York authorities insisted on demands that would have prevented the ratification of a treaty. Both the English and the French wanted the Iroquois to be recognized as their subjects, and for this reason the English opposed any peace treaty in which they did not participate. Thus, New York officials constantly attempted to prevent Iroquois diplomats from going to Canada.[55] Even some of the

51. Leder, ed., *Livingston Indian Records*, p. 178.

52. Wraxall, *Abridgment*, ed. McIlwain, August 29, 1700, p. 34.

53. Bellomont to the Board of Trade, October 17, 1700, in *NYCD*, 4: 714.

54. Innis, *Fur Trade in Canada*, pp. 75, 82–83.

55. Indian Conferences at Montreal, July 18, September 3, 1700, in *NYCD*, 9: 708–11, 715–20; *Journal of the Votes and Proceedings of the General Assembly of the Colony of New York [1691–1765]*, 2 vols. (New York, 1764–66), April 7, 1699, 1: 99; Wraxall, *Abridgment*, ed. McIlwain, June 12, 1699, p. 32; Leder, ed.,

less important English demands would have prevented a peace treaty had the Iroquois accepted them.

While delegates from the Five Nations negotiated with Callières in the summer of 1700, another group of sachems was meeting with Bellomont in Albany. Acknowledging the importance of the fur trade to the Iroquois, he advised them to make peace with the Ottawas and other far Indians, but in the same breath he told them to imprison any Jesuits entering their territory and to encourage the return of the Caughnawagas or Praying Indians, who were deserters from the Iroquois Confederacy living near Montreal. The shrewdness of Iroquois diplomacy was illustrated in their reply: "These three heads do not well consist and agree together therefore we are of Opinion it will be more Advisable, first to conclude a firm Peace with the Dowagenhaw and remote Indians, and then see to draw back our Indians from Canada that are debauched thither before we meddle with or disturb the Jesuits . . . ."[56] A few days later in Montreal, Iroquois representatives were telling Callières: "When we came here last, we planted the tree of Peace; now we give it roots to reach the Far Nations, in order that it may be strengthened; we add leaves also to it, so that good business may be transacted under its shade."[57] Apparently, nothing was more important to them than the successful conclusion of a peace treaty with the Ottawas.

Although constantly engaged in efforts to circumvent English obstructionism, the Iroquois still found time to use the situation for their own economic advantage. At almost all diplomatic conferences the Five Nations complained about high prices and urged that they be lowered. Explanations by Englishmen about the law of supply and demand seemed to fall on deaf ears.[58] Now that the English wanted to attract the trade of the far Indians to Albany, Iroquois spokesmen lost no opportunity to tell them that this would not occur unless prices were reduced.[59] Like his Indian counterparts, Bellomont knew that political means could be used to influence the prices of goods, and he recommended to the Board of Trade the removal of all customs duties on furs "both here and

Livingston Indian Records, p. 178; Bellomont to the Board of Trade, October 24, 1700, in *NYCD*, 4: 768.

56. Wraxall, *Abridgment*, ed. McIlwain, August 29, 1700, p. 35.

57. Indian Conference, September 3, 1700, in *NYCD*, 9: 716. On the general desire of the Iroquois to achieve a lasting peace, see Paul A. W. Wallace, "The Return of Hiawatha," *New York History* 29 (1948): 385–403.

58. Indian Conference, August 29, 1715, in *NYCD*, 5: 442; Wraxall, *Abridgment*, ed. McIlwain, June 10, 1711, pp. 88–89.

59. Wraxall, *Abridgment*, ed. McIlwain, July 22, 1698, August 13, 1700, pp. 29, 37.

in England, both for the advantage of our 5 Nations, and to draw the remote nations to trade with us . . . ." He also suggested legislation requiring a certain amount of beaver fur to be included in all hats.[60] In addition to demanding lower prices, the Iroquois at conferences in 1700 and 1701 used the English fear of a French alliance with the Five Nations to increase the supply of presents always given to them on these occasions. The governors did not mind giving an abundance of presents, because the Iroquois usually gave skins in return. On one occasion, at a conference with Bellomont, the Indians sold some of their presents to Albany merchants for beaver skins, which they then used to get more presents from the governor.[61] While they assured themselves of the New York market, the Iroquois opened up other sources of trade by negotiating a commercial treaty in 1699 with William Markam, Lieutenant Governor of Pennsylvania. As a form of economic security, they also arranged to have a store of inexpensive goods kept for them at Fort Frontenac.[62]

When Lieutenant Governor John Nanfan, replacing the deceased Bellomont, learned that a great peace conference had been set for the summer of 1701 in Canada, he called for a meeting in July with the Iroquois, who resolved the conflict by sending delegations to both Montreal and Albany. Although the larger and more distinguished group went north, the diplomats who went to New York possessed powers that they used to good purpose.

At Montreal a magnificent assemblage gathered with representatives from numerous tribes, including the Ottawas, Miamis, Illinois, Winnebagos, and Potawatomis—more than one thousand Indians in all. After having spent nearly three years on preliminary negotiations, the French and Indians needed less than two weeks to arrive at final terms, and on August 4 Callières presided over a ceremony that brought an end to more than fifty years of warfare. For the Iroquois Confederacy, the terms of the peace treaty with Canada appeared very favorable. Considering their weakened condition, they must have been pleased to accept the French requirement that they remain neutral in case of another war between England and France. By having to make peace with all the French allies, they lost the opportunity to single out any particu-

---

60. Bellomont to the Board of Trade, November 28, 1700, January 10, 1701, in *NYCD*, 4: 789, 834.

61. Robert Livingston to the Board of Trade, May 13, 1701, ibid., p. 876.

62. Wraxall, *Abridgment*, ed. McIlwain, August 23, 1699, p. 33; Governor Callières and Intendant Champigny to Pontchartrain, October 18, 1700, in *Royal Fort Frontenac*, ed. Preston and Lamontagne, p. 201.

lar tribe for revenge, but this agreement was probably to their long-range benefit. In approving the only other explicit requirement, they opened the way for Jesuits to take up residence in their territory.[63]

The Iroquois diplomats could justly look upon this peace treaty with a sense of accomplishment. They had given their people a peace that was to last with only a few minor incidents for more than half a century. At a cost of neither pride nor independence, the Five Nations now found themselves in a position of being able to play off one group of Europeans against another. Nevertheless, the sachems knew that they had given up more than what appeared in the terms of the treaty. They were fully aware that peace would enable the French to execute their plans to build a fort at Detroit—a strategic location that would greatly strengthen Canada's position in the fur trade.[64] By allowing the French to build on lands claimed by the Iroquois through right of conquest, they were tacitly admitting, as they had done in the negotiations with the Ottawas during the previous summer, that they did not actually own the territory but simply possessed the right to hunt on it. Sharing these hunting grounds with the Ottawas, mainly a trading people, was one thing, but allowing their ancient European enemy to build forts there was quite another. Although they wanted peace and knew that only warfare could prevent the French from building at Detroit, they did not accept the matter gracefully.

While one delegation from the Five Nations participated in the peace conference with Callières, the Iroquois who had gone to Albany sought ways to hinder the French efforts to construct fortifications at Detroit. "What shall we do," they asked Nanfan, "if the French continue to draw away our People and encroach upon our Country, they build Forts round about us and pen us up." Although clearly recognizing the inevitability of such encroachments on these lands, they refused to admit in principle that the French could build forts there without permission.[65] The New Yorkers feared the effects of French trading posts on their plans to attract the trade of the western Indians and to build forts of their own in the wilderness, but they were in no better position than the Iroquois to prevent the Canadians from doing as they pleased.[66] Nanfan could do nothing but exhort the Indians to prevent the French from establishing

63. Peace Conference, August 4, 1701, in *NYCD*, 9: 722–25. For an account of this conference, see Anthony F. C. Wallace, "Origins of Iroquois Neutrality: The Grand Settlement of 1701," *Pennsylvania History* 24 (1957): 223–35.

64. Wraxall, *Abridgment,* ed. McIlwain, July 21, 1701, p. 41.

65. Ibid., pp. 41–42.

66. Bellomont to the Board of Trade, October 17, 1700; Robert Livingston to the Board of Trade, May 13, 1701, in *NYCD*, 4: 716, 872.

themselves at Detroit. "I wonder," he said, "that . . . you are not more zealous to oppose . . . their building a Forte at Tjughsaghrondie [Detroit] . . . the principle pass where all your Beaver hunting is." [67] A glance at a map illustrates the significance of Nanfan's statement. Since Indians paddling canoes could not risk crossing one of the Great Lakes, the various tribes were able to travel between Canada and areas to the south only by circling the eastern end of Lake Ontario or by passing near either Niagara or Detroit. Urging the Iroquois sachems not to believe the French governor's promises of inexpensive goods at Detroit and of protection from their enemies, Nanfan argued, "when the Forte is made then he will command you and your beavers too, Nay you shall never hunt a beaver there without his leave . . . ." [68]

The Iroquois sachems had come well prepared to answer the English arguments. Rather than face the embarrassment of having to protect this territory, they simply deeded it all to the King of England. Excluding the homelands of the Five Nations in New York, the territory comprised all the country formerly owned by the Hurons and other conquered tribes. Detroit, Niagara, and Irondequoit, the place where the Genesee River flows into Lake Ontario, were specifically mentioned as part of the vast land grant. [69] The terms of the deed left the Iroquois with all the privileges of using the land while presenting the problems of protecting it to the English: "wee are to have free hunting . . . forever and that free of all disturbances expecting to be protected therein by the Crown of England . . . ." [70] To insure that the importance of the deed would not be overlooked, they asked that "our Secretary Robert Livingston" be sent to England personally to present the document to the king. [71]

Undoubtedly Livingston, New York's Secretary of Indian Affairs, played a significant role in these negotiations. He had apparently drafted the deed for the Indians and also seems to have influenced its content. Although for two years he had been advocating the building of English forts in the wilderness, the French obviously now had a substantial lead in undertaking such efforts. Both he and the sachems must have realized that nothing could be done to prevent a French fort at Detroit, which was already under construction, but they may have believed that the English government would prevent the French from building at even more threatening places such as Niagara or Irondequoit. Such reasoning

67. Indian Conference, July 18, 1701, ibid., 4: 900.
68. Ibid.
69. Deed from the Five Nations to the King, July 19, 1701, ibid., pp. 908–9.
70. Ibid., pp. 909–10.
71. Indian Conference, July 19, 1701, ibid., p. 905.

was consistent with Livingston's thinking during the previous two years. In 1699 he had proposed a fort at Detroit. Then, in the spring of 1701, he modified his proposals and only advocated a post as far west as Onondaga country.[72]

The results of the conference at Albany complemented those at Montreal to a degree that proved most significant for the future of the Five Nations. By turning over their lands to the English, the Iroquois greatly reduced the danger of a conflict with the French. The combination of Iroquois ownership and French determination to construct forts would have made the maintenance of peace a virtual impossibility, and those imperial-minded authorities in New York who wanted to challenge the French could have used this source of irritation to secure Iroquois participation in the wars with France. The responsibility, however, for protecting the lands had been transferred to the English, and Iroquois diplomats could thus use New York's failure to take action against the French as their excuse for not aiding the English in Queen Anne's War and later in King George's War. Nevertheless, the deeding of the Iroquois hunting grounds to the Crown did bring the Iroquois closer to dependence on the English, with the result that New York authorities considered the conference a success.[73] After 1701, young Iroquois warriors would have to travel many miles to win their fighting honors, for the sachems had succeeded in establishing a peace with their neighbors that lasted for more than half a century.

72. Robert Livingston to Bellomont, April 12, 1699, in *Calendar of State Papers,* 17: 140; Livingston to the Board of Trade, May 13, 1701, in *NYCD,* 4: 873–74.
73. Nanfan to the Board of Trade, September 24, 1701, in *NYCD,* 4: 915.

3

THE IROQUOIS IN AN AGE

OF PEACE AND PROSPERITY

WHILE DIPLOMATS of the Five Nations were facing problems of peace-making in 1701, the Iroquois hunters and traders sought ways of rebuilding an economy that had been badly disrupted by the long years of almost continual warfare. For the traders among the Five Nations, the idea of establishing themselves as middlemen between the far Indians and the English presented great difficulties. Not only had the Iroquois been constantly at war with these western tribes for at least fourteen years, but in the peace of 1701 the Ottawas earned the privilege of traveling through Iroquois country for the purpose of bringing their skins to Albany. An even greater difficulty for the Indian traders involved the increasing competition from the colonists in both New York and Canada. The Iroquois hunters, on the other hand, had far fewer problems than the relatively small number of traders, because hunting had never been entirely disrupted, and the Iroquois could now travel in Canada without fear of meeting hostile war parties. They seem to have immediately taken advantage of the situation.[1]

Every year after the first signs of autumn, small parties of Iroquois hunters left their villages for wilderness places as far as a thousand miles away, where they would spend the winter collecting pelts of practically any fur-bearing animal that crossed their paths. The beaver, being valuable and easy to catch, attracted the most attention. As a result, the unfortunate creature often became extinct in many hunting areas in spite of attempts at conservation measures by the Iroquois and other Indians. Upon discovering a beaver pond, the hunters, only oc-

1. Instructions of the Council and Assembly to John Schuyler and John Bleeker, April 7, 1699; Answer of the Five Nations to Bellomont, May 9, 1699; Message from the Onondagas to the Commissioners of Indian Affairs, September 21, 1699; Indian Conference, July 18, 1701, in *Documents Relative to the Colonial History of the State of New York*, ed. Edmund B. O'Callaghan and Berthold Fernow, 15 vols. (Albany, 1856–87), 4: 499, 565, 597, 900, hereafter cited as *NYCD*.

casionally using their guns, either drained most of the water out of it by breaking the dam with axes, or in winter they chopped holes in the houses, forcing the animals to leave and surface through the ice at air holes. At times nets were used, but steel traps did not appear on the scene until the last decades of the eighteenth century.[2]

The Iroquois men enjoyed hunting deer nearly as much as they did beaver. The pursuit of these wary animals gave them great pleasure, and after feasting on the meat, they sold the skins, which usually brought a decent price. On occasion, hunting parties would laboriously build two long fences that eventually ran together and became a trap for the deer driven ahead of pursuers. When faced with larger animals such as moose, elk, and bear, guns proved to be far superior to stone-age weapons, but for catching minks, raccoons, muskrats, martens, and other small animals, the hunter used a variety of traditional methods including snares, nets, and cage-traps.[3]

By the end of February the Indians began the long trek home, probably dragging sleds over the ice that prevented the use of canoes. After arriving at their villages, they waited until the ice had melted before going to Albany or, in later years, to Oswego. When the rivers began flowing again, some men went fishing and let the women take the furs to market, where they were likely to be more successful than their husbands, who frequently were cheated while in a state of intoxication.[4] Heavy skins from elk, moose, and bear were often traded at the nearest post regardless of whether it was English or French, but the Indians did not mind carrying the lighter skins to wherever they could obtain the best price. If necessary, canoes as long as forty feet were used to carry loads of over six thousand pounds.[5]

Upon arriving at a trading post, the Iroquois faced one of their most

2. Bellomont to the Board of Trade, February 28, 1700, ibid., p. 608; Father Nau to Father Bonin, October 2, 1737; Father Vivier to Father ———, June 8, 1750, in *Jesuit Relations and Allied Documents: Travels and Explorations of the Jesuit Missionaries in New France, 1619–1791*, ed. Reuben G. Thwaites, 73 vols. (Cleveland, 1896–1901), 68: 275, 69: 147; Louis Armand Lahontan, *New Voyages to North America*, ed. Reuben G. Thwaites, 2 vols. (Chicago, 1905), 2: 481–84.

3. Lahontan, *New Voyages to North America*, ed. Thwaites, 1: 109–13; Lewis H. Morgan, *League of the Ho-Dé-No-Sau-Nee or Iroquois* (New York, 1904), pp. 335–37.

4. Evert Wendell, Jr., Account Book, 1695–1726 (in Dutch, partially translated by Dingman Versteeg), New-York Historical Society, New York City. Approximately 20 percent of the Indians doing business with Wendell at Albany were women.

5. Clerambault d'Aigremont to Pontchartrain, November 14, 1708, in *NYCD*, 9: 821; George Irving Quimby, *Indian Culture and European Trade Goods* (Madison, Wis., 1966), p. 164.

difficult economic problems—receiving a "good pennysworth" for their peltry. Although the Albany traders possessed an unsavory reputation, the Indians were better off in the days before Albany lost its monopoly in the 1720s. Since the law required that trading be conducted within the walls of the city, a certain amount of order had to be maintained. Thus, the magistrates often vigorously enforced the ordinances against fraudulent trading practices. If a particularly zealous sheriff—who received a share of the fines—happened to be in office, then the Indians could expect to receive a reasonable amount of protection.[6] In addition, they could at least make their complaints known to the Commissioners of Indian Affairs, who were responsible to the governor and, as leading citizens of Albany, had a stake in maintaining order. After the founding of Oswego on Lake Ontario in the 1720s, however, the traders had much greater opportunity to do as they pleased, and many of them took advantage of the situation by cheating their customers.

In attempting to get a fair deal, the Indians suffered mainly from their weakness for rum and their inability to receive much satisfaction under English law. After accepting a gift of rum, many Indians soon became intoxicated, and then the traders could get from them an entire winter's work for a few yards of cloth and a small keg of rum, well diluted with water. If an Iroquois chose to take legal action against a trader, he first had to find a lawyer, file charges, and then wait sometimes for a year or more before the case came before the courts. Even then, he could not expect justice since his own testimony was usually not admissible. Juries, filled with frontiersmen, seldom favored the Indians, while the offender could often expect assistance from his creditors, who had an investment to protect and could not afford to see the defendant spend a trading season in jail.[7]

In view of the harsh criticisms leveled at the Albany Dutch for their trading practices, it is unfortunate that so few records are available describing the everyday transactions between the traders and the Indians. An account book kept by one Albany trader, Evert Wendell, Jr., between 1695 and 1726 provides us with the best source of information. The book does not contain all of his transactions, but only those that

6. Joel Munsell, ed., *Annals of Albany*, 10 vols. (Albany, 1850–59), 4: 182–83, 192.

7. Cadwallader Colden, "The present state of the Indian affairs . . . ," August 8, 1751, in *The Letters and Papers of Cadwallader Colden*, 10 vols., New-York Historical Society *Collections*, 50–56 (1917–23), 67–69 (1934–35) (New York, 1918–36), 4: 276, hereafter cited as *Colden Papers*; William Johnson to the Board of Trade, June 28, 1766, in *NYCD*, 7: 838.

involved credit to Indians. Wendell kept the accounts not in money but in terms of bears, beaver, and marten. Thus, if an Indian agreed to pay him twenty-five beaver skins, Wendell drew crude sketches of each beaver so that at a future date the customer would be able to look in the book and see for himself the amount owed. In return for the credit extended, the Indian apparently agreed to do all his trading with Wendell and promised that a violation of the agreement would add an extra amount of peltry to his debt. Although Wendell did not mind extending credit to a stranger, he sometimes required a debtor to leave a gun as security for his return with the furs. Wendell often violated the law by providing some of the Iroquois with goods to sell for him in their villages. As with most other traders, the bulk of his merchandise consisted of textiles and rum.[8]

After the introduction of European goods, life for the inhabitants of the Five Nations changed dramatically. By the beginning of the eighteenth century the Iroquois were purchasing almost every kind of merchandise imaginable, from basic utensils to beaver hats and lace coats, but in the fur trade there were three essential types of merchandise—gunpowder, woolen goods, and rum.[9] The constant demands from the Iroquois to lower the price of gunpowder indicates how important a commodity this was to them. Gunpowder, however, did not play as large a role in the fur trade as woolens and rum, because the Indians obtained much of their powder supply in the form of presents from both the British and the French. The tribesmen also received a large portion of their guns in this way and had ready access to French and British blacksmiths, who lived in their villages and kept the guns in good repair. Even with these extensive gifts of ammunition, the Iroquois still needed to buy substantial quantities from the traders, because each of the hunters, who were "continually discharging their pieces at every little Object," may have annually used as much as eight pounds of powder and twenty pounds of lead.[10] At such a rate, the Senecas alone at the middle of the eighteenth century would have used over eight thousand pounds of powder and twenty thousand pounds of lead per year. Of all the important merchandise sold in the fur trade, the only French article

<hr />

8. Evert Wendell, Jr., Account Book, 1695-1726.

9. Johnson to Governor George Clinton, May 30, 1747, in *The Papers of Sir William Johnson*, ed. James Sullivan et al., 14 vols. (Albany, 1921-65), 1: 95, hereafter cited as *Johnson Papers*.

10. Board of Trade to the Privy Council, December 20, 1739; George Clarke to the Board of Trade, May 28, 1711; William Johnson to General Jeffrey Amherst, August 25, 1763, in *NYCD*, 6: 156, 5, 237, 7: 543.

that the Indians preferred was gunpowder, and they usually purchased each year "from twenty to twenty-five thousand weight" of this commodity in Canada.[11]

Ironically, just as the Dutch traders depended on fashions in Europe to create a demand for their furs, so did their trade with the Iroquois and other tribes depend on fashion trends among the Indians. To be fashionable, the Indians favored particular kinds of woolen garments, accentuated with accessories made from a wide variety of textiles and ornaments. Duffels, named after the place near Antwerp where they originated, were pieces of coarse woolen cloth from which the Indians made blankets. Strouds, produced in the English town of Stroud, were even more popular and were "universally in fashion among the Indians."[12] The stroud cloth could be used for a greater variety of purposes than duffels, including leggings and women's skirts. In selecting the red and blue strouds, Indian shoppers were fickle and would not buy a single yard unless it had a thick nap and a dark shade. In answering a commercial firm in London that had asked for his advice, Albany trader Philip Livingston wrote, "Send our traders Such goods as you think they Require . . . tho Some sorts as Strowds be dear If they really be good they Covit them Especially those who trade themselves with the Indians for those Savages who come to trade here will have good Choise goods, and do understand them to perfection."[13] Except when buying black cloth for funerals, the Indians purchased only red or blue strouds with black selvages. If the cloth was too coarse, they would not buy it, but the single most important criterion was for the blue strouds to be "Dark blue—almost Black."[14]

The desire of the Iroquois for woolen garments was equalled by their passion for rum, and by the middle of the eighteenth century they were trading at least as many furs for liquor as for woolens. When contemporary observers reported that the Indians were "supplyed with Rum by

11. Memoir from Governor Philippe de Rigaud de Vaudreuil to the Duke of Orleans, February [?], 1716; Cadwallader Colden, Memoir on the fur trade, November 10, 1724, ibid., 9: 870, 5: 729.

12. Minutes of the Commissioners of Indian Affairs (microfilm), November 12, 1724, 1: 108, Public Archives of Canada, Ottawa, hereafter cited as Minutes of the Indian Commissioners.

13. Philip Livingston to Storke and Gainsborough, November 28, 1734, in Miscellaneous Manuscripts, vol. 5, New York State Library, Albany.

14. Ibid., November 1, 1736; Cornelius Cuyler to Samuel Baker, July 4, 1733; Cuyler to Joseph Mico, November 12, 1736; Cuyler to Champion and Hayley, September 20, 1759, in Cornelius Cuyler Letter Books, 1724–1736, 1752–1764 (microfilm), American Antiquarian Society, Worcester, Mass.

the traders in vast and almost incredible quantities," they did not seem to have been exaggerating.[15] In earlier years alcoholics among the Iroquois did not exceed the number that might be expected in any society, but over the years an increasingly large proportion of the Iroquois became addicted.[16] In 1687 the Albany fur traders sold approximately eight thousand gallons of rum—a rather high figure considering the relatively limited number of customers at that time, but this amounted to an almost negligible quantity when compared to the number of gallons used during later years.[17] In 1773 the merchants of Montreal imported 378,633 gallons of rum in addition to 98,605 gallons of molasses; and a year later, in order to avoid some new duties, they imported 701,305 gallons of rum plus 193,559 gallons of molasses.[18] These Canadian imports of rum, however, probably represented only a fraction of the total amount of strong liquor going into Indian country, because the traders of Pennsylvania, Virginia, and New York were notorious for the amount of rum that they sold. Complaining about these "great cargoes of Rum," Sir William Johnson stated, "many Traders carry little or nothing else, because their profits upon it are so considerable . . . ."[19] In addition, large quantities were sold to the Indians by the settlers living on the frontiers.[20]

Although very important as an article of exchange, rum had at least three additional roles in the fur trade. First, the desire for it caused Indian hunters to put much greater effort into their hunting and to kill many more animals than they would have if they had only been interested in purchasing dry goods, of which they could obtain a year's supply for a relatively small amount of peltry.[21] Second, their great weakness for rum and the likelihood of becoming intoxicated substantially decreased their chances of getting full value for their furs. As one of the River Indians of New York explained, "When our people came from Hunting . . . and acquaint the Traders and People that we want Powder and Shot and Clothing, they first give us a large cup of Rum . . . so that in fine all the Beaver and Peltry we have hunted goes for

15. Proceedings of the Albany Congress, July 9, 1754, in *NYCD*, 6: 888.

16. Anthony F. C. Wallace, *The Death and Rebirth of the Seneca* (New York, 1970), p. 199.

17. Stephen Van Cortlandt and James Graham to William Blathwayt, 1687, in William Blathwayt Papers (microfilm), Colonial Williamsburg, Williamsburg, Va.

18. Haldimand Collection, Calendar III, p. 6, in *Report on Canadian Archives, 1888*, ed. Douglas Brymner (Ottawa, 1889).

19. William Johnson to the Earl of Hillsborough, August 14, 1770, in *NYCD*, 8: 226.

20. Alexander McKee, Account of merchandise brought to Fort Pitt, 1767, in *Johnson Papers*, 13: 396.

21. William Johnson to Colden, August 9, 1764, in *Colden Papers*, 5: 365–66.

drink, and we are left destitute either of Clothing or Ammunition . . . ."[22]
Third, the effects of rum on the Indians greatly obstructed the chances
of establishing good relations between them and the traders. The digni-
fied bearing of the Indians commanded respect, but when this quality of
character completely broke down in fits of drunkenness, the white
traders looked upon them with contempt, and in turn the Indians deeply
resented having their weaknesses exposed.[23]

Because of its effect on their economy and the disruption it caused
within their society, the Iroquois sachems vigorously struggled to control the amount of rum that reached their people through the fur trade.
They were mainly concerned with the terrible fighting that occurred
during drunken brawls. At an Indian conference in 1728 they told Governor John Montgomerie that they had "Already lost many men through
Liquor which . . . Occasions our people killing one another."[24] And to
New York's Commissioners of Indian Affairs, a sachem lamented, "You
may find graves upon graves along the Lake all which misfortunes are
occasioned by Selling Rum to Our Brethren."[25]

The sachems frequently urged the British authorities to regulate the
liquor traffic, and they even threatened to use force if action was not
taken. Unfortunately, they were fighting a losing battle. After Oswego
developed into the main trading center in the 1720s, the task of keeping
the fiery spirits out of their country became even more difficult because
traders were constantly passing back and forth between there and Albany. The sachems asked Governor William Burnet to prohibit the sale
of intoxicants at Oswego, but he insensitively told them that "you need
not buy the rum unless You please."[26] Lacking cooperation from the
New York authorities, the Iroquois then threatened to prevent anyone
from carrying rum through their country, but they relented when
promised that the Oswego traders would be prohibited from selling
any of their liquor supplies along the way.[27]

Probably the main difficulty for the sachems in their fight against
alcohol was that the young hunters demanded it as recompense for
spending winters in the northern wilderness far from the comforts of

22. Indian Conference, August 31, 1722, in *NYCD*, 5: 663.
23. Johnson to Lord Loudoun, September 17, 1756, in *Johnson Papers*, 9: 531;
Lewis O. Saum, *The Fur Trader and the Indian* (Seattle, 1965), p. 211.
24. Indian Conference, October 4, 1728, in *NYCD*, 5: 863.
25. Minutes of the Indian Commissioners, July 4, 1730, 1: 231a.
26. Indian Conference, September 13, 1726, in *NYCD*, 5: 796–98.
27. Peter Wraxall, *An Abridgment of the Indian Affairs Contained in Four Folio
Volumes, Transacted in the Colony of New York, from the Year 1678 to the Year
1751*, ed. Charles H. McIlwain (Cambridge, Mass., 1915), October 4–5, 1728,
pp. 173–75.

their long houses. Although the sachems were reluctant to speak of dissension between themselves and any of their people, sometimes it appeared that the temperance issue was a serious internal problem. On one occasion in 1716, Dekannissora, one of the greatest leaders in Iroquois history and a strong advocate of temperance, asked the New York legislature through the Commissioners of Indian Affairs to reenact an old law against the sale of rum to the Indians. The assembly promptly agreed to his request, but within four months Dekannissora returned to Albany wanting to know who had asked for such a prohibition. When faced with the obvious answer, he replied that he and the Five Nations had changed their minds and wanted the law repealed.[28] On another occasion, a sachem told Burnet that rum "produces all Evil and Contention between man and wife, between the Young Indians and the Sachims."[29] Obviously any authority, either Iroquois or British, would have had difficulty in denying to the Indian hunters what they craved most, and the task became even more difficult when the French began to relax their restrictions on the sale of brandy in the second decade of the eighteenth century.[30]

In addition to the three main items in the trade, the Indians also purchased large quantities of knives, assorted textiles, ornaments, and wampum. Silver jewelry was a popular item, as was vermilion, used as body paint. Until about 1630 the Iroquois obtained their supply of wampum from coastal Indians, who made the small purple and white beads out of clam and conch shells. After this date the Dutch and English monopolized the supply, as the French never learned how to produce it. Although ownership of wampum symbolized wealth, it was not used as money by the Indians. After being strung together in belts, it served to formalize the results of Indian ceremonies, especially those involving diplomatic negotiations.[31]

While the hunters were taking advantage of the new peace treaties of 1701, the traders among the Five Nations were again looking for ways to establish themselves as middlemen between the English and the

---

28. Ibid., June 13, 15, September 14, 1716, pp. 113, 115; *Colonial Laws of New York from the Year 1664 to the Revolution*, 5 vols. (Albany, 1894–96), June 30, 1716, 1: 888–90.

29. Indian Conference, September 13, 1726, in *NYCD*, 5: 796–97.

30. Gustave Lanctot, *A History of Canada*, 3 vols. (Cambridge, Mass., 1964), 3: 13–14.

31. Morgan, *League of the Iroquois*, 2: 51–53; Allen W. Trelease, *Indian Affairs in Colonial New York: The Seventeenth Century* (Ithaca, N.Y., 1960), p. 48; Johnson to Governor George Clinton, September 20, 1749, in *Johnson Papers*, 9: 51; Cuyler to William Darlington, January 20, 1753, in Cornelius Cuyler Letter Book, 1752–1764.

western Indians. Although the Ottawas had been allowed the privilege of passing through their country to Albany, numerous other tribes could still be considered potential customers, and Iroquois traders hoped to exploit the situation. The lack of support given to them by the sachems indicates that their numbers were not great and that their chances of success were small.

In the eighteenth century a few of the Iroquois, who considered themselves to be traders, carried large quantities of goods deep into the interior to trade with the western Indians. Evert Wendell, Jr.'s, account book shows that he employed numerous Indians to sell goods for him, and it also indicates that Indians purchased merchandise from him to sell for their own profit. Some of these people seem to have been trading goods for Wendell in order to obtain credit for their own business ventures. In one instance, he noted that Schadseeaaei, the daughter of the "chief sachem of the Seneca country," had purchased a large supply of goods and had also agreed to dispose of a few items for him.[32] As late as 1770 some sachems complained to Sir William Johnson, that they strongly opposed "Indians coming and trading among us." "When we had White Traters," they exclaimed, "Goods Seemed [to] be Something reasonable and right; but Indians devour us, they extort from us every thing we get with pain and Labour in the Woods, for little or nothing . . . ." After explaining that Indian traders were "destitute of the fear of God" and paid no attention to their pleas for lower prices, they asked Johnson to prohibit trade between Indians in order "that there by we may be Strengthened to oppose Indian Traders."[33]

Even before the end of King William's War, a party of Iroquois traveled to the area around Detroit with a large supply of goods, and in 1700 Robert Livingston reported that Iroquois traders were competing with the French for the peltry of the western Indians.[34] Although coming from the smallest of the Five Nations, the Mohawk traders took advantage of their proximity to Albany and seem to have been the most ambitious of the Iroquois businessmen. Some of the French allies complained that the Mohawks had "told the Miamis whom they found with the French of Detroit that if they would remove, they will furnish them goods at a cheap rate, and do them every sort of kindness."[35] Much to

32. Evert Wendell, Jr., Account Book, 1695–1726.

33. Sachems of Oquaga to Johnson, January 22, 1770, in *Johnson Papers*, 7: 348–49.

34. Anonymous, "An Account of the most remarkable Occurrences in Canada . . ." (1695–96); Robert Livingston, Observations, May 3, 1700, in *NYCD*, 9: 646–47, 4: 650; Allen W. Trelease, "The Iroquois and the Western Fur Trade: A Problem in Interpretation," *Mississippi Valley Historical Review* 49 (1962): 43–44.

35. Indian Conference with the French, July 14, 1703, in *NYCD*, 9: 752.

the chagrin of the French, Mohawk traders even sold English goods to the Caughnawaga Indians living near Montreal.[36]

After establishing Detroit in 1701 the Canadians found that they had to face competition from the Iroquois even though this location was a considerable distance from the nearest village of the Senecas. One French observer noted that if Canada wanted to establish a good trade with the Indians near Detroit, it would be necessary to make French "goods as cheap to them as the Iroquois sell those of the English." He did not fear that the English would establish a post near Detroit, because the Iroquois would not allow it: "They are quite willing for the English to do this trade, but want it to be done through them so that they may share the profit on it with them."[37]

The Senecas controlled the Niagara portage and used their position to trade with numerous people who passed by this strategic crossroads. During King William's War, Iroquois attacks had forced the French to evacuate their fort at Niagara. Although they considered rebuilding it after the war, they did not feel any need to rush due to their belief that the Iroquois would not allow the English to build at this location. Governor Vaudreuil and Intendant Raudot explained, "the Iroquois is too skillful, and understands his interests too well, to permit it. If the English-man were settled there, the Iroquois would find himself deprived of the profit he makes out of the people of the lakes . . . from the beaver-skins they trade in with them." Vaudreuil and Raudot also pointed out that the Iroquois could make some profits from the people passing through their lands to Albany, but if the English established themselves at Niagara, most of this traffic would be eliminated. Furthermore, they believed that the Iroquois would oppose an English post at Niagara for diplomatic reasons: "the people of the lakes would no longer have need of the Iroquois for trading with the English, who would attract to them all the tribes of the lakes, so that, in this way, the Iroquois would be between the English and the lake tribes, who would always side with the English . . . ."[38] One of the reasons why the French authorities themselves hesitated to build a fort at Niagara was their fear that the western Indians would be drawn to the post but would trade with the Iroquois for English goods in preference to the more expensive, lower quality French merchandise.[39]

36. Pontchartrain to Vaudreuil, June 6, 1708, ibid., p. 813.

37. Clerambault d'Aigremont to Pontchartrain, November 14, 1708, in "Cadillac Papers," *Michigan Historical Society Collections* 33 (1904): 445, 441.

38. Vaudreuil and Raudot, Report on the Colonies, November 14, 1708, ibid., pp. 415, 415–16.

39. Ibid., p. 416.

These anxieties of the French did not prove to be justified. The Iroquois traders, though they persisted until the end of the colonial period, never reached the point of endangering the trade of either Canada or New York, and they never became successful enough to be described as middlemen. In fact, they did not become a very important element even within the Iroquois economy. The hunters continued to be the major source of the peltry that enabled the Iroquois families to purchase European goods. In all the years of peace after 1701, no Iroquois trader ever became well known among the New Yorkers as a businessman, although several diplomats and other leaders achieved recognition for their abilities. New Yorkers did not view the Iroquois as competitors and seldom gave any consideration to the traders among them. In one of the most significant statements indicating the limited size of the Iroquois trading establishment among the Five Nations, Lieutenant Governor Richard Ingoldsby told several sachems in 1709 that the French encroached "upon your Rights and Libertyes by building Forts upon your land against your wills, Possessing the Principall Passes and hunting Places, whereby all your hunting (your only Support) was rendered not only Precarious, but dangerous."[40]

Throughout the first half of the eighteenth century, Iroquois diplomats followed a foreign policy that militated against the possibility of their traders achieving middleman status. The policy of allowing the far Indians to pass through Iroquois country for commercial purposes may not have necessarily meant that Iroquois traders exerted little influence at the council fires but, rather, that the sachems were simply yielding to the inevitable. After the Five Nations had opened the door for the Ottawas to travel to Albany with peltry, the New York governors almost constantly pressured them to allow other tribes the same privilege. By increasing the number of Indians coming to British trading posts, the governors not only helped the colony's economy but also weakened the influence of the French among the western tribes. When deciding whether or not to grant one of the frequent English demands, the Iroquois had to weigh the effects of the decision on their economy against its influence on their military security.

In the first decade of the century the Iroquois hesitated to "open the path" for western tribes. Possibly they feared the economic consequences of doing so, but more likely they were irritated by Governor Cornbury's inept handling of Indian affairs. During this time, they did honor their agreement with the Ottawas, who readily took advantage of

40. Indian Conference, July 14, 1709, in Livingston Family Papers (microfilm), Franklin D. Roosevelt Library, Hyde Park, N.Y.

it.[41] Governor Robert Hunter, arriving at New York in 1710, vigorously cultivated friendly relations with the Five Nations, and almost immediately the road to Albany became available to a larger number of western tribes. Hunter not only stressed this issue at Indian conferences, but also sent missions to the villages of the Five Nations, requesting them to allow free passage for the western Indians through their territory.[42] To one of the British emissaries, Dekannissora promised, "We now assure you that we shall not in any wise hinder them, but promise to afford them every possible encouragement, and assist them forward . . . ."[43] The sincerity of his statement soon became apparent as the western Indians greatly increased their visits to Albany in the years near the end of Hunter's administration. By the 1720s the Iroquois were even sending out ambassadors to distant nations for the purpose of encouraging them to bring their peltry to the British.[44] Except for the possibility of trading with some of the tribes in the Ohio Valley, the Iroquois had clearly abandoned their hopes of establishing themselves as middlemen.

In giving up these aspirations, the Iroquois leaders were mainly concerned with the future security of their people. In the middle of the seventeenth century, they had been able to indulge in the dream of an economic empire, but within fifty years their very existence had been threatened. They now needed to adjust their policies accordingly. In 1701 they had established themselves as neutrals between the two European powers, and for more than half a century they attempted to use this neutrality to their best advantage. Allowing the western Indians to pass through their territory was an important part of this policy.

By promoting friendly relations with the western tribes, the Iroquois hoped to establish alliances with them in order to strengthen their bargaining position between the British and the French.[45] In a speech to the Iroquois sachems, Governor Hunter attempted to explain this situation: "it is for your advantage and security that the farr nations have a free passage throw your Countrey to come and trade here, you could not see throw it at first but the only way to strengthen you and us and

41. Herbert L. Osgood, *The American Colonies in the Eighteenth Century,* 4 vols. (New York, 1924–25; reprinted, Gloucester, Mass., 1958), 1: 476; Wraxall, *Abridgment,* ed. McIlwain, September 29, 1706, p. 48; Evert Wendell, Jr., Account Book, 1695–1726.

42. Proceedings of the Commissioners of Indian Affairs, July 17, 1716, in New York Colonial Manuscripts, 60: 122, New York State Library, Albany.

43. Hendrick Hansen, Journal of a mission to Onondaga, September 10–22, 1713, in *NYCD,* 5 :375.

44. Wraxall, *Abridgment,* ed. McIlwain, May 20, 1711, p. 87, passim.

45. Minutes of the Indian Commissioners, September 15, 1724, 1: 91.

weaken the Enemy is, to have as many brought into the Covenant Chain as possible . . . ."[46] The Iroquois understood the situation with far greater clarity than Hunter imagined, but their viewpoint differed considerably from his. At about the time of Hunter's speech, Dekannissora was advising his people that they must support neither the French nor the British, because if the Iroquois hoped for survival, they needed to maintain a balance of power between these two opponents. When the day came that they were no longer a significant factor in the struggle for North America, the prophetic Dekannissora warned that the British would enslave them as they had the Indians of southern New York and Long Island.[47]

Although the Iroquois continued to have closer relations with New York than with Canada, they recognized that both of these powers threatened their existence. In fact, they even harbored suspicions that the French and British might unite in a war of extermination against them so that, as they told their trusted friend Peter Schuyler, Europeans could "settle their Lands because Land is very scarce in Europe."[48] In describing the Iroquois attitude toward the struggle between France and Great Britain, Peter Wraxall, the Secretary of Indian Affairs between 1750 and 1759, explained, "Our Six Nations . . . are apprehensive that which ever Nation gains their Point will become their Masters not their deliverers—They dread the success of either and their ablest Politicians would very probably rather wish us to continue destroying each other than that either should be absolute conquerors . . . ."[49] After the conquest of Canada, Sir William Johnson likewise noted, "they did not appear to have wished that one power should swallow up the other, they were desirous to preserve a kind of equilibrium between us, and inclined occasionally to throw their weight into the lightest scale . . . ." Johnson concluded that they could not be blamed "for a way of thinking so exactly correspondent with that of the most Civilized Nations, for, (as they often declared) they saw, that the White people were for reducing them to nothing, that the views of both Nations tended to one and the same object . . . ."[50]

In order to maintain themselves as a significant weight in the balance of power, the Iroquois worked to rebuild their military strength. They

46. Indian Conference, August 16, 1710, in *NYCD*, 5: 221.
47. Colden, Account of a conference between Governor Burnet and the Five Nations, 1721, in *Colden Papers*, 1: 129.
48. Wraxall, *Abridgment*, ed. McIlwain, May 8, 1711, p. 83.
49. Peter Wraxall, "Some Thoughts Upon the British Indian Interest . . ." [January 9, 1756], in *NYCD*, 7: 18.
50. Johnson, "a Review of the progressive State of Trade . . ." [September 22, 1767], ibid., p. 958.

increased their population by remaining at peace and by inviting other peoples to live with them—the most notable being the adoption of the Tuscaroras of North Carolina in the third decade of the century, after which they became known as the Six Nations. By 1763 they had increased their numbers from a low of around 1100 warriors at the end of King William's War to approximately 2000.[51] Their policy of allowing the western Indians to peacefully travel through their lands was so successful that in 1740 they could report that "All the Indians which were formerly our enemies are now entered into the Covenant with us, almost as far as the river Mississippi."[52] The sachems must have been in complete agreement with Governor George Clinton when he told them in 1751 that, because of these policies, the Iroquois could command the respect of "all their Neighbors" who could "see and understand the Strength and numbers of your Brethren, all over this great Continent."[53] Naturally, the Iroquois hoped that the Europeans would have an equally high respect for their strength. They may have wanted Clinton to take the hint when they mentioned that with the aid of their allies they could "overcome any Enemy whatever."[54]

The diplomatic gains of Iroquois policy in these years outweighed any regrets that they might have had over giving up the possibility of achieving middleman status, but they did not view the passage of other tribes through their lands as being entirely an economic disadvantage. There were profits to be made from having so many foreigners traveling through their lands, and they seldom, if ever, disputed British assurances that peaceful relations with the western Indians would "prove profitable to you in Commerce."[55] Unfortunately, the nature of the trade that developed remains obscure, although at least part of it involved an exchange of provisions with the weary travelers in return for peltry.[56]

In addition to the trade with the western Indians, the Iroquois discovered several other ways of using the commercial relations between these tribes and the European colonies to their own economic advantage. Since the British and the French both sought to maintain the friendship of the Six Nations in order to carry on an undisturbed trade with the western Indians, the Iroquois obtained a considerable amount of merchandise

51. Johnson, "Present State of the Northern Indians . . . ," November 18, 1763, ibid., p. 582.

52. Indian Conference, August 12, 1740, ibid., 6: 178.

53. Indian Conference, July 6, 1751, ibid., p. 718.

54. Wraxall, *Abridgment*, ed. McIlwain, June 20, 1744, pp. 234–35.

55. New York Executive Council Minutes, June 9, 1720, vol. 12, New York State Library, Albany, hereafter cited as Council Minutes.

56. Minutes of the Indian Commissioners, November 23, 1730, in *NYCD*, 5: 911; Trelease, "The Iroquois and the Western Fur Trade," pp. 45–46.

from both sides in the form of presents. Many New York officials considered themselves victims of extortion, and as early as 1702 Governor Cornbury had told the Board of Trade that if the English could conquer New France, the "constant charge of presents to the Indians will cease, for then the Indians must depend upon you for what they want, so you may do with them as you shall think fit . . . ."[57]

Fortunately for the Iroquois, more than sixty years passed before they had to face the situation envisioned by Cornbury. In the meantime, the New York authorities recognized that the only method of preserving friendly relations with the Six Nations was "that of feeding them with presents, which the French never fail to give them yearly to intice them from us."[58] The presents, provided by both the colonial legislature and the British government, had to be given at every Indian conference, and the Iroquois expected each new governor to meet with them shortly after his arrival in the colony. Usually the smallest transactions between the Commissioners of Indian Affairs and the Indians required some presents, and at major conferences the total value often amounted to £1000, with gunpowder being the largest single item.[59]

Not only were the Iroquois able to obtain free supplies of merchandise, but they also received the services of blacksmiths from the French and British, who were anxious to have their representatives living among the Iroquois villages. For the Six Nations, these blacksmiths were a tremendous asset to their economy, and they constantly demanded that more of them be sent to live in their country. The Indians themselves seem to have initiated the process of receiving free repairs when they arrived at a conference called by Governor Hunter in 1710 with all of the broken guns and hatchets that they wanted repaired by the Albany blacksmiths.[60]

Although the Senecas were unable to prevent the establishment of a French fort at Niagara in 1720, they exacted a high price for this privilege by insisting that only they would have the right to carry goods over the portage. Through the use of this monopoly, the Senecas earned a considerable income by charging high prices to carry the goods of both Frenchmen and western Indians. Some of them even owned horses to

57. Cornbury to the Board of Trade, September 29, 1702, in *NYCD*, 4: 977–78.

58. Lieutenant Governor George Clarke to the Duke of Newcastle, December 30, 1742, ibid., 6: 223. On Indian presents, see Wilbur R. Jacobs, *Diplomacy and Indian Gifts: Anglo-French Rivalry Along the Ohio and Northwest Frontiers, 1748–1763* (Stanford, Calif., 1950).

59. John Champante to the Board of Trade [November 10, 1715?]; Board of Trade to the Privy Council, December 20, 1739, in *NYCD*, 5: 457, 6: 156; Council Minutes, July 28, 1720, vol. 12.

60. Indian Conference, August 14, 1710, in *NYCD*, 5: 220.

lighten their work.[61] Niagara, according to one Englishman, was "a Store house for bribery for the Indians, at which place the Senecas were taken particular notice."[62] To a lesser extent, the Oneidas procured a similar type of income by transporting goods over the portages between the Mohawk River and Lake Ontario, and they used threats of violence to force the traders to pay as much as three times the rate charged by the Palatine Germans who lived nearby.[63]

With these several methods of obtaining European goods in addition to their hunting trips every winter, the Iroquois assured themselves of a high standard of living that they could enjoy in peace. The diplomats had been successful in adjusting to the realities of the political and economic situation that developed after the great peace of 1701, and they were not willing to risk renewed warfare in an effort to achieve the elusive goal of establishing themselves as middlemen. Having been unable to fulfill their aspirations in over fifty years of violent conflict, they recognized that in their weakened condition they could not hope to turn back the ambitions of the European powers; they could only make the best of the situation. They succeeded so well in their efforts that Sir William Johnson could justly tell the Board of Trade in 1763: "The Indians, I do assure your Lordships are no wise inferior to us in sagacity and stratagem, qualities most essentially necessary in this Country . . . ."[64]

61. *Journal of the Votes and Proceedings of the General Assembly of the Colony of New York [1691–1765]*, 2 vols. (New York, 1764–66), October 29, 1751, 2: 318; Wraxall, *Abridgment,* ed. McIlwain, May 29, 1736, p. 196; Johnson to General Thomas Gage, January 27, 1764, in *Johnson Papers,* 4: 308–9; Peter Kalm, *Peter Kalm's Travels in North America,* ed. Adolph B. Benson, 2 vols. (New York, 1937), 2: 696.

62. Johnson to John Vaughan, April 18, 1765, in *Johnson Papers,* 11: 701.

63. Indian Conference, August 12, 1740, in *NYCD,* 6: 177; Council Minutes, June 18, 1754, vol. 23.

64. Johnson to the Board of Trade, September 25, 1763, in *NYCD,* 7: 561.

4

THE ALBANY MONOPOLY

WHENEVER THE IROQUOIS wanted to sell their furs or conduct negotiations with the British, they paddled down the Mohawk, pulled their canoes ashore at Schenectady, where the river ceased to be navigable, and traveled overland the remaining sixteen miles to Albany. For them, this city on the Hudson continued to be the center of diplomatic conferences with New York until the middle of the eighteenth century, and not until the founding of Oswego in the 1720s did it cease to be their market place. Although nearly all of their contact with the British colonies occurred at Albany, the Iroquois usually dealt not with Englishmen, but rather with Dutch citizens of the city, who remained the dominant influence in Indian affairs until the middle of the eighteenth century.

In the first hundred years of its existence, most of Albany's wealth came from the fur trade, and every wealthy inhabitant of the area owed much, if not all, of his fortune to this commerce. Even the local aristocracy, composed of men such as Peter Schuyler, Robert Livingston, and Kiliaen Van Rensselaer, who all owned vast tracts of land, depended on commercial relations with the Indians for their major source of income. Undeniably, the residents of Albany considered trade to be the most important factor in their lives, and they devoted much of their energy to business and to the protection of their commercial interests. Notoriously frugal, they seldom missed an opportunity to save a penny, and even their most personal correspondence usually contained references to business matters. In one short letter to his friend Jacob Wendell of Boston, for example, Cornelius Cuyler consoled him for the death of his son, Jacob, Jr., ordered some furniture, announced the marriage of his daughter Elizabeth to James Van Cortlandt, and asked Wendell to use his political influence in Massachusetts to arrange a business deal for himself.[1]

During the first two decades of English rule, therefore, the major

1. Cuyler to Jacob Wendell, March 21, 1754, in Cornelius Cuyler Letter Book, 1752–1764 (microfilm), American Antiquarian Society, Worcester, Mass.

concern of Albany officials was the protection of their trade from the residents of a new town several miles to the west. Although Albany did not have an official monopoly, the city's residents had gradually gained control of the major part of the colony's fur trade, and they were determined not to relinquish it. In 1661 a small group of farmers had settled on the fertile lands known as the Mohawk Flat and founded the town of Schenectady in a perfect position to intercept the Indians carrying furs to Albany, but the province had forbidden them to participate in the fur trade. Almost immediately, the Dutch governor, Peter Stuyvesant, received complaints that these farmers had "taken the liberty to sell strong liquor to the savages" in direct defiance of his orders.[2] To prevent this violation of the regulations under which the town was founded, he warned the people of Schenectady that their lands would not be officially surveyed until they signed a pledge promising "that we shall have no dealings with the savages."[3]

The farmers, displaying their intentions of also being traders, refused to sign the pledge on the grounds that other patents had been granted without such a self-denying proscription. Though agreeing to obey all "the published ordinances," they could not understand why they should be treated "in a different manner or with less consideration" than other residents of the province.[4] Arent Van Curler, a close friend of the Mohawks and founder of Schenectady, fully intended to do at least some fur trading and complained to Stuyvesant "that those who support themselves by agriculture ought not to have less than those who entirely support themselves by trade . . . ." Although agreeing that the people of his town would not sell liquor to the Indians, Van Curler argued that they should not be "prohibited from bartering any beavers from the Indians in exchange for bread, milk, the products of the soil or other allowable commodities . . . while there is no likelihood that within any conceivable time such trade with the Indians may be carried on at Shinnechtade as advantageously as by those of Fort Orange . . . ."[5] Such pleading did

2. Stuyvesant to Vice Director Johannes La Montagne, May 9, 1663, in *Documents Relative to the Colonial History of the State of New York*, ed. Edmund B. O'Callaghan and Berthold Fernow, 15 vols. (Albany, 1856–87), 13: 244, hereafter cited as *NYCD*. For a full account of this controversy, see Ruth L. Higgins, *Expansion in New York: With Especial Reference to the Eighteenth Century* (Columbus, Ohio, 1931), pp. 12–16. Also see John Romeyn Brodhead, *History of the State of New York*, 2 vols. (New York, 1859–71), 1: 732; and Edmund B. O'Callaghan, *History of New Netherland; or, New York Under the Dutch*, 2 vols. (New York, 1846–48; reprinted, Spartanburg, S.C., 1966), 2: 438–42.

3. Stuyvesant to La Montagne, May 9, 1663, in *NYCD*, 13: 244.

4. Petition of the settlers at Schenectady, May 18, 1663, ibid., p. 253.

5. Van Curler to Stuyvesant, May 21, 1663, in *Minutes of the Court of Albany,*

not change Stuyvesant's mind, but by the end of 1664 neither he nor the Dutch were in control of the province.

Although Schenectady's location made it impossible to completely keep the residents from fur trading, Albany, as long as the law was on its side, could prevent any major breaches of the trade regulations. Geographical necessity required most merchandise bound for the interior to pass through the city. The English conquest presented the possibility of a change in the law, but the conquerors had no extensive plans to reshape the economy of the colony. When Albany agreed to surrender terms, Governor Richard Nicolls provided the residents with official assurances that the people of Schenectady would not be allowed "to trade with the Indyans for Beaver."[6] In spite of continued English cooperation, the people of Albany remained uneasy, and frequent violations of the law in Schenectady did not help to relieve their anxieties.[7]

The greatest advantage enjoyed by Albany in struggling to protect its economy was that Schenectady lay within Albany County. Consequently, the city magistrates could enact restrictive ordinances and have them enforced by the sheriff. In 1675 Governor Edmund Andros formally sanctioned the legal powers of the city by establishing a general court consisting of five or more magistrates from Albany and Rensselaerswyck, the commander of the fort at Albany, and two or more magistrates from Schenectady.[8] Taking advantage of this recognition of their power, the city magistrates immediately passed an ordinance that required the inspection of all wagons traveling between Albany and Schenectady. Three years later they empowered the sheriff, who received a percentage of fines and confiscated goods, to enter houses in random searches for merchandise used in the Indian trade. In one instance, Sheriff Richard Pretty even searched the house of Jan Van Eps, a Schenectady magistrate, and seized some trading goods. Van Eps pleaded economic hardship and was allowed to dispose of his merchandise in Albany, but he was fined one hundred florins as a reward to Sheriff Pretty.[9]

In addition to establishing a general court for Albany County, Andros also pleased Albany residents by vigorously supporting their efforts to control traffic between their city and Schenectady.[10] He performed an

Rensselaerswyck and Schenectady, ed. A. J. F. Van Laer, 3 vols. (Albany, 1926–32), 3: 495–96, 496.

6. Articles of Agreement with Albany, October 10, 1664, in NYCD, 14: 559.

7. Minutes of the Court of Albany, ed. Van Laer, October 25, 1678, 2: 361–62.

8. Ibid., August 30, 1675, p. 24. Arthur James Weise, The History of the City of Albany, New York (Albany, 1884), p. 160.

9. Minutes of the Court of Albany, ed. Van Laer, December 9, 1675, October 25, 1678, November 22, 1676, 2: 57, 361, 370.

10. Ibid., June 26, 1676, p. 123.

even greater service by refusing to cooperate with the Van Rensselaers, who in 1678 had won approval in London of an English patent for their manor of Rensselaerswyck that would have included the city of Albany. Not only were the people of Albany disturbed by the prospects of having to pay rent to the Van Rensselaers, but they were also concerned about the part of the patent that included the land route between Albany and Schenectady.[11] "The rumor of such a remarkable change," wrote Nicholas Van Rensselaer, the main advocate of this claim, "immediately alarmed the Albanians, everyone being afraid of loss and damage to the beaver trade, which might be transferred to Schangeghtade . . . ."[12] The Albany magistrates vehemently protested to Andros, who assured them that "all Indian Trade is strictly Prohibited at Schaenhechtady as in all other Out Places." As for the land claims made by the Van Rensselaers, he eased their fears by telling them, "The Duke intends the family of Renselaers there just Rights formerly Enjoyed . . . but without wronging any others of which all Care and Regard shall be had and therefore the Court and officers are to take Care, there be no disturbance, or needlessee Expenses made by the Inhabitants upon Reports or Rumors to their Prejudice."[13] These were his true sentiments, for when he left the colony in 1681, Andros still had not executed the Van Rensselaer warrant.[14]

During Andros's administration, Albany succeeded in making its control of the trade more effective by placing restrictions on the outsiders who arrived at the beginning of each trading session to do business within the city walls. On August 7, 1676, the magistrates enacted an ordinance taxing the merchandise of the "several persons who come up the river to trade and sell in this city by the small measure . . . without their paying any charges, impost, taxes or assessments for the maintenance and support of this place . . . ."[15] Two years later, on July 2, 1678, the magistrates prohibited anyone except year-round residents of the city from engaging in the fur trade. In achieving this legal establishment of a monopoly, Albany had to pay a high price, as Andros appeased the New York City merchants by prohibiting Albany merchants from participating in overseas commerce. Though often accused of being shortsighted, the Albany merchants could see the effect of this prohibition on

11. S. G. Nissenson, *The Patroon's Domain* (New York, 1937), pp. 288–91, 303.

12. Nicholas Van Rensselaer to Jan Baptist Van Rensselaer, October 16, 1678, in *Correspondence of Maria Van Rensselaer, 1669–1689*, ed. A. J. F. Van Laer (Albany, 1935), p. 25.

13. *Minutes of the Court of Albany*, ed. Van Laer, October 31, 1678, 2: 363.

14. Nissenson, *Patroon's Domain*, p. 291.

15. *Minutes of the Court of Albany*, ed. Van Laer, August 7, 1676, 2: 137.

the economic future of the city, and they protested that it would result in "the entire ruin of this place."[16] Their dire prediction proved to be exaggerated, but this restriction on overseas trade did help to shape the economic development of the colony.

On the whole, the policies carried out by Edmund Andros were highly beneficial to the fur traders of Albany. They had not only established a complete monopoly, but had also developed the means for effectively prosecuting violators. Although they desired a stronger legal basis for the monopoly than simply the orders of Governors Nicolls and Andros, they had beaten back all the efforts of Schenectady to break it. The only immediate threat to the city's economic future was the possibility that the new governor, Thomas Dongan, might grant a favorable patent to the Van Rensselaer family.

If the citizens of Albany had apprehensions about Dongan, he put their minds at ease soon after his arrival in 1683. He strongly believed that Albany could be of extreme importance in preventing the French from forming alliances with the tribes of eastern North America and thus endangering the security of the English colonies. Accordingly, he sought to strengthen Albany, which at the time contained only about two thousand inhabitants.[17] Thus, when the Van Rensselaers asked him in 1684 to confirm the patent that included the city within Rensselaerswyck, Dongan took no action until the Van Rensselaer family agreed in 1685 not to ask either for the inclusion of Albany or for the strip of land running to Schenectady.[18]

Shortly after winning Albany's friendship by settling the patent dispute, Dongan took an ever more significant step in deciding the future of the city by granting it a charter on July 22, 1686, that gave Albany a more effective municipal government and guaranteed it a monopoly over the fur trade. Albany was raised from the status of town to city, with a mayor, recorder, town clerk, six aldermen, and six assistants, who were collectively to be described as "the mayor, aldermen, and commonality of the city of Albany." Several lesser officials included a treasurer and sheriff. Although Dongan filled all the offices temporarily, the charter provided for the election of the aldermen from their respective wards, the appointment of the mayor and sheriff by the governor, and the ap-

---

16. Ibid., July 2, August 23, 1678, April 30, 1679, pp. 336, 403, 406.

17. Arthur H. Buffinton, "The Policy of Albany and English Westward Expansion," *Mississippi Valley Historical Review* 8 (1922): 343–45; Population statistics of New York, in *Documentary History of the State of New-York*, ed. Edmund B. O'Callaghan, 4 vols. (Albany, 1850–51), 1: 468, hereafter cited as *New York Documentary History*.

18. Nissenson, *Patroon's Domain*, p. 203.

pointment of the recorder and town clerk by the Crown or by the governor if the government in England did not care to make a selection. The mayor and three or more aldermen along with three or more assistants constituted a common council with the power to make city ordinances "for the preservation of government, the Indian trade, and all other commerce."[19]

Before defining the extent of the fur trade monopoly, the charter—clearly showing Dongan's concern for the strategic importance of good Indian relations—explained the reasons for granting such a privilege to Albany. The document described at considerable length the advantages that the colony derived from confining the trade to one location and asserted that "orderly management" of the trade under the watchful eyes of the city magistrates was "the sole means" of remaining at peace with the Indians. "Whereas on the other hand, it has been no less evident, that whenever there has been any slackness or remissness in the regulation and keeping the Indian trade within the walls of the said city . . . this government has lost much of the reputation and management amongst the Indians, which it otherwise had and enjoyed." Consequently, Dongan, who apparently drafted much of the document himself, granted to Albany "the right, privilege . . . and advantage of the sole and only management of the trade with the Indians."[20]

The monopoly could hardly have been more complete. Only "actual inhabitants within the said city and within the now walls or stockadoes" could trade in Albany or "to the eastward, northward and westward thereof so far as his majesty's dominion here does or may extend." The city officials had complete power in deciding cases of disputed residency, and no one except "free citizens" of Albany could engage in any kind of "art, trade mystery or manual occupation" within the city. The fee for being accepted as a merchant of Albany amounted to £3 12s., and admission as an artisan required the payment of thirty-six shillings. No New Yorkers living outside of Albany could keep "in their houses or elsewhere, any Indian goods or merchandize" including beaver skins,

19. Albany Charter, in *Albany Chronicles*, ed. Cuyler Reynolds (Albany, 1906), pp. 90, 94–98. For more on the structure of the Albany government, see David A. Armour, "The Merchants of Albany, New York, 1686–1760" (Ph.D. diss., Northwestern University, 1965), pp. 1–10; and Peter Wraxall, *An Abridgment of the Indian Affairs Contained in Four Folio Volumes, Transacted in the Colony of New York, from the Year 1678 to the Year 1751*, ed. Charles H. McIlwain (Cambridge, Mass., 1915), pp. liii–lxi.

20. Albany Charter, in *Albany Chronicles*, ed. Reynolds, pp. 103–4. For Dongan's Indian policies, see Allen W. Trelease, *Indian Affairs in Colonial New York: The Seventeenth Century* (Ithaca, N.Y., 1960), pp. 176, passim; and Broadhead, *History of New York*, 2: 466–67, 474–96.

furs, gunpowder, lead, rum, and duffels, with the only exceptions being Indian corn, dressed deerskins, and venison.[21]

The charter also provided the city officials with all the machinery necessary to prevent circumvention of the law. Violators, who faced fines up to £20 and the confiscation of their merchandise, could be tried in Albany courts even if they had been trading in another county or in the wilderness. In order to plug even the smallest of possible loopholes, the charter prevented any colonial official from issuing a license for anyone to hunt in Albany County or in the wilderness without first obtaining the permission of an Albany magistrate.[22]

Albany's citizens, who paid Dongan £300 for his efforts, were delighted with the charter and wasted no time in putting it to use.[23] On September 14, 1686, the Common Council issued an ordinance that barred all outsiders in almost the same language as used in the charter. All trading had to be conducted within the city walls, and not even a resident of the city would be allowed to engage in trade with the Indians outside of the stockades. A violation of this section of the ordinance would result in a fine of £20. No one outside of the city could keep in their possession "Gunns, Strouds, Blanketts, Rumm, Pouder, Lead or other Indian Goods or Merchandizes whatsoever, on pain and penalty, of forfeiting" all of these articles with one-third of them going to the complainant or informer. To prevent the development of a class of bush-lopers, the equivalent of the French *coureurs de bois*, the Common Council ordered, "that no Person or Persons whatsoever within this Citty, shall send out or make use of any Broakers, whether Christians or Indians, in the management of the Indian Trade . . . ."[24]

In helping Albany to strengthen its commercial position, Governor Dongan must have been at least partly motivated by the need to construct a bulwark against the increasing competition from neighboring English colonies. The greatest outside problem came from Pennsylvania traders, who as early as the 1680s had pushed their way up the Susquehanna River into Iroquois country in search of peltry. In a message to the Iroquois, dated April 25, 1687, Governor Dongan complained, "I take it Verry ill that those Indians that the [Iroquois] Brethren hes given leave to live upon the Skuylkill and the Susquehanne should Bring Bever and Peltry to Philadelphia, which is Contrary to the agreement the

21. Albany Charter, in *Albany Chronicles*, ed. Reynolds, pp. 102–4.

22. Ibid., pp. 105, 107.

23. Thomas Dongan, Report on the state of the province [1687?], in *NYCD*, 3: 411; Weise, *History of Albany*, p. 203.

24. Joel Munsell, ed., *Annals of Albany*, 10 vols. (Albany, 1850–59), 8: 206–8, 208–9.

Brethren has made with us, I Desyre of the Brethren not to suffer any Indians to live there Longer but on Condition not To trade any where but at albany." If the Indians found any French or English traders "goeing up those Rivers" without a license from Dongan, he asked them to "bring them tyed to Albany," where the Iroquois would receive all the goods confiscated by the city magistrates.[25] The Iroquois agreed to honor his request but probably had little desire to anger the Pennsylvanians, with whom they made a commercial treaty several years later.[26]

In 1691 the New York Council and Richard Ingoldsby, who had taken over the reins of government after the death of the recently arrived Governor Henry Sloughter, wrote a letter to King William complaining about encroachments of East Jersey, Connecticut, and especially Pennsylvania on New York's trade. They maintained that the Iroquois Confederacy had surrendered "themselves and their lands" to the protection of Albany during the period of Dutch rule and afterwards to the Crown of England; therefore, "the Sinnekes Country in which is the Susquehannah River" and the rest of the Iroquois lands belonged within the colony of New York. They claimed that the Iroquois had "always reckoned themselves subjects to your Majesties Crowne, and are not willing to submitt or have any trade or Commerce with any of your Majesty's subjects but those att Albany . . . ."[27] Influenced by the knowledge that the fur trade either directly or indirectly provided England's only significant source of revenue from New York, the English authorities in 1692 ordered Benjamin Fletcher, the new governor, to prevent any other colony from transporting Indian goods up the Hudson River.[28]

Fletcher's instructions, of course, had no effect on the Pennsylvania traders, who continued to compete with New York throughout the rest of the colonial period. Nevertheless, Albany residents considered them to be a far lesser threat than the people of Schenectady. Although Pennsylvania occupied a position suitable for tapping the peltry sources of the Ohio Valley, the Albany traders were mainly concerned with obtaining the prime skins of beaver, marten, and otter from the Great Lakes region. The development of Oswego on Lake Ontario in the 1720s gave New York an even greater geographical advantage, and as long as the

25. Lawrence H. Leder, ed., *The Livingston Indian Records, 1666–1723* (Gettysburg, Pa., 1956), p. 112; Trelease, *Indian Affairs*, pp. 254–55.

26. Leder, ed., *Livingston Indian Records*, pp. 113–16; Wraxall, *Abridgment*, ed. McIlwain, p. 33.

27. Richard Ingoldsby and the Council to King William, August 6, 1691, in *New York Documentary History*, 1: 268.

28. Ibid., p. 269; Stephen Van Cortlandt and James Graham to William Blathwayt, 1687, in William Blathwayt Papers (microfilm), Colonial Williamsburg, Williamsburg, Va.

Pennsylvania traders did not establish a similar post, they could not hope to compete successfully for the northern furs. Their one possibility of obtaining a share of these pelts involved the establishment of strong trade agreements with the Iroquois Confederacy, but Pennsylvania's efforts along these lines were greatly hampered by the long tradition of conducting Indian affairs at Albany and by the insistence on the part of New York governors that any outside meddling with the Iroquois Confederacy constituted a threat to the military security of all the English colonies. As a consequence of these difficulties, the Pennsylvanians put much of their energy into developing a trade in deerskins.[29]

The people of Albany therefore seldom complained about threats from other colonies, but within three years after receiving their charter in 1686, they again had to face a serious intra-colonial challenge from Schenectady. When Jacob Leisler seized control of the New York government in 1689 during the confusion caused by the Glorious Revolution, he expected Albany citizens to recognize the legality of his position as most others had done. Instead, they formed themselves into a convention that decided to take no action until instructions arrived from England. In November 1689 Leisler sent a force of militia to Albany and, at the same time, gained support from Schenectady by offering the residents the privileges of flour bolting and fur trading. Greatly alarmed, Albany stiffened its resistance with the aid of some Connecticut troops, who had arrived to protect the frontier city against possible French attack.[30]

King William's War had a damaging effect on the growth of Albany, but it did literally wipe out Leisler's threat to the city's monopoly in the form of the French-Indian destruction of Schenectady on February 9, 1690. Albany residents claimed that responsibility for this massacre rested at the feet of Leisler, because the people of Schenectady had listened to his siren song rather than heeding the warnings or orders from

29. William Johnson, "a Review of the progressive State of the Trade . . ." [September 22, 1767], in *NYCD*, 7: 953. For an interpretation that puts more stress on the importance of Pennsylvania's competition with New York, see Gary B. Nash, "The Quest for the Susquehanna Valley: New York, Pennsylvania, and the Seventeenth-Century Fur Trade," *New York History* 48 (1967): 3–27. On the activities of James Logan in the early Pennsylvania trade, see Francis Jennings, "The Indian Trade of the Susquehanna Valley," *Proceedings of the American Philosophical Society* 110 (1966): 406–24.

30. Albany Convention Records, November 10, 1689; Hendrick Cuyler to the people of Schenectady, November 2, 1689, in *New York Documentary History*, 2: 66; Brodhead, *History of New York*, 2: 578–81, 585–89; Lawrence H. Leder, *Robert Livingston, 1654–1728, and the Politics of Colonial New York* (Chapel Hill, 1961), pp. 61–63. For a general account of the Leisler controversy, see Jerome R. Reich, *Leisler's Rebellion: A Study of Democracy in New York, 1664–1720* (Chicago, 1953).

Albany. "Thus," wrote Robert Livingston, "had Leyler perverted that poor people by his seditious letters now founde all bloody upon Shinnechtady streets, with the notions of a free trade, boalting &c and thus they are destroyed; they would not watch, and wher Capt: Sander commanded, there they threatened to burn him upon the fire, if he came upon the garde."[31] On the other hand, Leislerians claimed that Albany had in some way encouraged the Indians to attack Schenectady.[32]

At the end of King William's War Albany traders became concerned over the possibility of other townships being formed to the north and west of the city and becoming equally as troublesome as Schenectady. "The City of Albany," explained Robert Livingston, "always practised to hinder such settlements, because they have ingrossed the Indian trade in this Province, and having built large houses and made good farms and settlements near to Albany care not to leave them . . . and will not suffer others to goe beyond them to intercept the trade . . . ."[33] The people of Albany were particularly upset when Governor Benjamin Fletcher in 1697 granted a patent to Evert Bancker, Dirk Wessels, Godfrey Dellius, William Pinhorne, and Peter Schuyler for lands that included a stretch along the Mohawk River two miles on each side and fifty miles long. In addition, they opposed a grant to Hendrick Van Renssalaer for lands at the Indian village of Scaticook to the north of the city, where he would be in a perfect position to intercept furs on the way to Albany from Montreal.[34]

Early in 1698 the Albany magistrates, knowing that Fletcher was soon to be replaced by the Earl of Bellomont, opened fire in a battle to abrogate the grant of the Mohawk lands, which threatened not only their monopoly, but also the good relations of the colony with the entire Iroquois Confederacy. They faced formidable opposition. Peter Schuyler, extremely influential among the Iroquois, had been Albany's mayor from 1686 to 1694 and was followed in that office a year later by Evert Bancker, who in turn was succeeded by Dirk Wessels. Domine Godfrey Dellius, who had built up a following among the Mohawks due to his missionary work, held the influential post of minister in the Dutch Re-

31. Robert Livingston to Edmund Andros, April 14, 1690, in *NYCD*, 3: 708. For the details on the Schenectady massacre, see Brodhead, *History of New York*, 2: 606–12; and William Smith, Jr., *The History of the Late Province of New-York from Its Discovery to the Appointment of Governor Colden in 1762*, 2 vols. (New York, 1829–30), 1: 90–92.

32. Jacob Leisler and the Council to Johannes de Bruyn and others, March 4, 1690, in *NYCD*, 3: 702.

33. Robert Livingston to the Board of Trade, May 13, 1701, ibid., 4: 874.

34. Board of Trade to the Privy Council, October 19, 1698, ibid., p. 391; Munsell, ed., *Annals of Albany*, 3: 32, 34–35.

formed Church of Albany, and William Pinhorne was a member of both
the New York Council and the Supreme Court. Unintimidated by this
imposing array of politicians but considerably intimidated by their
angry constituents, the aldermen, according to Mrs. Robert Livingston,
"summoned the minister and Dirk Wessels to the courthouse and asked
them if they wanted to transfer the patent to the town, but they refused
. . . and threatened to establish a trading company there."[35] After several
more fruitless discussions with Schuyler, Dellius, and Wessels, the
Common Council on February 17 passed a resolution appointing Henry
Hansen and David Schuyler as the city's agents "to goe for Yorke" and
seek a redress of their grievances against this patent, which was "so
Destructive to the gennerall good of this Place." Every member of the
Common Council except Hendrick Van Rensselaer and Dirk Wessels
signed the resolution.[36]

Hansen and Schuyler received no satisfaction when they presented
a petition to Fletcher, but shortly after Governor Bellomont's arrival in
April, he promised to give them a hearing. Upon receiving this agreeable
news, the Common Council strengthened the prestige of their delegation
in New York by replacing Hansen and Schuyler with Robert Livingston
and Johannes Janse Bleeker, the recorder.[37] At this point, Wessels and
Peter Schuyler relinquished their claim to the grant and thus did much
to redeem themselves in the eyes of their neighbors while at the same
time weakening the position of the other claimants.[38] Livingston apparently declined the appointment, and was replaced by Ryer Schermerhorn, who along with Bleeker presented Bellomont with a petition on
June 6, 1698, claiming that the land grant would force the Mohawks to
move to Canada as allies of the French: "Then in what imminent danger
must the Provence be in upon another warr, if those that fought our
Battles for us become our Enemies . . . ." The petition concluded by
asking Bellomont either to intercede "with his Majestie for the vacateing
the said grant" or risk the danger of alienating the Indians and destroying
Albany's economy.[39]

35. Alida Livingston to Robert Livingston (in Dutch), January 25, 1698, in
Livingston Family Papers (microfilm), Franklin D. Roosevelt Library, Hyde Park,
N.Y., quoted in Leder, Robert Livingston, p. 127.

36. Munsell, ed., Annals of Albany, 3: 31–32.

37. Ibid., p. 33.

38. Bellomont, Account of a meeting with Godfrey Dellius, August 2, 1698, in
Calendar of State Papers, Colonial Series, America and West Indies, ed. W. N.
Sainsbury et al., 43 vols. to date (London, 1860–), 16: 436, hereafter cited as
Calendar of State Papers.

39. Memorial of J. Janse Bleeker and Ryer Schermerhorn, June 6, 1698, in
NYCD, 4: 330, 330–31.

Bellomont then decided to view the situation at closer range and traveled to Albany in July for a conference with the Iroquois, who at first treated him very coldly. He attributed this "cold behavior and doggedness of the Indians" to the schemes of Dellius, who in 1696, along with Schuyler, Bancker, and Wessels, had been conveniently appointed by Fletcher as the only Commissioners of Indian Affairs.[40] After winning the confidence of the Indians, Bellomont learned from some Mohawk sachems that Dellius had fraudulently obtained a deed for the lands by leading them to believe that he and the others would hold this territory "in trust for the use of them and their posterity, and to hinder the said land being disposed of to other hands, that would probably dispossesse them thereof . . . ."[41] At the end of the conference, Bellomont promised to have the patent vacated, and in 1699 the colonial legislature passed an act to this effect.[42]

Although the act vacating the patent was not enforced until ten years later, Dellius and his friends gave up their efforts to acquire the western trade. Albany also succeeded in overcoming the threat of Van Rensselaer's patent to the north, which included five hundred acres near the Indian village of Scaticook that had been granted to the city of Albany by the charter of 1686. The people of Albany hoped that the various tribes known as River Indians and wandering tribesmen from New England or Canada would permanently settle in that region, where they would act as a buffer against possible war parties traveling down the Lake Champlain route into New York. Albany officials also complained that "if Private men shall setle there than the trade of the Toune with those Indians is Ruined."[43] It went without saying that much of their concern over Scaticook involved the possibility that with the ending of the war these Indians could be used as carriers in developing a lucrative trade with Montreal. In May 1698 the Common Council offered either to give Van Rensselaer £50 for his claims to the six square miles or to let him have fifty acres near Scaticook in exchange for his patent rights and an agreement "that he does not setle it before the Citty, setle theres." The Common Council accepted his counter offer of £100 for his claims in the area, but disagreement on a minor issue prevented the bargain from being concluded. Finally, in August 1699 the city officials

---

40. Instructions from Benjamin Fletcher, August 10, 1696; Bellomont to the Board of Trade, September 14, 1698, ibid., pp. 177, 362–63.

41. Bellomont to the Board of Trade, September 14, 1698, ibid., p. 363.

42. Wraxall, *Abridgment*, ed. McIlwain, July 27, 1698, p. 30; *Colonial Laws of New York from the Year 1664 to the Revolution*, 5 vols. (Albany, 1894–96), May 16, 1699, 1: 412–17, hereafter cited as *Laws*.

43. Munsell, ed., *Annals of Albany*, 3: 34–35, 35.

purchased the patent from Van Rensselaer and thus succeeded in protecting their northern flank for many years to come.[44]

In the first two years of Bellomont's administration, the people of Albany actively supported his land policies, but many of them turned against him in 1700, when he unveiled a plan to develop a forest products industry and to exploit the fur trade more effectively through a policy of westward expansion. One of the most important features of this plan was the building of a fort in Onondaga country, and Bellomont immediately ran into opposition from both Albany and the Iroquois. He blamed the reluctance of the Iroquois on the influence of Schuyler and his disgruntled partners in the aborted land deal, but he was probably mistaken, as these men certainly did not oppose westward expansion. The Iroquois had their own reasons for opposing a fort that would have been built two hundred miles into the wilderness near the central council fires at Onondaga, where the Confederacy held its conferences and entertained ambassadors from other tribes. Many prominent citizens in Albany sent Bellomont a petition asking that the forts in Schenectady and their own city be repaired before he began any other expensive projects. Greatly underestimating the cost of building such a fort, Bellomont requested a grant of £1500 from the New York assembly. At first, the legislators seemed reluctant and only appropriated £1000, with the provision that commissioners be appointed to take charge of the fort's construction. Later, they became more cooperative by providing Bellomont with the additional £500 and eliminating the requirement of appointing construction supervisors.[45]

Whether or not the fur trade would be conducted at the Onondaga fort was a question that concerned both Albany and the Iroquois. Although maintaining that the trade would be confined to Albany and assuring the Indians that the fort was only for their protection, Bellomont would not have opposed extending the fur trade to this post had such a move proved advantageous to his imperial plans. In fact, he told the Board of Trade that since his fort could be reached by river from Lake Ontario, the far Indians would be able to travel over the lake in order to "trade at our Fort there, in spight of our Five Nations."[46] Bellomont may or may not have been implying that the Iroquois planned to open a trade with the far Indians themselves. He did know, however, that they opposed a trading post in the wilderness and favored keeping

44. Ibid., pp. 34–35, 55–56.

45. Bellomont to the Board of Trade, October 17, November 28, 1700, in *NYCD*, 4: 716, 782–83; *Laws*, August 9, November 2, 1700, 1: 432–33, 445–46.

46. Indian Conference, August 28, 1700; Bellomont to the Board of Trade, October 17, 1700, in *NYCD*, 4: 731–33, 717.

the fur trade confined to Albany, because they claimed that whenever traders came into their country "wee must pay a Bever skin for a few spoons full of rum, and a Bever for a pair of childrens stockings."[47] If an outpost had been completed, a fur trade probably would have developed there, but any immediate hopes of building the fort died with Bellomont in the early spring of 1701. Part of the money appropriated for the project went into repairs of the fortifications in Albany County, and nearly a quarter of a century passed before the Albany traders again had to concern themselves with the possible effects of a wilderness trading post.[48]

During Queen Anne's War, which broke out a year after Bellomont's death, the people of New York managed to establish an unofficial neutrality between themselves and Canada. Thus, instead of having to fight off Indian attacks, Albany continued to nurture the trade with Montreal that had been renewed and greatly expanded at the end of the first intercolonial war. In all probability, Albany merchants throughout Queen Anne's War received the majority of their furs from Canada. Although the Dutch fur traders kept few records concerning their sources of peltry, the estimates of the French authorities in the early years of the century were that from one-half to two-thirds of all beaver skins purchased from the Indians in Canada were smuggled out of the colony. At this time, Albany's only major source of peltry from the west came in the canoes of the Iroquois, who did not begin to allow the far Indians, except the Ottawas, to travel through their territory until after 1710, when Governor Robert Hunter encouraged them to grant this privilege. In the years after Queen Anne's War, the number of western Indians coming to Albany increased greatly. At the same time, the Canadian government opened an attack on the Albany-Montreal trade, which was illegal in Canada, by taking such measures as stationing troops along the shores of Lake Champlain during the trading season. Naturally, many Albany residents then began to give greater consideration to the trade with western Indians.[49]

As increasingly large numbers of canoes pulled ashore at Schenectady, with strange Indians looking for a place to sell their furs, the town's residents sought ways of turning this situation into profits for themselves. As a result, Albany launched a vigorous campaign to protect its monopoly. In 1717 the Common Council reissued the ordinance affirming the

47. Indian Conference, August 31, 1700, ibid., p. 741.
48. Nanfan to the Board of Trade, October 20, 1701; Cornbury to the Board of Trade, July 12, 1703, ibid., pp. 921, 1064.
49. Jean Lunn, "The Illegal Fur Trade out of New France, 1713–1760," *Canadian Historical Association Report, 1939* (1939), pp. 61–76.

city's monopoly privileges and specifically asserted in the same words used in 1686 that only inhabitants of Albany could participate in the trade.[50] In this year, Albany also tightened the regulations concerning the transportation of Indians to the city after they reached the end of navigable waters at Schenectady, where the residents made some extra money each spring by using their wagons to carry the Indians and their furs over the last sixteen miles of their journey. The citizens of Albany complained that not only did the farmers charge the Indians for this service, but also managed to get "an extravagant price" from the traders by driving the Indians to particular houses. Consequently, the Common Council prohibited the drivers from bringing the western Indians any closer to the city than the houses that served as living quarters for the tribesmen on the hill outside of town. As for the Iroquois, who in many cases were exempt from the law requiring Indians to lodge themselves outside of the city, the new regulation required the wagoners to discharge them at least five hundred yards from the stockades. Several years later, the Common Council established a price of nine shillings as the charge for carrying Indians from Schenectady to Albany.[51] For the most part, these ordinances concerning transportation reflected Albany's desire to prevent Schenectady from draining away a percentage of the profits, but to some extent the regulations answered Indian complaints that the wagoners cheated and overcharged them.[52]

In 1719 Albany residents witnessed the first breach in the legal barricades they had so carefully constructed to protect their monopoly. Their difficulties started when the sheriff seized a hogshead of rum from Johannes Myndertse, who carried on a trade with the Indians at Schenectady. Gilbert Livingston, the son of Robert Livingston and the farmer of the excise in New York, went before the assembly with a complaint that such actions limited the amount of revenue that could be raised from the liquor excise. Livingston may have been following the orders of his father, who wanted to expand New York's western frontier. Declaring that Albany's seizure of the rum was "illegal and of pernicious Consequence, and an Obstruction to the Farming the Excise in that Part of the Province," the assembly resolved that the Albany officials could not legally seize liquor from anyone in Schenectady who had a license to sell it.[53]

50. Munsell, ed., *Annals of Albany*, 7: 67–68.
51. Ibid., pp. 64–65, 8: 281.
52. Minutes of the Commissioners of Indian Affairs (microfilm), May 31, 1723, 1: 28–30, in Public Archives of Canada, Ottawa.
53. *Journal of the Votes and Proceedings of the General Assembly of the Colony of New York [1691–1765]*, 2 vols. (New York, 1764–66), June 25, 1719, 1: 438.

Angered by this setback, the magistrates in December passed another ordinance reasserting their monopoly rights.[54] Less than a year later, they received an entirely new opportunity for combating the Schenectady menace. In November 1720 Governor William Burnet succeeded in securing a law prohibiting the export of Indian trading goods to Canada. Under this new law, which carried a penalty of up to £100, it became illegal for anyone to transport trading goods to the north of Albany.[55] Schenectady, though to the west of Albany, is also located slightly to the north, and Albany traders quickly realized that the new law could be used against their competitors. Possibly fearing Burnet's wrath, the magistrates at first seemed reluctant to use the law to their advantage. Nevertheless, Philip Livingston, another of Robert's sons, who was just beginning to rise in colonial politics, did not dare to sell to a customer in Schenectady, "for I may easely know what joy there would be if I should be Catched in such trade . . . ."[56]

Livingston's caution proved to be justified. In the late summer of 1721 the magistrates sent Sheriff Henry Holland to Schenectady, where he seized a quantity of strouds from one of the traders, who was then convicted of violating the law against trading with Canada and ordered to pay the full penalty of £100. Outraged by this blatant attempt of Albany to turn the law to its special advantage while many of its citizens were violating it themselves, Burnet intervened in the case, and the offender escaped without paying any part of the fine. In answer to this rebuff, the Common Council sent Burnet a petition, requesting that he "lett the Law have its course, which if not duely observed we humbly conceive will tend to the ruin and distruction of the Inhabitants of the said City . . . ." [57] Burnet paid little attention to their pleas, and the Albany officials did not again use this law against the residents of Schenectady.

Realizing that they could not expect any assistance from provincial authorities, the undaunted Albany magistrates continued their efforts to harrass the Schenectady traders. In April 1723 they again issued the ordinance prohibiting outsiders from trading with the Indians, and this time they specifically provided "that no person or persons whatsoever at the Township of Schinectady" could participate in the trade. To demonstrate that the new ordinance was not an idle threat, the Common Council on May 18 ordered the sheriff "to make diligent search in all

54. Munsell, ed., *Annals of Albany*, 8: 239.

55. *Laws*, November 19, 1720, 2: 9–10.

56. Philip Livingston to Robert Livingston, February 8, 1721, in Livingston Family Papers.

57. Munsell, ed., *Annals of Albany*, 8: 269.

houses barns warehouses . . . and to seize all Bever, Peltry or other Indian comodities as also all Trading Guns, Strowds, Blankets, Rum, Powder, Lead or other Indian goods . . . ."[58]

While conducting this spring offensive in 1723, the Albany officials again ran afoul of Johannes Myndertse, who had caused them so much embarrassment four years later. On June 15 Johannes E. Wendell and Robert Roseboom swore under oath that two days earlier they had seen "Indians with beaver and Peltry" enter Myndertse's house. Having failed to learn their lesson about tangling with this pugnacious Schenectady trader, the magistrates immediately issued a warrant for his arrest.[59] Without hesitation, Myndertse confessed to having Indians in his house for the purpose of trading with them, but refused to pay the fine of £10. The magistrates then ordered the sheriff to lock Myndertse in the city jail until he agreed to pay the fine. Obtaining his release through a writ of *habeas corpus* from the Supreme Court, Myndertse then proceeded to sue the Albany aldermen in the same court for "trespass and false imprisonment."[60] The case dragged on for several years, but finally the Supreme Court decided in his favor, and by the beginning of the trading season in 1727 Albany's monopoly had reached its end.[61]

In reality, the decision of the Supreme Court against the monopoly was anticlimactic, because for several years the Indian traders from both Schenectady and Albany had been conducting their business activities at Oswego on Lake Ontario. Some of the larger merchants became suppliers for the Oswego traders, and others continued to trade with Montreal. Increasingly, however, the large fur merchants turned to other business pursuits and longed for the day when their investments on the exposed frontier would be secure from the French menace to the north.

58. Ibid., p. 282.
59. Ibid., p. 286. For more on the controversy involving Myndertse, see Armour, "Merchants of Albany," pp. 158–61.
60. Munsell, ed., *Annals of Albany*, 8: 287–89.
61. Ibid., 9: 16; Armour, "Merchants of Albany," p. 161.

5

TRADE REGULATIONS AND

FRONTIER SECURITY

DURING THE FIRST HALF-CENTURY of colonization, the city officials of Albany handled most of the colony's Indian affairs routinely as matters of little more than local concern, and commercial relations with the Iroquois Confederacy, complicated by the involvement of French Canada, compelled the people of Albany to develop a certain amount of skill in diplomacy. The larger questions of imperial policy, however, did not trouble them greatly until after the arrival of Governor Thomas Dongan in 1683 and, a short time later, the outbreak of war with France. Dongan's policies, involving the use of the fur trade to acquire Indian allies, quickly propelled New York into a leading role in the struggle with France for control of North America. Never again could New Yorkers view the Iroquois Confederacy as simply a source of peltry, and Albany officials soon began to consider the regulation of the trade as simply a part of their overall policy to achieve military security.

Thus the fur trade became irretrievably tied to questions of imperial politics and frontier security. Due to their exposed position, the residents of Albany were inclined to put the greatest stress on the latter. Never feeling very comfortable as Great Britain's most advanced outpost in the imperial conflict with France, the Albany Dutch provided an indispensable service in regulating the colony's Indian affairs until the middle of the eighteenth century. Throughout these years, the Iroquois received constant inducements from French emissaries to ally themselves with Canada; but Albany officials, despite their limited resources and lack of support from other New Yorkers, succeeded in maintaining the friendship of this powerful Indian confederation.

Long before the outbreak of the first intercolonial war, the Dutch leaders of Albany had come to recognize the necessity of good relations with the Indians and thus had provided regulations to protect them from overzealous traders and frontier rogues. Consequently, upon receiving the city's charter from Dongan in 1686, the Albany Common Council passed a comprehensive regulatory ordinance on September 14 that not only contained provisions to protect the monopoly but also established the rules by which the fur trade was to be regulated for about forty years. To a large extent, the ordinance of 1686 was simply a compilation of rules that had been developed over the years. Although the city officials placed emphasis on maintaining orderliness in the commerce that was confined within the city walls, they also designed the regulations to give the Indians some protection in their desire to receive a "good pennysworth."

One of the problems concerning the competition among the individual traders resulted from their efforts to compete for customers "by making great promises of gifts and presents" to the Indians. The ordinance of 1686, therefore, prohibited any merchant or trader from giving any presents worth over ten shillings.[1] An even greater problem occurred when Indians arriving in the city were immediately confronted by a swarm of traders, ready to use practically any means of persuading them to do business at a particular place.[2] The ordinance, therefore, declared that upon the arrival of Indians no one could "addresse themselves or speake to them . . . concerning Trade" and no trader could "entice them either within or without the gates of the said Citty, by Signs or oyrwise howsoever, to trade with themselves or other Persones . . . ." If a trader disobeyed this law while outside of the city, he could receive a fine of £10, but only six shillings for doing so within the walls.[3]

Although the ordinance prohibited any commercial transactions after the ringing of the church bell at eight in the evening, it inexplicably failed to mention the standard rule against the lodging of Indians in the houses of the inhabitants, where a night of tippling often resulted in the cheating of the guests. Having as recently as 1684 renewed the prohibition against allowing Indians to sleep within the city, it seems unlikely that the magistrates intended to abandon this regulation, and in 1689 they passed a law that went so far as to prevent the traders from bringing any Indians, except sachems, Mohawks, and members of small neighboring tribes, into their houses with peltry at any time. Indians could sleep in Albany homes from the first of December to the first of

1. *Minutes of the Court of Albany, Rensselaerswyck and Schenectady*, ed. A. J. F. Van Laer, 3 vols. (Albany, 1926–32), July 5, 1681, 3: 143; Joel Munsell, ed., *Annals of Albany*, 10 vols. (Albany, 1850–59), 8: 209–12.
2. *Minutes of the Court of Albany*, ed. Van Laer, July 5, 1681, 3: 143.
3. Munsell, ed., *Annals of Albany*, 8: 208.

April, but during the trading season they had to stay in the dwellings provided for them on the hill outside the city.[4]

The Albany Common Council "had found by experience" that violations of trade laws were difficult to prosecute, because most of the illegal business transactions were conducted in secrecy unknown to anyone "butt the delinquents themselves or Indians," whose testimony was not "valid in law." Therefore, they made a provision in the ordinance of 1686 that allowed an Indian to give information against a trader to a magistrate, who would then call the offender in and ask him to take an oath that he had not broken the law. If he refused to do so, a certificate of this refusal from the magistrate could be entered in court as positive proof of his guilt. The ordinance also provided that even though there might not be "any legal proof of delinquency" a Christian could make an accusation if there was "a violent presumption" that the man might be guilty. Thereupon, the fur trader would be called upon to take an oath, the refusal of which would result in conviction of the offense.[5]

These regulatory sections of the ordinances of 1686 and 1689 provided the Albany officials with a legal foundation for building the city into an orderly market place. Yet, critics of the Albany Dutch have depicted the city as an ugly quagmire of avaricious merchants, corrupt officials, and brutish traders, whose greatest pleasures in life came from beating drunken Indians. Few groups of people in the history of North America have been so severely vilified by their neighbors as were the residents of Albany. "It is hardly possible," wrote Peter Wraxall, "to keep ones Pen within the Bounds of Moderation, when these Vermin come in ones way."[6] Although much of the criticism stemmed from Albany's contact with the French traders in Canada, even more of it involved their alleged mistreatment of the Indians, which supposedly made it difficult for New York authorities to conduct Indian affairs in the best interests of the English colonies. During the eighteenth century, nearly every commentator upon life in Albany criticized the Dutch for the methods they used in their commercial relations with the Indians.

Robert Livingston, who married Alida Schuyler Van Rensselaer and acquired much of his fortune through the fur trade at Albany, became their earliest prominent critic. In 1701 he lamented that the government of the province had fallen "into the hands of the meanest of the people,

---

4. Ibid., 2: 108–9; *Minutes of the Court of Albany*, ed. Van Laer, June 11, 1684, 3: 462.

5. Munsell, ed., *Annals of Albany*, 8: 212–13.

6. Peter Wraxall, *An Abridgment of the Indian Affairs Contained in Four Folio Volumes, Transacted in the Colony of New York, from the Year 1678 to the Year 1751*, ed. Charles H. McIlwain (Cambridge, Mass., 1915), p. 135n.

most of a foreign nation, who are prejudiced against the English, and strangers to government, and the richest and most considerable part of the people turned out of all offices in government."[7] Ten years later he allied himself with Governor Robert Hunter, who described the Albany traders as a "vile race," and in 1720, as speaker of the assembly, Livingston became a strong supporter of Governor William Burnet in his efforts to abolish the trade between Montreal and Albany.[8]

Cadwallader Colden, one of Burnet's closest advisers, moved to New York in 1718 and shortly afterwards also began a campaign of vilification against Albany that lasted for more than half a century. He never relented in his accusations that the Albany Dutch were "a low ignorant set of mankind who were capable of no other views but that of promoting their private profit in Trade and which they have done by the most shamefull means so as to become contemptible in the eyes of the Indians."[9] On one occasion, he confided to a friend that "strong proofs remain still in being in their families" that "sometimes when an Indian came into some of their houses to trade rather than that he should go to try the market at a neighbours house they would suffer the Indian to turn into bed to their wives." According to Colden, these "particular facts" could not be made public because of the delicate nature of the subject.[10]

For a while in the 1730s men with such visibly hostile views toward Albany did not play important roles in New York politics, but in the next decade Colden joined forces with William Johnson, who had risen to prominence as a fur trader on the Mohawk River and who eventually became northern Superintendent of Indian Affairs. Although Johnson sometimes made unkind statements about his Dutch neighbors, he never matched the vitriolic prose of Peter Wraxall, who was his close friend and, as Secretary of Indian Affairs, wrote an abridgment of New York's Indian records that was well spiced with footnotes denouncing the Dutch fur traders. "The People of Albany," he declared, "are extremely Ignorant and Illiterate and so enslaved to the love of Money that they

· 7. Robert Livingston to the Board of Trade, May 13, 1701, in *Documents Relative to the Colonial History of the State of New York*, ed. Edmund B. O'Callaghan and Berthold Fernow, 15 vols. (Albany, 1856–87), 4: 877, hereafter cited as *NYCD*.

8. Robert Hunter to the Board of Trade, September 29, 1715, ibid., 5: 436; Lawrence H. Leder, *Robert Livingston, 1654–1728, and the Politics of Colonial New York* (Chapel Hill, 1961), pp. 252–55.

9. Colden to Governor William Shirley, July 25, 1749, in *The Letters and Papers of Cadwallader Colden*, 10 vols., New-York Historical Society *Collections*, 50–56 (1917–23), 67–69 (1934–35) (New York, 1918–36), 4: 126, hereafter cited as *Colden Papers*. For the only biography of Colden, see Alice M. Keys, *Cadwallader Colden: A Representative Eighteenth Century Official* (New York, 1906).

10. Colden to Peter Collinson, May –, 1742, in *Colden Papers*, 2: 259.

have no other Principle of Action." Although claiming in one footnote not to be conscious of "any ungrounded Prejudice," he described the Albany residents on another page as "Dutch Reptiles" who "considered nothing but their present profit, and were animated by no Views to Posterity, which is the genuine Character of true Dutchmen."[11]

Most of the Albany critics, including Robert Livingston, Colden, Johnson, Wraxall, and governors Hunter, Burnet, and Clinton, were identified with a faction in New York politics that advocated an aggressive policy to meet the threat presented by French expansion in the interior of North America. Much of their dislike for the Dutch resulted from their belief that these businessmen actively worked to subvert such a policy; but in view of their obvious ethnic prejudices and their connection with a particular political faction, their criticism was scarcely disinterested. Nevertheless, the testimony of at least two other critics —Philip Livingston and Peter Kalm—seems to carry a great deal more weight.

As the son of Robert Livingston, Philip might have become a leading member of the imperial faction in New York politics, but he had been educated for a career in business, and even during his father's lifetime he demonstrated more enthusiasm for building his fortune than for opposing commercial relations with the French.[12] In the late 1740s he became one of Governor Clinton's severest political opponents. Though never criticizing anyone for being Dutch, Livingston considered many of the fur traders to be "unreasonable brutes," and in 1737 he thought about abandoning his business as a fur merchant, "for a man cant do any thing with pleasure while those one trades with have and do use all the black art they are Master of to Cheat and deceive as if they had no Conscience nor Religion even much worse than our Savages."[13] Philip Livingston's correspondence indicates that he was usually courteous and agreeable toward his associates, so his comments should be viewed as more than just everyday grumblings from an ill-tempered merchant.

Because of his clear attempts to be fair, the statements against Albany by Peter Kalm, the Swedish naturalist, who toured New York in the mid-eighteenth century, add considerable weight to the body of evidence indicating the disreputable character of these fur traders: "The avarice,

11. Wraxall, *Abridgment*, ed. McIlwain, pp. 132n, 154n, 180n.

12. Lawrence H. Leder, "Robert Livingston's Sons: Preparation for Futurity," *New York History* 50 (1969): 242; Philip Livingston to Robert Livingston, March 15, May 15, 1724, August 25, 1725, in Livingston Family Papers (microfilm), Franklin D. Roosevelt Library, Hyde Park, N.Y.

13. Philip Livingston to Storke and Gainsborough, July 21, 1735, July 14, 1737, in Miscellaneous Manuscripts, vol. 5, New York State Library, Albany.

selfishness and immeasurable love of money of the inhabitants of Albany are very well known throughout all North America, by the French and even by the Dutch, in the lower part of New York Province . . . . I likewise found that the judgment which people formed of them was not without foundation." As for the methods that they used to cheat the Indians, Kalm stated, "The merchants of Albany glory in these tricks, and are highly pleased when they have given a poor Indian, a greater portion of brandy that he can stand, and when they can, after that, get all his goods for mere trifles." Although Kalm may have been influenced by his brief friendship with William Johnson, his other comments indicate that he had no bias against the Dutch people and actually had a good deal of respect for them. In an effort to explain the behavior of the Albany residents, he argued that possibly during the early Dutch period "a pack of vagabonds" may have been sent up the Hudson in order to establish an outpost in the wilderness and to get them away from the better colonists. "I cannot in any other way account for the difference between the inhabitants of Albany and other descendants of so respectable a nation as the Dutch, who are settled in the lower part of New York province. The latter are civil, obliging, just in prices, and sincere . . . well meaning and honest and their promises may be relied on."[14]

In spite of all the criticism leveled against them, the Dutch residents of Albany made no effort to defend themselves, and as the historian Arthur Pound succinctly explained, "Being merchants, they were content to say it in ink on their ledgers and so left no apologies."[15] Consequently, the only objective way to evaluate the Albany Dutch is to measure the criticism directed against them by their actions: their commercial contacts with the Indians, their administration of Indian affairs, and their attitudes toward the struggle with France.

All too frequently the majority of people in a community receive a bad reputation as a result of misbehavior on the part of a troublesome minority. Such was the case in colonial Albany. Although the city had its share of disreputable characters, the honest citizens did reasonably well, considering the adverse circumstances, in their efforts to maintain friendly relations with the Indians. No particular social group deserves all the praise or all the blame in considering Albany's treatment of the Indians. The poorer people had the misfortune of having among their ranks the usual complement of riffraff that congregate on any frontier, but Lawrence Claessen, a man of only modest means, performed ad-

14. Peter Kalm, *Peter Kalm's Travels in North America*, ed. Adolph B. Benson, 2 vols. (New York, 1937), 1: 344, 343, 345.

15. Arthur Pound, *Johnson of the Mohawks* (New York, 1930), p. 15.

mirable diplomatic services for over forty years in his position as an official Indian interpreter.[16] On the other hand, Evert Wendell, Jr., one of the most substantial Indian traders and a supplier of furs to the New York exporter Stephen DeLancey, frequently violated the various trading laws, especially the ones against sending brokers into the wilderness and the acceptance of personal items from the Indians as security for the payment of debts. On several occasions, he and members of his family were defendants in cases involving violations of the trade ordinances.[17]

Undoubtedly, the Indians who traded at Albany often ran afoul of unscrupulous traders, who invited them in for a drink of rum and then took their furs for practically nothing when the victims became intoxicated.[18] Although the records indicate that many people had few qualms about cheating the Indians, they also show that the city officials made sincere attempts to prevent these illegal activities and provided themselves with legal machinery for doing so

The nature of local politics prevented the establishment of any well-defined policy, but Albany consistently attempted to maintain good relations with the Iroquois and other tribes. At least for a while in Albany courts, Indians had the unusual right of accusing a trader and causing him to take an oath. To encourage the discovery of trade violations, the sheriff or the informer was given one-third to one-half of all fines or goods confiscated. In 1700 the Common Council agreed to provide complainants with the entire amount of the fine in certain types of violations, such as bringing Indians into trader's houses, and in 1704 the sheriff made an agreement that allowed him two-thirds of fines involving all fur trade regulations. The Common Council frequently republished the trade ordinances and often added clauses to make them more effective. In 1717, for example, the magistrates empowered the sheriff or his deputies to search the city houses after sunset in order to discover if any Indians were being lodged by the residents.[19]

The effectiveness of law enforcement often depended on who hap-

16. Claessen seems to have gone on his first mission on June 14, 1700. Lawrence H. Leder, ed., *The Livingston Indian Records, 1666–1723* (Gettysburg, Pa., 1956), p. 177. He died either in late 1741 or early 1742. Minutes of the Commissioners of Indian Affairs (microfilm), January 11, 1742, 2: 22a, Public Archives of Canada, Ottawa, hereafter cited as Minutes of the Indian Commissioners.

17. Evert Wendell, Jr., Account Book, 1695–1726, New-York Historical Society, New York City; Wendell to Stephen DeLancey, August 14, 1718, in Stephen De-Lancey Papers, Miscellaneous Manuscripts, New-York Historical Society; Munsell, ed., *Annals of Albany*, 4: 182–83, 5: 118–19; *Minutes of the Court of Albany*, ed. Van Laer, 2: 271.

18. Evert Wendell, Jr., Account Book, 1695–1726.

19. Munsell, ed., *Annals of Albany*, 4: 110–11, 192, 7: 65, 8: 207–13.

pened to occupy the office of high sheriff in the county of Albany. When the trade began to revive after King William's War, Sheriff Jacob Turke not only enforced the laws, but frequently urged the Common Council to strengthen the ordinances and to increase the penalties. Apparently very much interested in the revenue from the fines, he often asked to have his percentages increased. When Henry Holland became sheriff in 1706, the situation changed considerably, and a number of inhabitants began to complain that he and his deputy had entered into some kind of clandestine agreement with several traders. Consequently, the Common Council enacted a law that established a fine of £3 to be taken from a sheriff or deputy who made any arrangement by which a trader might have to pay "a Less sum of mony then the fine or fines Specified" by the ordinances.[20]

Since Indians could not stay within the stockades at night, Albany officials had found it necessary to provide houses for them outside the city. The task of maintaining these places developed into a constant problem, because whenever the wooden shacks became uninhabitable, the traders used this as an excuse to allow the Indians to stay in their homes. The first of these structures, built in the shape of Iroquois long houses and being sometimes as lengthy as seventy feet, had been con-structed before 1666 and were repaired from time to time or completely rebuilt when necessary. The law required the Indian traders to provide firewood and occasionally to pay a special assessment for repairs or new construction.[21] In 1705, when the houses had deteriorated to the point of being uninhabitable, the Common Council changed the law and al-lowed Indians to stay in the city. Many traders immediately complained that such a policy damaged the trade, and so the city officials reinstated the regulation, along with a provision for repairing the houses. In this instance, Evert Wendell, Jr., claiming that the houses were "Prejudicial to him," refused to pay the assessment for the cost of repairs and was fined nine shillings. Until 1716 the city of Albany maintained the houses on its own initiative, but in this year the provincial legislature ordered the building of two houses at the expense of the traders, and in 1723 it provided the money for rebuilding them.[22]

One of the most vexing problems for the Albany magistrates and other

20. Ibid., 4: 110, 177, 192, 5: 116–17, 164.

21. Allen W. Trelease, *Indian Affairs in Colonial New York: The Seventeenth Century* (Ithaca, N.Y., 1960), p. 221; *Minutes of the Court of Albany*, ed. Van Laer, 2: 105, 106; *Colonial Laws of New York from the Year 1664 to the Revolution,* 5 vols. (Albany, 1894–96), June 30, 1716, 1: 890–97, hereafter cited as *Laws*; Munsell, ed. *Annals of Albany*, 2: 97, 3: 54.

22. Munsell, ed., *Annals of Albany*, 5: 118; *Laws*, June 30, 1716, 1: 890–91; Gov-ernor William Burnet to the Board of Trade, December 16, 1723, in *NYCD*, 5: 701.

New York authorities concerned the sale of liquor to the Indians. In both the Dutch and English periods, the provincial authorities provided Albany with guidelines for controlling the liquor traffic, and until 1720 no other legal aspect of the fur trade received so much attention from outside of Albany Country. Unfortunately, the hodgepodge of city ordinances, executive proclamations, and short-term laws added to the complexity of a problem in which the victims often insisted upon being exploited. So many people violated the liquor laws that the authorities had little chance of effectively handling the situation. Referring to the fur traders of New York City before the establishment of the Albany monopoly, Jasper Danckaerts, a visitor to the colony in 1679, noted, "Although it is forbidden to sell the drink to the Indians, yet every one does it, and so much the more earnestly, and with so much greater and burning avarice, that it is done in secret."[23] At times in the seventeenth century, colonial officials completely outlawed the sale of liquor to Indians, but they usually found that excise taxes and other restrictions in addition to local ordinances were more practical.[24]

When the fur trade revived after King William's War, neither the provincial authorities nor the Albany magistrates appeared eager to pass restrictive liquor regulations, although a city ordinance of 1703 did prohibit the selling of rum to the Indians in exchange for their clothing or firearms. During Queen Anne's War the problems of negotiating with the Iroquois, who remained neutral, increased because of drunkenness, and for this reason the New York assembly enacted a law completely prohibiting the sale of strong liquor to the Indians from June 1 to September 1, 1709. Except for a period between 1710 and 1711, this law continued to be renewed until 1713 with the approval of the Albany magistrates, who, in 1712, during a brief lapse in the provincial law, passed an ordinance outlawing the liquor traffic, which they described as "very prejudiciall in time of war."[25] In 1716 the legislature, at the insistence of the Iroquois sachems, passed a law against the sale of liquor to the Indians, but it was soon discontinued when the Indian leaders changed their minds.[26]

From 1716 until the French and Indian War no group of New Yorkers made a successful attempt to oppose the sale of rum to the Indians on

23. Jasper Danckaerts, *Journal of a Voyage to New York in 1679–80* (New York, 1913; reprinted, Upper Saddle River, N.J., 1967), p. 153.

24. Trelease, *Indian Affairs*, pp. 223–24.

25. Munsell, ed., *Annals of Albany*, 4: 181, 6: 272; *Laws*, May 24, November 12, 1709, August 4, November 24, 1711, June 26, 1712, 1: 657–58, 685–86, 740, 751, 755.

26. Wraxall, *Abridgment*, ed. McIlwain, June 13, 14, September 14, 1716, pp. 113, 115; *Laws*, June 30, 1716, 1: 888–90.

the frontier. Certainly no moral force with the power of the Jesuits in Canada rose to work effectively against the dispensing of rum to the tribesmen, who were clearly being damaged by its effects. Often rum made up nearly the entire stock of a small or illegal trader, and many farmers earned a little cash by keeping a supply of the fiery liquid for their Indian neighbors. Because of the Indian habit of destroying fences and devouring the cattle of the frontiersmen, these small farmers should have attempted to limit such transgressions by trying to keep the Indians as sober as possible, but many of them could not resist a quick profit.[27] "They brought forward this excuse," observed Jasper Danckaerts, "that if they did not do it, others would, and then they would have the trouble and others the profit, but if they must have the trouble, they ought to have the profit; and so they all said, and for the most part falsely, for they all solicit the Indians as much as they can . . . ."[28]

Despite all the criticism of the Albany inhabitants over their treatment of the Indians, the responsible city officials displayed more concern for the welfare of these people than any other politicians in the colony. While the Dutch in the southern part of New Netherlands and the New England immigrants on Long Island had been slowly destroying the indigenous populations, the Albany Dutch had established a system that allowed the two races to live in reasonable harmony. Almost all the protection afforded the Indians came from Albany ordinances, and until about the middle of the eighteenth century the responsibility for enforcing protective laws belonged to officials in Albany.

With the exception of William Johnson, none of the leading critics of the Dutch traders demonstrated any great concern for the welfare of the Indians. Usually the critics, mainly members of the imperialist faction, were only interested in using the tribesmen as wilderness soldiers in conflicts with France. Unfortunately for the Iroquois, Peter

27. Stuyvesant to La Montagne, May 9, 1663, in *NYCD*, 13: 244; *Minutes of the Court of Albany*, ed. Van Laer, August 5, 1684, 3: 475; Johnson to Jeffrey Amherst, August 1, 1762; Johnson to Cadwallader Colden, October 9, 1764, in *The Papers of Sir William Johnson*, ed. James Sullivan et al., 14 vols. (Albany, 1921–65), 10: 478, 4: 566, hereafter cited as *Johnson Papers*. In his well-known dissertation, Beverly McAnear assumed that the small farmers advocated restrictions on the sale of liquor to the Indians. Thus, he concluded that the provincial laws restricting liquor sales during Queen Anne's War should be interpreted as indications of conflict between the agrarian and business classes on the frontier. He did not, however, present any evidence to demonstrate agrarian support of restrictive laws, and he overlooked the evidence indicating that farmers often sold rum to the Indians and that the Albany merchants supported wartime prohibitions on the liqour trade. "Politics in Provincial New York, 1689–1761" (Ph.D. diss., Stanford University, 1935), pp. 274–75.

28. Danckaerts, *Journal of a Voyage*, p. 274.

Wraxall correctly predicted that after the conquest of Canada the British would be able to "gradually possess . . . the valuable country on the South side of Lake Erie." Although Cadwallader Colden based much of his political strategy on opposition to Albany, he made few, if any, suggestions designed to improve the lot of the Indians. During the entire history of colonial New York only three white men—Arent Van Curler, Peter Schuyler, and William Johnson—completely succeeded in winning the friendship of the Iroquois, and the first two of these men were Dutch leaders. The insistence of the Iroquois on calling all New York governors by the name "Corlaer" illustrates the influence of Van Curler, who died in 1667. During Schuyler's long career as mayor of Albany and member of the New York Council, the Iroquois sachems, as Colden complained, often "addressed themselves to Quider (that is Peter Schuyler) as well as to Corlaer."[29]

Even though Albany policy frequently worked to the advantage of the Iroquois, there is no reason to believe that the policy-makers were altruistically concerned with the welfare of their Indian brethren. Albany officials were simply acting to protect the economic and political interests of their city. Fortunately for the Indians, Albany viewed them as valuable assets both as customers and as military allies. Thus, when the magistrates passed protective ordinances, they acted for "the good of this country" and not simply to assist abused Indians. In one instance of this kind of attitude, the Common Council made a regulation against taking in trade from the Indians "cloathing and other necessaries," because such a practice rendered them "incapable to go hunting."[30] Almost without exception, the people of Albany schemed to keep the prices of trading goods high enough so that the Indians could not obtain all of their needs for just a few beaver skins. In 1681, for example, a group of traders complained "that the Indians make no effort at all to catch any beavers, as 4 or 5 beavers sufficiently supply their needs, because the goods are given to them scandalously cheap, which causes a considerable loss in revenue to our Sovereign Lord, the King."[31] Thus,

29. Wraxall, "Some Thoughts upon the British Indian Interest . . ." [January 9, 1756], in NYCD, 7: 28; Colden, "Continuation of Colden's History of the Five Indian Nations for the Years 1707 through 1720," in Colden Papers, 9: 381. In referring to Schuyler's influence among the Indians, the eighteenth-century historian William Smith, Jr., explained, "This power over them was supported, as it had been obtained, by repeated offices of kindness, and his singular bravery and activity in defence of his country." The History of the Late Province of New-York from Its Discovery to the Appointment of Governor Colden in 1762, 2 vols. (New York, 1829–30), 1: 109.
30. Munsell, ed., Annals of Albany, 4: 181, 8: 268.
31. Minutes of the Court of Albany, ed. Van Laer, July 5, 1681, 3: 143–44.

the ordinance of 1686 placed a limit on the value of Indian presents and also attacked the problem of surpluses by restricting the number of people allowed to import merchandise into the city.[32] In later years even William Johnson gave his approval to this kind of exploitation by advocating the sale of rum to the Indians for the purpose of encouraging them to bring in more pelts.[33]

To counter these sharp business practices, the Iroquois were not reluctant to exploit New York's fears of both Canada's commercial and military threats. Consequently, New Yorkers did not have a free hand in dealing with the Iroquois as long as the French possessed Canada. And not even the most shortsighted Albany trader wanted to drive the Iroquois into the arms of the French and thus ruin the economy and expose the frontier to the ravages of an Indian war.

After King William's War, the fear of attack from New France as much as the desire to exploit the fur trade shaped Albany's policies toward the Iroquois. As the years passed and as the fur trade became proportionally less significant, the concern for security in Albany became more important than any other issue. Albany occupied a distinctive position in British North America, and in order to survive the inhabitants had to adapt to their peculiar strategic situation. Seldom receiving support from the main base of the colony nearly 150 miles to the south, Albany from the very beginning of its existence stood as an outpost in the wilderness. Other English colonies began by establishing beachheads on the seacoast, gradually pushing inland, and exterminating the Indians as they went. By contrast, the Albany merchants, having little need for Indian hunting territory as farm land, established a peaceful economic relationship with the Iroquois Confederacy that remained unbroken for nearly a century and a half. Albany, however, continued to be extremely vulnerable to swift raids down the Lake Champlain route from Canada. Even at the middle of the eighteenth century, only the village of Saratoga, north of Albany, stood in the path of a French attack.

During King William's War, Albany had witnessed a bitter demonstration of its vulnerability when residents of the surrounding countryside fled into the city, leaving butchered relatives and burning farms behind them. Unquestionably, this bloody war had a profound effect on the inhabitants of the city, who up until this time had been unaccustomed to the horrors of frontier warfare. Even before the brutal massacre at Schenectady on the night of February 9, 1690, the Albany Common Council had found it necessary to issue an ordinance prohibiting

32. Munsell, ed., *Annals of Albany*, 8: 209–10.
33. William Johnson to Colden, August 9, 1764, in *Colden Papers*, 5: 365–66.

adult males from leaving the county, but at the end of the war about a quarter of the population had fled to safer locations. They could hardly be blamed; rumors frequently circulated that the French were preparing the same treatment for the people of Albany that they had given to the residents of Schenectady.[34]

By the end of this first war with the French, the exhausted New Yorkers were ready to leap at a chance to avoid a resumption of hostilities. Before long the opportunity arose, and they did not hesitate to take advantage of it. Upon the conclusion of the Iroquois treaty with the French in 1701, New Yorkers recognized that they, too, should establish themselves as neutrals, because without Iroquois assistance a war with Canada was unthinkable for a small and already weakened colony.[35] Even with active Iroquois participation in King William's War, New York had been lucky to avoid disaster.

The French, who had no desire to arouse the Iroquois by conducting military expeditions through their territory, also accepted the idea of a neutrality. Although neither side requested a written agreement, the frontier inhabitants of New York were thus spared the devastating effects of a renewed war. Undoubtedly, Albany's businessmen viewed the prospects of peace as an opportunity to continue their trade with Montreal, and some of the traders actually conducted negotiations with the French governor. This tacit neutrality agreement, however, was a general policy of New York and not simply of Albany. Except for an abortive military excursion in 1709, the sentiment for neutrality dominated New York politics throughout the war.[36] In a speech to the New

34. A proclamation from the Albany magistrates, August 7, 1689; Population statistics of New York, in *Documentary History of the State of New-York*, ed. Edmund B. O'Callaghan, 4 vols. (Albany, 1850–51), 2: 48, 1: 468; Peter Schuyler to Governor Benjamin Fletcher, October 5, 1693; Fletcher to the Committee of Trade, October 9, 1693, in *NYCD*, 4: 65, 57; New York Executive Council Minutes, December 2, 1695, vol. 7, New York State Library, Albany, hereafter cited as Council Minutes; Leder, ed., *Livingston Indian Records*, p. 174; Arthur H. Buffinton, "The Policy of Albany and English Westward Expansion, *Mississippi Valley Historical Review* 8 (1922): 347–48. On New York's participation in the war, see Howard H. Peckham, *The Colonial Wars, 1689–1762* (Chicago, 1964), pp. 27–36, 38–41, 45–46, 48–49, 53.

35. Buffinton, "Policy of Albany," pp. 350–51. A half-century later, when New York had become far more powerful, William Johnson still insisted on obtaining the services of Indian warriors before advancing northward even as far as the French fort at Crown Point on Lake Champlain. "Without Indians," he declared, "I think it will be madness to attempt Crown Point." Johnson to Thomas Pownall, July 31, 1755, in *Johnson Papers*, 1: 805.

36. See chapter 8; Council Minutes, October 18, 1711, vol. 11; Robert Hunter to Gurdon Saltonstall, October 15, 1711, in New York Colonial Manuscripts, 56:

York assembly lamenting that there was "neither Money in the Treasury, nor Forts . . . Arms or Men for our Defence," Governor Robert Hunter exclaimed, "we are forced to rest contented with a precarious Security, under a suspicious Neutrality, that hath no firmer Foundation than the Faith of Savages, whilst our Neighbours Frontiers are on Fire, and the Inhabitants inhumanly butchered."[37]

As long as the Iroquois remained content with a policy of neutrality, which allowed them to hunt in distant lands and to extract special favors from both of the European powers, the province of New York could not undertake an aggressive course of action against the French without more help than either Britain or the other colonies were willing to supply in the first half of the eighteenth century. New York could only attempt to provide security for its own frontiers and to challenge the French economically while keeping in mind the long-range goal of winning the allegiance of the tribes living in the west. The maintenance of friendly relations with the Iroquois Confederacy was essential for the success of such a policy or any policy dealing with the struggle for control of North America. Consequently, the problem of dealing with the Iroquois became not only a provincial but also an imperial question.

Because of its strategic location and position as a market place for the Indians, Albany had naturally developed as the center of diplomatic conferences. On occasion, New York governors and commissioners from other colonies journeyed up the Hudson in order to converse with the sachems, but these visits did not fill the need for closer communications on everyday problems. In the seventeenth century the city magistrates had usually taken it upon themselves to handle the difficulties that arose, but after the beginning of the wars with France, the importance of the issues called for a more formal conduct of official business. A system developed by unplanned evolution rather than by design, and eventually the Albany Dutch found themselves in the role of diplomats serving to protect the British Empire from the threat of French expansion.

By the third quarter of the seventeenth century, the people of Albany and the governors of the province had come to realize that when dealing with the Indians the city magistrates were accepting responsibilities transcending their ordinary duties as municipal officials, but none of them held a special commission authorizing them to handle such matters.

126, New York State Library, Albany; G. M. Waller, "New York's Role in Queen Anne's War, 1702–1713," *New York History* 33 (1952): 44–46.

37. *Journal of the Votes and Proceedings of the General Assembly of the Colony of New York [1691–1765]*, 2 vols. (New York, 1764–66), September 1, 1710, 1: 272, hereafter cited as *Assembly Journal*.

Although the Albany officials were occasionally referred to as commissaries of Indian affairs, the word "commissaries" was merely another term for magistrates.[38] In the 1660s the city began to keep separate records of its negotiations with the Indians, and in 1675 a step toward better organization was undertaken when Robert Livingston, a new arrival in the colony, who was fluent in both Dutch and English, received an appointment as Secretary of Indian Affairs—a post that he and then his son Philip held for seventy-four years.[39]

This system for dealing with the Indians continued unchanged until 1696, when Governor Benjamin Fletcher presented Peter Schuyler, Godfrey Dellius, Dirk Wessels, and Evert Bancker with a formal commission "to treat confer and consult with the Five Indian Nations . . . and to hold a correspondence with them pursuant to such instrucçôns as you shall from time to time receive from me, so as by your endeavours they may be confirmed in their fidelity and allegiance."[40] From then on, the men charged with these responsibilities owed their appointments directly to the governors, and they soon became known as the Commissioners of Indian Affairs, which through tradition developed into the official name of the board. In 1698 Governor Bellomont changed the composition of Fletcher's commission by appointing the city's magistrates to take charge of Indian relations. With the exception of Wessels, this action automatically removed all the old commissioners, whom Bellomont disliked because of their attempts to claim the lands belonging to the Mohawks, but he recognized Schuyler's invaluable influence among the Indians and again made him a commissioner along with Robert Livingston.[41]

Over the years the number of commissioners and their qualifications varied according to the whims of incumbent governors, but the majority always consisted of the leading citizens in the Albany area, who were the only people in the colony with the inclination to undertake this task. Usually, the board had from nine to twelve members, but on occasion it contained as many as twenty.[42] In the early years of the century,

38. Wraxall, *Abridgment*, pp. lv–lvi; Trelease, *Indian Affairs*, p. 207–8; Albany Charter, in *Albany Chronicles*, ed. Cuyler Reynolds (Albany, 1906), p. 89.

39. Leder, *Robert Livingston*, pp. 15–16; Trelease, *Indian Affairs*, p. 208.

40. A commission, August 10, 1696, in *NYCD*, 4: 177.

41. Bellomont to the Board of Trade, September 14, 1698, ibid., p. 365; Instructions to Peter Schuyler, Robert Livingston, and the mayor of Albany, August 1, 1698, in *Calendar of State Papers, Colonial Series, America and West Indies*, ed. W. N. Sainsbury et al., 43 vols. to date (London, 1860–), 16: 433; Leder, *Robert Livingston*, p. 134.

42. Minutes of the Indian Commissioners, January 21, 1730, 1: 311.

most commissioners came from the ranks of the Albany aldermen and assistants, but later governors reduced the participation of these elected officials in order to free the board from dependence on the voters of the city. The most drastic departure from tradition came in November 1720 when Governor Burnet, seeking to find support for his efforts to abolish the Montreal-Albany trade, appointed Peter Schuyler, Hendrick Hansen, John Cuyler, Peter Van Brugh, Evert Bancker, Henry Holland, Philip Livingston, John Collins, Johannes Wendell, and John Bleeker as Commissioners of Indian Affairs.[43] None of them was an Albany alderman, and elected city officials never again played more than a minor role as commissioners.[44]

Burnet's successor, John Montgomerie, increased the number of Indian Commissioners to twenty, but the general character of the board remained unchanged. Several years later in 1738 the assembly asked Lieutenant Governor George Clarke to decrease the number in order to reduce the cost of the expense accounts that they presented each year. Clarke attempted to make the selection of commissioners more orderly in the future by decreeing that the board should consist of the nine men holding the positions of Indian Secretary, commander of the military forces at Albany, mayor, recorder, and sheriff of the city, and the representatives to the assembly from Schenectady, Rensselaerswyck, and Albany City and County. In little more than a year, however, the number of commissioners had again increased.[45]

The difficulty in keeping the board down to a manageable size indicated that it had become a position of prestige, which the governors could award to their friends in Albany County without incurring any great expense or jealousy from politicians elsewhere in New York. During the early years of the century many of the most important men in Albany sought positions on the Common Council, but as they became more prosperous and influential in colonial politics they were no longer so enthusiastic about being city councilmen. Almost all of Burnet's appointees to the board, for example, were more politically and socially prominent than the magistrates of Albany. At some time in their lives, six of the ten received appointments as mayors of the city. Many of them had acquired a great deal of property, and Philip Livingston soon

43. Council Minutes, November 12, 1720, vol. 13.
44. Munsell, ed., *Annals of Albany*, 8: 289.
45. Minutes of the Indian Commissioners, January 21, 1730, October 7, 1738, December 17, 1739, 1: 311, 2: 154–55, 178a–79; *Assembly Journal*, October 18, 1738, 1: 744; Edward Collins to Daniel Horsmanden, October 21, 1745, in Selections from the Daniel Horsmanden Papers (microfilm), New-York Historical Society, New York City.

became one of the wealthiest men in the colony. His uncle Peter Schuyler had obtained numerous honors in his life, including the presidency of the New York Council. Both Henry Holland, the sheriff of Albany, and John Collins, who was Robert Livingston's brother-in-law and a prominent attorney, wielded considerable influence from behind-the-scenes political activities.[46]

Some of the commissioners looked upon their position as little more than an honorary title and seldom attended a meeting, but others, including Philip Livingston, Peter Schuyler, John DePeyster, Nicolas Bleecker, Barent Sanders, and Myndert Schuyler, who served for approximately forty years, put a considerable amount of time and effort into their duties. Receiving no financial remuneration for their services, these men displayed very little desire to use their positions to make profits. The New York assembly paid for expenses incurred in the line of duty, but the commissioners seldom padded their accounts; and even in the eventful year of 1746, their personal expenditures came to less than £300. On one occasion, during the early years of the century when the colony was in particularly dire financial straits, the commissioners paid about £200 out of their own pockets for the costs of Indian affairs.[47] Although their critics actually seem to have believed that they used their official powers to increase the size of their trade with the Indians, the commissioners after 1720 seldom conducted any business transactions with the tribesmen, and those among them who engaged in the fur trade devoted their energies to the importation of woolen goods and the exportation of peltry received either from the Dutch Indian traders or from Canada.[48]

In addition to prestige and a sense of civic duty, the commissioners were motivated by their interest in bringing security to the frontier and thus protecting the property and investments that they and their families had built up over the years. Contrary to the invective directed against them by numerous critics throughout the first half of the century, the commissioners and other Albany leaders were not disloyal to the British cause against France but actually ranked among the severest colonial

46. Leder, *Robert Livingston*, pp. 233, 238, 256; *Albany Chronicles*, ed. Reynolds, p. 201; Leder, ed., *Livingston Indian Records*, p. 229.

47. Minutes of the Indian Commissioners, June 27, 1746, 2: 386a; *Assembly Journal*, August 28, 1708, 1: 220.

48. Wraxall, *Abridgment*, ed. McIlwain, pp. 140–41n; Colden, "The present state of the Indian affairs . . . ," August 8, 1751, in *Colden Papers*, 4: 276; Minutes of the Indian Commissioners, November 27, 1746, 2: 405; David A. Armour, "The Merchants of Albany, New York, 1686–1760" (Ph.D. diss., Northwestern University, 1965), pp. 252–53.

opponents of French policies in North America. Their desire to remain neutral during wars in which the province was woefully unprepared to fight did not indicate any more disloyalty than that demonstrated by the efforts of Massachusetts to establish a neutrality in Queen Anne's War.[49] The main difference between the two situations was that the New Yorkers achieved success due to their friendly relations with the Iroquois while the people of Massachusetts had nothing but hostile Indians on their borders. The persistence of Albany in trading with Canada was merely a reflection of the times, differing very little from the trade engaged in by other cities with the French West Indies or from the attitude of Governor Joseph Dudley in Massachusetts, who condoned a sea-borne trade carried on by his political friends with Quebec and Nova Scotia during Queen Anne's War.[50]

Two early leaders among the Indian commissioners, Peter Schuyler and Robert Livingston, led the colony in advocating the use of strong measures in dealing with the French threat, and many of the latter's ideas were incorporated into Burnet's novel trading policies. Although not as much of a strategist as Livingston, Schuyler displayed no less vehemence in his feelings toward the French. William Smith, Jr., the eighteenth-century historian of New York, described Schuyler as a man who believed in "the absolute necessity of reducing Canada to the crown of Great-Britain," and Smith asserted, "we had not a man in this province, who had more extended views of the importance of driving the French out of Canada . . . ."[51] At an early date, the commissioners recognized the intercolonial significance of their actions. Writing to Governor Hunter in 1717, they complained about French agents among the Iroquois and warned, "if they become our Enemies [it] will probably not only be the Ruin of our out Settlements but also of those of his majestys neighbouring Colonies . . . ." In a complete departure from Albany's

49. Vaudreuil, Proposed treaty with New England, October —, 1705; Vaudreuil to Pontchartrain, April 28, 1706, in *NYCD*, 9: 770–72, 775–76; Arthur H. Buffinton, "The Colonial Wars and Their Results," in *History of the State of New York*, ed. Alexander C. Flick, 10 vols. (New York, 1933–37; reprinted, Port Washington, N.Y., 1962), 2: 217–18; G. M. Waller, *Samuel Vetch: Colonial Enterpriser* (Chapel Hill, 1960), pp. 80–81. Although the Massachusetts legislature eventually rejected the proposed treaty with New France, it did so on the grounds that the French claims to Arcadia would threaten the Massachusetts fishing industry. Ibid., p. 81.

50. For the connections between Governor Dudley, the illegal traders, and the attempts to establish a neutrality, see Waller, *Samuel Vetch*, pp. 80–93. Also see Herbert L. Osgood, *The American Colonies in the Eighteenth Century*, 4 vols. (New York, 1924–25; reprinted, Gloucester, Mass., 1958), 1: 420–23.

51. Smith, *History*, 1: 173–74. For an interesting comparison of Schuyler and Livingston, see Trelease, *Indian Affairs*, pp. 209–10.

earlier opposition to Bellomont's plans for building a fort in Onondaga country, they urged the governor to establish a fort at Irondequoit on the shores of Lake Ontario for the purpose of extending British influence among the Iroquois.[52]

When Schuyler as president of the Council became executive head of the New York government for a year between 1719 and 1720, the mayor, recorder, magistrates of Albany, and the Commissioners of Indian Affairs wrote him a letter expressing their desire that the French traders be removed from Niagara and that British forts be built there and at Irondequoit in order "to defeat the intreagues of the French and secure and preserve the Five nations to the British interest." Such drastic steps were necessary, they argued, because, "the said Five nations are the balance of the continent of America." They added the dire warning that if "proper persons, Officers and Souldiers" were not posted in the wilderness, the Five Nations would "unavoidably go over to the French interest," and this would prove to be "the ruin and destruction of the greatest part of this continent."[53]

In matters of military security during the next thirty years, the Commissioners of Indian Affairs often acted as spokesmen for Albany politicians, who frequently sent warnings to the governors about French expansion and who almost constantly complained about the inadequacy of the colony's defenses.[54] The commissioners' correspondence in these years demonstrated that they clearly understood the connection between the fur trade and the security of the frontier. In 1724 they told Governor Burnet that nothing but the fur trade could do as much "to keep the five Nations of Indians firm in their faith and allegeance to his Majesty and the Enlarging of his Majesties Empire in America and to keep them strictly united to the Interest of the Inhabitants of this and neighbouring Provinces." Ten years later, they warned Governor William Cosby that it would be "very prejudiciall and Fatall to the British Plantations in

52. Indian Commissioners to Robert Hunter, March 27, 1717, in New York Colonial Manuscripts, 50: 156.

53. Officials of Albany to Peter Schuyler, September 14, 1720, in NYCD, 5: 572, 571.

54. Minutes of the Indian Commissioners, November 12, 1724, August 7, 1732, January 2, 1738, August 25, 1738, January 4, 1746, [May –, 1746], 1: 108, 361a–62a, 2: 124–24a, 141, 322–22a, 379–81a; Wraxall, Abridgment, ed. McIlwain, July 4, 1722, February 8, 1731, May 3, 1742, July 6, 1744, May 17, 1745, pp. 140, 182, 225, 236–37, 238; Indian Commissioners to John Montgomerie, May 26, 1730; Indian Commissioners to George Clarke, August 30, 1738, in NYCD, 5: 908, 6: 131; Assembly Journal, October 20, 1738, March 27, 1739, 1: 747–48, 750; Philip Livingston to Jacob Wendell, January 14, 1746, in Livingston Papers, Museum of the City of New York.

America" if the French were able to lure away the Iroquois.[55]

These impassioned words from the commissioners sounded very similar to statements made by Colden, William Johnson, Peter Wraxall, and others in the imperial group of New York politicians, who were the inveterate opponents of the Albany Dutch. The difference in the attitudes of the two groups involved their long-range goals. The imperial-minded faction envisioned a day when the Union Jack would fly over Canada, and so they emphasized military expeditions, such as the ones in Queen Anne's and King George's wars, aimed at Montreal over the Lake Champlain route. Reflecting their practical business instincts, most residents of Albany, with some notable exceptions, would have been satisfied to surround themselves with sturdy forts while continuing their success in the fur trade by using inexpensive goods and rum to attract the various tribes to Oswego.

Both groups often criticized the New York assembly, controlled by members from the southern counties, who cared little about frontier defenses or imperial adventures.[56] In criticizing the assembly, Albany demanded more money for Indian presents and better fortifications with larger garrisons. Telling of their "unspeakable dread" of a French attack, the Indian Commissioners and the officials of Albany in 1732 complained to Governor Cosby that they had "made Severall Applications to the Legislative Power Entreating their Assistance" without satisfaction.[57] In 1745 the commissioners told Governor Clinton that "the People of our Country are daily exposed to and must expect . . . Barbarous Cruelties, to prevent which the general Assembly have not taken any one step that we know of . . . ."[58]

The reluctance of the assembly to appropriate money for frontier defenses made the work of the commissioners difficult, but they did not despair and continued to perform a wide variety of duties involving the fur trade and diplomacy. During wars, they also provided various military services ranging from the supervision of spies and scouts to the construction of forts.[59] In a humanitarian endeavor, they even arranged

55. Minutes of the Indian Commissioners, November 12, 1724, March 4, 1734, 1: 108, 2: 51.

56. George Clarke to the Board of Trade, February 17, 1738, August 24, 1742, June 19, 1743, in *NYCD*, 6: 113–14, 215, 225; *Assembly Journal*, December 1, 1743, May 14, 1745, 2: 9, 61; Minutes of the Indian Commissioners March –, 1746, 2: 343; Philip Livingston to Storke and Gainsborough, June 2, 1738, in Miscellaneous Manuscripts, vol. 5.

57. Minutes of the Indian Commissioners, August 7, 1732, 1: 316a.

58. Wraxall, *Abridgment*, ed. McIlwain, July 17, 1745, p. 239.

59. Ibid., September 25, 1708–March 17, 1709, p. 63; Leder, ed., *Livingston*

to provide the Indians with emergency food supplies during the famine that spread through numerous tribes in 1741 and 1742.[60] Their source of authority as direct agents of the governor and their political influence among both the Indians and the whites gave them a great deal of practical power. In conducting Indian negotiations, they were at the height of their power, and other colonies could seldom effectively negotiate with the Iroquois Confederacy without their assistance—a service that the commissioners readily provided for them.[61]

In addition to renewing treaties and conducting frequent discussions with visiting Indians, the commissioners spent much of their time coordinating the activities of New York Indian agents, who in conjunction with blacksmiths lived among the Iroquois during the winters in order to offset the effects of French diplomats. Before the end of the seventeenth century, the practice of sending diplomatic missions into Iroquois country had been long established; but after the beginning of the struggle with France, New York sent out larger numbers of agents, who spent longer periods of time with the Indians. During the early years of the eighteenth century, the interpreters Jan Baptist Van Eps and Lawrence Claessen did most of this work with assistance from prominent Albany citizens, who occasionally traveled to the council fires at Onondaga for official talks.[62] Later, the governors used the Iroquois demand for blacksmiths as an opportunity to accomplish diplomatic goals. By the middle 1720s smiths and armorers were spending every winter in Seneca country. The commissioners had little difficulty in finding men willing to undertake the journey, because the workers not only received wages of £25 but also had such lucrative trading opportunities that for a two- or three-year period in the early 1730s many "smiths" volunteered to go without asking for financial renumeration from the government.[63] The

Indian Records, p. 219; Minutes of the Indian Commissioners, December 31, 1744, January 4, February 18, June 19, 1746, 2: 310a, 321a–23a, 337–38a, 385.

60. Assembly Journal, May 28, 29, 1741, 1: 804, 805; Minutes of the Indian Commissioners, June 18, 1741, May 14, 1742, 2: 210, 227.

61. Wraxall, Abridgment, ed. McIlwain, May 31, 1723, June 10, 1724, September 10, 1725, May 28, 1735, March 9, 1737, August 25, 1738, September 13, 1745, pp. 146, 151, 160, 191, 198, 211, 241; Minutes of the Indian Commissioners, August 18, October 21, 29, 1729, May 11, 1730, 1: 296–97, 312–16a.

62. Aigremont to Pontchartrain, December 14, 1708; Peter Schuyler to Robert Hunter, May 27, 1711, in NYCD, 9: 823, 5: 245; Colden, "Continuation of Colden's History," in Colden Papers, 9: 384; Warrant for payment of Peter Schuyler, Johannes Schuyler, and Dirk Wessels, June 6, 1704, in New York Colonial Manuscripts, 50: 26; Leder, ed., Livingston Indian Records, pp. 177–80; Council Minutes, June 20, 1701, [June 1, 1708], vols. 8, 10.

63. Council Minutes, November 2, 1725, vol. 15; Assembly Journal, November

problem of New York agents trading with the tribesmen continued, but the Indians seemed to be quite pleased with the arrangement and did not complain.[64] After the outbreak of King George's War, New York paid salaries as high as £100 per man to "Persons of Interest" who agreed to winter with the blacksmiths in the Seneca villages.[65]

Unfortunately for the Indians, the commissioners did not gain as much power to regulate the conduct of individual fur traders as they developed to handle diplomatic affairs. In possessing the right to require fur traders to take oaths attesting to the legality of their conduct, the commissioners had the necessary weapon to discover law violators, but they seldom used this power. Apparently they lacked the inclination to become involved in minor disputes between Indians and traders, and they left such matters in the hands of the Albany magistrates and the commissary at Oswego, who had the power of a justice of the peace.[66] In the matter of the liquor traffic, however, they actively worked to bring about stronger regulations and to see that the laws on this subject were enforced.[67]

The most frequent complaint made by the Indians concerned the prices of merchandise, but in such instances the commissioners were almost powerless—a situation that frustrated both them and the Indians. In asking that prices be lowered, a group of Iroquois once complained to the commissioners "The governor told us That he is not Master of the Trade, we therefore think That you are Masters of it . . . ." They could only reply in the usual manner: "We will recommend to the traders to sell their goods at Oswego as Cheap As they Can Afford it, but the prices of goods is generally regulated according to the Price of Furs in England."[68] In spite of their inability to control prices, the commissioners probably did help to lessen the anger of overcharged Indians by simply being there to listen to complaints and by occasionally taking some action against the offenders.

6, 1725, 1: 529; Minutes of the Indian Commissioners, September 14, 1726, September 20, 1729, August 24, 1730, 1: 170–70a, 194, 326–26a.

64. Council Minutes, March 25, 1734, vol. 16; Indian Conferences, September 13, 1726, September 11, 1733, in *NYCD*, 5: 797, 969; Johnson to Governor George Clinton, January 22, 1749, in *Johnson Papers*, 9: 38.

65. *Assembly Journal*, April 9, 1745, 2: 55; Council Minutes [October 28, 1751], vol. 23.

66. Minutes of the Indian Commissioners, June 11, 1725, March 24, 1732, 1: 136, 354–55; Summons from the Commissioners, July 17, 1743, in *Johnson Papers*, 1: 19.

67. Minutes of the Indian Commissioners, April 21, 1726, August 12, 1745, 1: 125a–26, 2: 88; Wraxall, *Abridgment*, ed. McIlwain, February 22, 1729, p. 176.

68. Minutes of the Indian Commissioners, January 26, 1742, 2: 223a, 224a.

Though never empire-builders, the commissioners, whose actions illustrated the best side of Albany politics, did an admirable job in carrying out their duties while receiving little support from other New Yorkers and having to live with the verbal abuse unleashed against them by Colden and others, who believed that these officials demonstrated too much enthusiasm for their own business interests and not enough for the public good. To Colden, Burnet, Johnson, and other imperialists, the public good meant the earliest possible expulsion of the French from Canada; whereas to the Dutch, it meant the maintenance of a diplomatic *status quo* until the British developed a clear economic and military superiority over their rivals. To the detriment of everyone in the colony, the avarice of some traders and the lack of cooperation from other provincial officials often hindered the Indian Commissioners in their efforts to maintain the friendship of the Iroquois Confederacy.

6

TRADERS AND MERCHANTS

A SURE SIGN of spring in colonial Albany was the arrival of the first Indians loaded down with packs of fur. Beginning early in April and lasting through the end of June, Indians from the west and north traveled to the Dutch city, where they bartered their furs and deerskins to the white men for woolens, rum, gunpowder, and other goods that by the eighteenth century had become essential for their survival. Most of the Indians from the north were Caughnawagas, who acted as carriers of merchandise for Frenchmen, illegally sending furs to New York. After the founding of Oswego in the 1720s, many of the Dutch and English traders transported their goods to Lake Ontario, where they usually completed the trading before the middle of July.[1]

During most of the colonial period, the province contained three identifiable groups of colonists participating in the peltry business—fur traders, merchants with moderate-sized businesses, and the great import-exporters, who usually lived in New York City. Until the early 1730s most fur traders did not ship the furs themselves. Instead, they used the peltry to pay off their debts to Albany or New York merchants, who sold some of the furs to colonial hatters and exported the rest to London in exchange for English manufactured goods. The majority of fur merchants ran businesses of moderate size; they should be distinguished from the small handful of great merchants, who from time to time controlled large percentages of the export trade in furs. The distinction between the great merchants and the others was usually clear, but fur traders frequently became merchants, and some of them played both roles.

In the regulatory ordinance of 1686 the Albany magistrates had legally distinguished between merchants and traders by ordering the latter not to import Indian goods "from England or any other part of Europe or

---

1. Minutes of the Commissioners of Indian Affairs (microfilm), September 2, 1725, 1: 142a–43, Public Archives of Canada, Ottawa, hereafter cited as the Minutes of the Indian Commissioners.

the West Indies into this Citty." They also had prohibited importers of merchandise from trading directly with the Indians. The magistrates had even attempted to make a distinction between the types of Indian traders by prohibiting anyone who sold "Duffells, Strouds, Blanketts, and other Indian goods of value" from selling any of the numerous small items, whose sale helped to provide "a comfortable livelyhood, to several . . . inhabitants within this Citty."[2] Fortunately for ambitious, younger entrepreneurs, no one seems to have enforced these regulations, and subsequent publications of the ordinances made no mention of them.

After exchanging their merchandise for peltry, Albany merchants could not simply load their skins on ships bound for Europe, because they were barred from any direct overseas trade.[3] New York City had officially become the colony's exclusive port in the 1680s, and all goods being exported or imported had to be unloaded there before being shipped elsewhere.[4] The confinement of the export trade to this channel did not prove inconvenient to the Albany merchants, who would have probably employed New York City agents to represent them even if it had not been legally necessary.[5] Among the more important New York City agents were Henry and Philip Cuyler, Isaac Low, and John Cruger, all closely related to the traders. Some of these Manhattan merchants, including the well-known Hayman Levy, maintained a direct interest in the fur trade and frequently offered to buy the furs of their clients.[6]

2. Joel Munsell, ed., *Annals of Albany*, 10 vols. (Albany, 1850–59), 8: 210–11, 212.

3. *Minutes of the Court of Albany, Rensselaerswyck and Schenectady*, ed. A. J. F. Van Laer, 3 vols. (Albany, 1926–32), August 23, 1678, 2: 403.

4. Petition of the Mayor and Common Council of New York to Governor Thomas Dongan, November 9, 1683, in *Documents Relative to the Colonial History of the State of New York*, ed. Edmund B. O'Callaghan and Berthold Fernow, 15 vols. (Albany, 1856–87), 3: 337–39; hereafter cited as *NYCD*; I. N. Phelps Stokes, *The Iconography of Manhattan Island*, 6 vols. (New York, 1895–1928; reprinted, 1967), 4: 326, 327.

5. Bill of Lading for Hendrick Ten Eyck, October 15, 1726; Henry Cuyler to Hendrick Ten Eyck, October 31, 1733, in Harmanus Bleecker Papers, New York State Library, Albany; Samuel and William Baker to Johannes R. Bleecker, October 13, 1747, in Johannes R. Bleecker Papers, New York State Library, Albany.

6. Cornelius Cuyler to John Cruger, October 30, 1725; Cuyler to Richard Jeneway, May 27, 1726; Cuyler to Philip Cuyler, November 6, 1755, in Cornelius Cuyler Letter Books, 1724–1736, 1752–1764 (microfilm), American Antiquarian Society, Worcester, Mass.; Robert and Peter Van Brugh Livingston and Company to Henry Van Rensselaer, Jr., June 23, 1735, in Van Rensselaer-Fort Papers, New York Public Library, New York City; Isaac Low to William Johnson, November 26, 1767, in *The Papers of Sir William Johnson*, ed. James Sullivan et al., 14 vols. (Albany, 1921–65), 5: 823, hereafter cited *Johnson Papers*.

In later years Schenectady traders used Albany businessmen as their representatives in a similar manner even though they were not required to do so.[7]

New York's position as the exclusive port encouraged the rise of great fur merchants, who often controlled the major part of the trade. In all of the years from the 1680s until the French and Indian War, three men alone—Frederick Philipse, Stephen DeLancey, and Philip Livingston—clearly belonged to this group. Only Livingston ran his business from outside of New York City. Seldom, if ever, dealing with Indians in business transactions, these men imported goods from England and resold them to Albany merchants and traders in exchange for peltry. Because of their desire to control as much of the fur import business as possible, they apparently never acted as shipping agents for other merchants.

In spite of strenuous efforts to corner the market, these three entrepreneurs never found a way to eliminate their competition. At various times in the first half of the eighteenth century, other New York City exporters, including Adolph Philipse, Ouzel Van Sweeten, and Rip Van Dam, along with up-river merchants such as Robert Livingston, Cornelius Cuyler, and William Johnson also shipped large quantities of peltry to Europe. This second group of substantial exporters, however, either were not consistent enough in their shipments or never controlled a large enough section of the market to be considered great fur merchants.

Frederick Philipse, who was a member of the New York Council and one of the wealthiest men in the colony's history, reached the height of his economic and political power before the end of the seventeenth century. Shortly before Philipse's retirement in 1698 at the age of seventy-three, Edward Randolph, Surveyor General of Customs in America, described him as "one of the most ancient inhabitants and the greatest trader to Albany."[8] Robert Livingston, as an influential politician in Albany who had established a substantial overseas trade, seemed in a good position to replace Philipse when the trade began to revive at the end of King William's War. Unfortunately for Livingston, his chances of becoming a great fur merchant at this time were severely impeded by his involvement in the aftermath of Leisler's Rebellion and by his absence from the colony during two trips to England from 1694

7. Phyn and Ellice to Hayman Levy, May 25, June 8, 1769, September 1, October 13, 1772, in Phyn and Ellice Letter Book (microfilm), 1: 186, 188, 2: 195, 217, Buffalo and Erie County Historical Society, Buffalo, N.Y.; John H. Lydius to William Johnson, October 25, 1748, in *Johnson Papers*, 1: 193.

8. Edward Randolph to the Board of Trade, May 16, 1698, in *Calendar of State Papers, Colonial Series, American and West Indies*, ed. W. N. Sainsbury et al., 43 vols. to date (London, 1860–), 16: 217, hereafter cited as *Calendar of State Papers*.

to 1696 and from 1703 to 1706.[9] Near the end of his second journey, however, he sent home a large amount of goods, including several bales of duffels and strouds. After receiving the returns on these woolens, Livingston sent several large shipments of peltry to England in 1707, but in the following year he shipped only a few skins. By then he had probably given up his own efforts to compete with the firmly entrenched fur merchants in order to boost the chances of his son Philip, who was about to enter this business. Within a few years Robert Livingston became content to handle only small quantities of peltry, probably obtained from some of his tenants, who like many frontier farmers played the additional role of Indian traders during the early spring.[10]

Although no one in the first decade of the eighteenth century took the place of Frederick Philipse, a small group of merchants, including Rip Van Dam, William Glencross, John Barberie, Ouzel Van Sweeten, Benjamin Faneuil, and Stephen DeLancey, controlled the majority of beaver skins shipped from the port. The numerous other export merchants, including four or five women, usually exported wide assortments of furs together with great loads of skins from deer, elk, and bear.[11]

During the second decade of the century DeLancey continually increased his share of the fur trade until he earned the reputation in the early 1720s of having "almost entirely engrossed the Indian trade of this province, and thereby acquired a very great Estate and Influence."[12] Except for Adolph Philipse, no other individual could even come close to matching the volume of his peltry exports. By 1721, in addition to a fourth interest in the ship *Beaver*, DeLancey owned the brig *Albany*

---

9. Lawrence H. Leder, *Robert Livingston, 1654–1728, and the Politics of Colonial New York* (Chapel Hill, 1961), pp. 38–53, 95, 117, 185, 199.

10. Invoices, January 15, 1706, February 28, 1707; Stephen DeLancey to Philip Livingston, July 20, 1710; Philip Livingston to Robert Livingston, March 27, July 8, 1717, in Livingston Family Papers (microfilm), Franklin D. Roosevelt Library, Hyde Park, N.Y.

11. Julius Bloch et al., eds., *An Account of Her Majesty's Revenue in the Province of New York, 1701–1709. The Customs Records of Early Colonial New York* (Ridgewood, N.J., 1966), passim.

12. J[ames] A[lexander] to Mr. P[eter] C[ollinson] in London, 1740, in Cadwallader Colden, *The History of the Five Indian Nations of Canada, Which are Dependent on the Province of New York in America, And Are a Barrier Between the English and French in That Part of the World*, 2 vols. (New York, 1902), 2: 58. There is no proof that Alexander was referring to DeLancey, but it probably could not have been any other person. Charles H. McIlwain also concludes that the subject of this letter was DeLancey. Peter Wraxall, *An Abridgment of the Indian Affairs Contained in Four Folio Volumes, Transacted in the Colony of New York, from the Year 1678 to the Year 1751*, ed. Charles H. McIlwain (Cambridge, Mass., 1915), pp. lxvii–lxviii.

and the snow *Sea-Nymph*. He employed all of these vessels as carriers of peltry to Bristol, London, and Amsterdam.[13]

The major part of DeLancey's beaver supply came to New York from Montreal, and his political opponents considered him to be a trader with Canada.[14] Technically, they were incorrect, because he had few, if any, direct connections with the French to the north. He acquired all of his furs from merchants in Albany, who viewed themselves as his customers, not his agents.[15] As long as the skins continued to flow down the Hudson into his warehouses, DeLancey did not care where they originated, and certainly some of his peltry did come from the west. In 1718 Evert Wendell, Jr., one of his best customers, reported to him that the trade with Canada had been slow and that residents of Schenectady were endangering Albany's western trade.[16] The versatile Wendell, who carried on a trade with Canada while at the same time trading with the Iroquois and buying furs from other Dutch traders, seemed in this letter to have been more concerned about the diminution of trade with the west than with the north.[17]

Unfortunately, very few of DeLancey's papers have withstood the ravages of time, and so the identity of his correspondents remains obscure. Besides Wendell, two of his other connections in Albany were Philip Livingston and Cornelius Cuyler at the beginning of their careers. Significantly, all three of DeLancey's identifiable customers traded primarily with Montreal, although like most Albany merchants they did not confine themselves exclusively to that branch of the fur trade.

Both Cuyler and Livingston had strong ambitions and eventually broke their connections with the New York merchant. Entering business sometime around 1723, Cuyler soon began exporting a great many furs, but he did not get completely out of DeLancey's debt for more than a decade.[18] Livingston's relationship with DeLancey came to an abrupt

13. Naval Office Lists for the Port of New York, in C. O. 5/1222 (microfilm), Public Record Office, London.

14. J[ames] A[lexander] to Mr. P[eter] C[ollinson] in London, 1740, in Colden, *History of the Five Indian Nations*, 2: 58; Alice M. Keys, *Cadwallader Colden: A Representative Eighteenth Century Official* (New York, 1906), p. 117.

15. Stephen DeLancey to Philip Livingston, July 20, 1710, in Livingston Family Papers; Cuyler to DeLancey, May 9, 1726, in Cornelius Cuyler Letter Book, 1724–1736.

16. Evert Wendell, Jr., to DeLancey, August 14, 1718, in Stephen DeLancey Papers, Miscellaneous Manuscripts, New-York Historical Society, New York City.

17. Evert Wendell, Jr., Day Book, 1717–1749, Ledger, 1711–1738, folio 73, New-York Historical Society, New York City; An account of goods purchased by Wendell from DeLancey, March —, 1715, in Stephen DeLancey Papers.

18. Cuyler to DeLancey, July 22, 1725, July 20, 1731, June 25, 1735, in Cornelius Cuyler Letter Book, 1724–1736.

conclusion almost as soon as it had begun in 1710 or shortly before. After receiving a complaint that two packs of beaver had little value due to their poor condition, Livingston replied that he had selected the two best packs out of four. In rebuttal, DeLancey quipped, "If you Pickt them out of four packs those you left behind must . . . be Extraordinary bad . . . ."[19] The older man must have enjoyed this battle of wits, but within twenty years Livingston proved to be a formidable competitor. Fortunately for Livingston, in the years while he was developing his peltry business, economic changes were forcing a reduction in the role played by DeLancey and the other merchants of New York City.

Most merchants, especially the larger ones, avoided the expense of carrying on the trade with the Indians. This burden fell on the shoulders of the traders, who had to bear the high cost of sending goods into the wilderness. Frequently, these were young men with high ambitions. Some of them, including Jelles Fonda, Jacob Glen, and David Vander Heyden, used their earnings to establish themselves as prosperous merchants.[20] In the early years, when the Indians brought their furs to Albany, the expenses of trading did not amount to very much, and all but the largest merchants dealt directly with the Indians. Later, as the center of the trade moved farther and farther to the west, the amount of money spent on transportation became substantial.

After 1726 the traders had to pay high duties on rum and strouds carried out of Albany. Wagoners charged nine shillings for every wagon load carried to Schenectady. From there, the traders had to transport their goods up the Mohawk, across the portages, and through the waterways to Oswego. In earlier years they used canoes that usually carried from ten to fifteen packs of skins, weighing about a hundred pounds each. Larger canoes could transport as many as twenty-five packs.[21] By the 1730s most traders switched to wooden battoes propelled by oars, poles, or sails. Although the battoes had to be rolled over the portages, they carried as much or more than the largest New York canoes and could withstand a great deal of abuse.[22]

In order to increase the size of their businesses, the traders, who usually banded together in small temporary companies, attempted to

19. DeLancey to Philip Livingston, January 13, 1711, in Livingston Family Papers.

20. Minutes of the Indian Commissioners, September 2, 1725, 1: 142–43.

21. Ibid.; Colden, Memoir on the fur trade, November 10, 1724, in *NYCD*, 5: 729.

22. Philip Livingston to Storke and Gainsborough, June 7, 1736, in Miscellaneous Manuscripts, vol. 5, New York State Library, Albany; Phyn and Ellice to John Stedman, July 12, 1774, in Phyn and Ellice Letter Book, 3: 105; Journal of Ferral Wade and C. Keiuser, May 13–June 10, 1770, in *Johnson Papers*, 8: 724.

attract hired hands, but wages often were too high. In 1726, for example, the average cost of having a battoe delivered to Oswego amounted to £8, and in 1762 a transportation company was paying each of its employees—usually Mohawk Indians—a wage of £4 for a trip from Schenectady to Fort Stanwix on the portage between the Mohawk River and Lake Oneida, only about two-thirds of the way to Oswego.[23] For the honest traders, one of the greatest burdens resulted from having to associate with a large band of frontier ruffians, described by Philip Livingston as "young wild brutes who for the most part have no breeding nor Education, no honour nor honesty and are governed only by an unruly passion of getting money by fair or foul means."[24]

Most surviving business records deal with the overseas transactions of the fur merchants and give the impression that the sale of textiles completely dominated the fur trade, but rum, which of course was never purchased in England, also played an extremely important part in the acquisition of peltry.[25] Indian traders and small merchants obtained most of their liquor supply from numerous New York distillers. The more substantial businessmen, including Hendrick Ten Eyck, Stephen DeLancey, Philip Livingston, and Cornelius Cuyler, established close connections in the West Indies, where they traded flour, bread, and dried peas in exchange for rum, sugar, and molasses.[26] Always asking that payment be made in one-half sugar and one-half rum, Cuyler usually sent his barrels of flour to Henry Bonnin on Antigua. One of Philip Livingston's sons, who set up a business in Jamaica, sent his father both molasses and rum.[27]

Ranking directly behind strouds, rum, and gunpowder in a scale of importance to the fur traders, wampum—another item that did not show up in many overseas business records—had a particular value to the

23. Minutes of the Indian Commissioners, May 5, 1729, 1: 283–83a; Account of persons employed by David Schuyler, Jr., February 9, 1762, in *Johnson Papers*, 3: 631.

24. Philip Livingston to Storke and Gainsborough, June 7, 1736, in Miscellaneous Manuscripts, vol. 5.

25. See chapters 3 and 11.

26. Naval Office Lists for the Port of New York, in C. O. 5/1222–1229; Philip Livingston, Invoice, July 29, 1730, in Miscellaneous Manuscripts, vol. 5; David [Minvielleo?] to Hendrick Ten Eyck, July 12, 1730, in Harmanus Bleecker Papers; Cuyler to David Van Brugh, May 21, 1736, in Cornelius Cuyler Letter Book, 1724–1736; Virginia D. Harrington, "The Colonial Merchant's Ledger," in *History of the State of New York*, ed. Alexander C. Flick, 10 vols. (New York, 1933–37; reprinted, Port Washington, N.Y., 1962), 2: 335–36, 338–41.

27. Cuyler to Henry Bonnin, September 26, 1752, July 27, November 17, 1753, October 19, 1754, in Cornelius Cuyler Letter Book, 1752–1764; Philip Livingston to Storke and Gainsborough, March 10, 1737, in Miscellaneous Manuscripts, vol. 5.

New Yorkers, especially since they produced almost the entire North American supply. "Many people at Albany," wrote Peter Kalm in 1749, "make wampum for the Indians . . . by grinding and finishing certain kinds of shells and mussels."[28] Writing about the "manufactorys for wampum" observed on his visit to Albany in 1744, Dr. Alexander Hamilton gave the best description of the manufacturing process: "They grind the beads to a shape upon a stone, and then with a well tempered needle dipt in wax and tallow, they drill a hole thro' each bead."[29]

In the middle of the century white wampum sold for about two-thirds the price of black or, more correctly, purple wampum, which ranged from four to six shillings per hundred beads.[30] Considering the amount of labor involved in its manufacture and the impossibility of monopolizing the industry in Albany, the merchandising of wampum could not have resulted in bountiful profits. Nevertheless, Canada traders such as Cornelius Cuyler and Robert Sanders handled large amounts of it in order to satisfy the Montreal merchants, who had to rely on Albany for their entire supply except for a little that they may have received from New England.[31] Possibly, Cuyler hired artisans to produce his wampum, because in 1753 he asked a correspondent in New York to send him forty thousand clam shells and five hundred conch shells.[32] The large size of his order was in keeping with the tremendous number of beads sold in the fur trade. Robert Sanders thought nothing of receiving orders from his French customers requesting from thirty thousand to fifty thousand beads, which he sold to them at the rate of 250 black wampum for one pound of beaver.[33]

With nearly complete control over the supply of strouds, rum, and wampum, the English successfully competed with Canada in spite of aggressive French commercial policies in the interior. The French traders attempted to substitute brandy for rum and various woolens for

28. Peter Kalm, *Peter Kalm's Travels in North America*, ed. Adolph B. Benson, 2 vols. (New York, 1937), 1: 343.

29. Carl Bridenbaugh, ed., *Gentleman's Progress: The Itinerarium of Dr. Alexander Hamilton* (Chapel Hill, 1948), p. 73.

30. Ibid.; Cuyler to ——, November 4, 1761, in Cornelius Cuyler Letter Book, 1752–1764; Robert Sanders to Judah Hays, March 22, 1756, in Robert Sanders Letter Book, 1752–1758 (microfilm), New-York Historical Society, New York City.

31. Johnson to Governor George Clinton, September 20, 1749, in *Johnson Papers*, 9: 51. See also the Robert Sanders Letter Book, 1752–1758, passim.

32. Cuyler to William Darlington, January 20, 1753, in Cornelius Cuyler Letter Book, 1752–1764.

33. Sanders to Monsieur A, June 23, 1753; Sanders to Monsieur D, July 12, August 11, 1753, in Robert Sanders Letter Book, 1752–1758. Sanders used various code symbols when corresponding with his French customers. I have arbitrarily assigned letters of the alphabet to each of his Montreal correspondents.

strouds, but less efficient manufacturing processes and high transportation expenses caused the prices of such goods to be much higher than
the corresponding articles in New York.[34] Brandy sold for as much as
six times the price of rum, and in 1724 Cadwallader Colden stated that
the price of strouds in Albany was £10 a piece compared to £25 in
Montreal.[35]

In view of Indian fastidiousness about styles and fashions, a serious
problem for the Canadians was the inability of French manufacturers
to produce an imitation of stroud cloth that the Indians could be persuaded to buy. In the spring of 1749 a Canadian observer noted that
the French West India Company "notwithstanding, the little success
which resulted from the repeated efforts it has made with cloths of our
manufacture . . . had again determined to make another trial."[36] The
company officials ordered several pieces of cloth from France, but this
new effort at duplication failed to such an extent that Governor La
Jonquière and Intendant François Bigot declared that "the article is
frightful; the red cloth is brown and unpressed; the blue, of a very inferior quality to that of England; [and] that as long as such ventures
are sent, they will not become favorites with the Indians."[37]

Partly because of poor marketing procedures in Europe, the French
also suffered from an oversupply of peltry. Consequently, the Canadians
could not pay the Indians or traders as much for their beaver as the
Albany traders, who at times paid nearly double the Montreal price.[38]
The combination of high prices for beaver and low ones for merchandise
permitted the New Yorkers to easily outbid the French for peltry even
after allowances were made for wide profit margins.[39]

34. Pontchartrain to Denis Riverin, June 3, 1708, in *Supplement to Dr. Brymner's
Report on Canadian Archives, 1899*, ed. Edouard Richard (Ottawa, 1901), p. 414.
Colden, Memoir on the fur trade, November 10, 1724, in *NYCD*, 5: 728–30.

35. A French list of price differences between Montreal and Albany, 1689;
Colden, Memoir on the fur trade, November 10, 1724, in *NYCD*, 9: 408, 5: 730.

36. Abstract of a dispatch from Canada, April 30, 1749, ibid., 10: 200.

37. La Jonquière and Bigot, Abstract of their dispatch from Canada, October 1,
1749, ibid.

38. Pontchartrain to Denis Riverin, June 3, 1708, in *Supplement to Dr. Brymner's
Report*, ed. Richard, p. 414; E. E. Rich, *Hudson's Bay Company, 1670–1870*, 3 vols.
(New York, 1961), 1: 402–15.

39. Note, for example, this French list of price differences between Montreal and
Albany, 1689, found in *NYCD*, 9: 408:

	beaver skins	
	At Albany	At Montreal
8 pounds of powder	1	4
a gun	2	5
40 pounds of lead	1	3

Although the people of Albany frequently expressed fear of French military and diplomatic advances, they seldom branded Canada as an economic threat. Since a large percentage of New York's peltry came from Montreal businessmen, the New Yorkers viewed at least some members of the French establishment as "no more than hands or instruments of carrying on this trade with the far Indians."[40] As long as the Six Nations remained loyal to New York, the Dutch traders knew that they would continue to get their share of peltry. Therefore, the most dangerous competition came from the Pennsylvania traders, who were in a better position than the French to attract the business of the Iroquois.

Taking advantage of the difficulties on the northern frontier in King William's War, the Pennsylvanians continued to carry out the policies introduced by William Penn in the 1680s to establish political and commercial relations with the Iroquois at the expense of the New Yorkers. Fortunately for Albany traders, when economic and political conditions stabilized at the end of the war, they had little difficulty in making up any ground that had been lost among the Five Nations. In 1700 the Iroquois strongly asserted their desire to have the Indian trade confined to Albany in preference to the Pennsylvania system of allowing traders to wander from village to village.[41]

Albany's dominance continued for the next three decades, with Pennsylvania seldom producing more than 5 percent of England's supply of furs while New York on several occasions exported between 35 and 50 percent of all English fur imports. By the 1730s, however, the Pennsylvanians had established trade routes into the Ohio Valley, and they began to acquire more beaver and other furs to go along with their

---

a red blanket	1	2
a white blanket	1	2
4 shirts	1	2
6 pairs of stockings	1	2

The list also shows that the English sold six quarts of rum for one beaver; and although it varied greatly, the French never gave as much as a quart of brandy for a beaver skin.

40. *Journal of the Commissioners for Trade and Plantations*, 14 vols. (London, 1920–38), May 13, 1725, 5: 175–76.

41. Lawrence H. Leder, ed., *The Livingston Indian Records, 1666–1723* (Gettysburg, Pa., 1956), p. 112; Governor Benjamin Fletcher to William Blathwayt, February 14, 1692; Indian Conference, August 31, 1700, in *NYCD*, 4: 2, 741; Wraxall, *Abridgment*, ed. McIlwain, August 23, 1699, p. 33; Francis Jennings, "The Indian Trade of the Susquehanna Valley," *Proceedings of the American Philosophical Society* 110 (1966): 411, 419. For a description of the Massachusetts system, in which the fur trade was conducted by the government, see Ronald Oliver MacFarlane, "The Massachusetts Bay Truck-Houses in Diplomacy with the Indians," *New England Quarterly* 11 (1938): 48–65.

large supply of deerskins. Although they did not come very close to surpassing New York's total fur exports, their peltry production in some years after 1730 became a significant factor on the London market.[42] Nevertheless, the people of Albany did not express any great concern. Their neighbors in traveling far down the Ohio River were tapping a source of beaver that had little effect on the New York trade.

Instead of being concerned with outside competition, businessmen in New York and Albany had greater reason to keep a wary eye on changing trade patterns within their own province. By 1710 considerable changes had taken place in the general economic structure of the trade since the beginning of the century. The most noticeable new development involved the growing number of traders who were exporting their own furs to England in exchange for trading goods. This involvement of traders in overseas commerce through shipping agents in New York City did not represent any kind of new phenomenon. Such a practice had been in existence for at least fifty years.[43] Until the middle 1720s, however, the number of traders doing their own exporting remained fairly consistent and then began to increase rapidly.[44]

The enumeration of furs in 1722 probably caused much of the rapid change. Now every cargo of peltry had to pass through a British port even if the actual destination was somewhere in Europe. With the disruption of old commercial patterns, the traders who had been dealing with merchants exporting to Holland had to find other ways of shipping their furs. Many of them took over the responsibility themselves. Frequently, the new exporters were young men such as Cornelius Cuyler and Hendrick Ten Eyck, who, with a good command of English, were better equipped than their fathers for entering into a direct trade with London.

Whatever the reasons, the accelerated growth of an overseas trade between Albany and England demonstrated that the merchants of New York City had lost the major part of the export trade in furs that they had enjoyed since the days of Governor Andros. In 1730 Alolph Philipse complained that the Albany businessmen "now have almost all their Indian goods from England on their owne accountes, whereas they formerly bought the same from merchants and factors at New York."[45] Within a few years after his statement, the New York City merchants,

42. Murray G. Lawson, "Extracts from Customs 3," in the possession of Lawrence A. Harper, University of California, Berkeley.
43. Munsell, ed., *Annals of Albany*, 8: 210.
44. Philip Livingston to Robert Livingston, June 10, 1724, in Livingston Family Papers.
45. Adolph Philipse to Peter Leheup, December 25, 1730, in *Calendar of State Papers*, 37: 420.

other than acting as shipping agents, had little to do with the fur exporting business.

By this time, however, the merchants on Manhattan Island did not have as much interest in handling fur exports as they had had in earlier years. The increase in the colony's population between 1700 and 1730—from about thirty thousand to fifty thousand—gave the city's merchants a large enough market to sustain their prosperity without a dependence on furs, and the thriving trade with the West Indies provided them with a means of making remittances to their factors in Great Britain. These merchants at the southern end of the Hudson simply had too many other interests to bother with an auxiliary enterprise that now stretched far into the interior. Changes in the pattern of the fur trade made Albany the logical and most convenient location for the shipment of furs.

In early years the Indians brought their furs to the city and the Albany traders sent them on to New York. After the founding of Oswego, the initial collection of peltry occurred far away on Lake Ontario, which meant increased transportation problems, larger numbers of men involved in the trade, and less control over the traders. Consequently, anyone with a large investment in the fur trade now had to play a more active role in such activities as building battoes, obtaining merchandise in time for transportation to Oswego, and keeping an eye on debtors, who were often frontiersmen with tendencies to wander away without paying their bills. In one demonstration of the risks of dealing with rootless traders, Philip Livingston lost a considerable amount of money in 1735 when Leonard Lewis fled the province owing him and a London merchant, Samuel Storke, several hundred pounds. At the time of his sudden departure, Lewis possessed more than enough money to have easily paid his debts.[46] By 1730 even Albany merchants began to feel the same influences which affected their counterparts to the south. The center of the fur trade was shifting toward Schenectady.

Although these economic changes would have eventually ended New York City's direct participation in the fur trade anyway, the emergence of Philip Livingston as a great fur merchant accelerated the process. Establishing a business in Albany before the end of Queen Anne's War, the second son of Robert Livingston concentrated for many years on the acquisition of peltry, developing connections both with the western traders and with Canada. Using his father's influence, he soon entered into the overseas trade.[47] After Robert Livingston died in 1728, Philip inherited Livingston Manor, but he still continued to pursue his busi-

46. Philip Livingston to Samuel Storke, June 2, June 14, 1735, in Miscellaneous Manuscripts, vol. 5.

47. Henry Douglas to Philip Livingston, April 18, May 27, December 27, 1709;

ness activities as vigorously as ever. In addition to his responsibilities as town clerk of Albany, Indian Secretary, second lord of the manor, and member of the New York Council, Livingston entered into numerous business ventures including land speculation, agriculture, overseas trade, and iron production at his foundry.[48] His fondest dream involved a desire to control the fur trade of the province.[49] In his pursuit of this objective, Livingston must have been spurred on by memories of his early career, when he had been overshadowed by Stephen DeLancey.[50]

In order to obtain enough capital to accomplish his goal, Livingston conducted much of his peltry business on the basis of joint ventures with the London firm of Storke and Gainsborough, who supplied half of the goods in return for half of the furs, on which the New Yorker charged them a commission of 5 percent for his role in making the purchases from the traders. The size of these transactions could be considerable. In 1736, for instance, the goods involved in a joint venture amounted to nearly £2000 sterling.[51]

Along with his London associates, the versatile second lord of Livingston Manor owned the brig *Charming Molly*, which was used to ship cargoes of peltry. In joint ventures not involving the fur trade, they sent shipments of New York foodstuffs to the West Indies and to Spain.[52] Livingston also continued to import Indian trading goods for his own account, and when prices reached high enough levels in England, he purchased peltry for cash.[53] Not satisfied with acquiring furs from just Canada and Oswego, Livingston urged Storke and Gainsborough to contact "a proper person in France," who in return for one-fourth of the profits would arrange for them to open a trade with the French on the

---

Philip Livingston to Robert Livingston, April 13, 1713, March 4, 1717, February 8, 1721, in Livingston Family Papers.

48. Philip Livingston to Jacob Wendell, January 12, 1739, January 15, 1742, December 22, 1746, in Livingston Papers, Museum of the City of New York.

49. Philip Livingston to Samuel Storke, May —, 1734, in Miscellaneous Manuscripts, vol. 5.

50. Stephen DeLancey to Philip Livingston, January 13, 1711; Philip Livingston to Robert Livingston, April 21, 1724, in Livingston Family Papers.

51. Philip Livingston, Invoices, October 23, 1734, July —, 1735, September 25, 1734; Philip Livingston to Storke and Gainsborough, June 7, 1736, in Miscellaneous Manuscripts, vol. 5.

52. Philip Livingston to Storke and Gainsborough, November 2, 1736; Livingston to Winder and Farrand at Barcelona, August 15, 1734; Livingston, Invoice, July 29, 1730, ibid.

53. Philip Livingston to Storke and Gainsborough, June 2, 1738, ibid.; Henry Van Rensselaer, Jr., Account Book, 1734–1742, p. 15, New-York Historical Society, New York City; Philip Livingston to Henry Van Rensselaer, Jr., May 4, 1730, in Letters and Papers of Harme Gansvoort, New York Public Library, New York City.

Mississippi for deerskins and low-priced beaver pelts. Although Livingston had "a great Inclination" to develop such a scheme, the cautious Londoners discouraged the idea.[54]

Realizing in the 1730s that his many competitors in Schenectady and Albany would prevent him from capturing the major part of the trade by ordinary business methods, Livingston attempted to obtain a piece of land that would "intercept all the northward trade from Canada to this place." At the same time, he tried to acquire territory along the Mohawk that would have allowed him to capture much of the trade from Oswego.[55] In a less grandiose manner, he strengthened his position in the western trade by establishing a strong business relationship with the youthful Henry Van Rensselaer, Jr., who became a Schenectady merchant in either 1729 or 1730. Van Rensselaer dealt in wheat and furs, and although he did not form a partnership with his older associate, they had some type of agreement under which Livingston received most of the furs obtained by his friend in Schenectady.[56] By 1735 Van Rensselaer had begun to export his own peltry, but he continued to act as Livingston's agent and performed such services as buying furs for him, collecting debts, and arranging for the transportation of goods to Oswego.[57]

Even with this assistance from Van Rensselaer, Livingston could not dominate the western trade, and his schemes for acquiring strategic land grants did not prove successful. As he became increasingly discouraged by his inability to make greater profits and by the "unreasonable brutes" who insisted on shipping their own furs to England, Livingston gave up his dream of controlling the trade. He even contemplated ending all of his involvement in the rough competition for peltry, and after 1737 he turned his attention to other business ventures, investing far less effort in the fur trade.[58]

54. Philip Livingston to Storke and Gainsborough, August 24, 1736, May 5, 1737, in Miscellaneous Manuscripts, vol. 5.

55. Philip Livingston to Samuel Storke, May —, 1734, ibid.; A petition from Samuel Storke and Peter and Peter Van Brugh Livingston to the king, October 9, 1734, in C. O. 5/1093.

56. John Richard to Henry Van Rensselaer, Jr., October 25, 1729; Philip Livingston to Henry Van Rensselaer, Jr., January 27, June 8, 1730, January 3, 1732, in Van Rensselaer-Fort Papers; Philip Livingston to Henry Van Rensselaer, Jr., May 4, 1730, in Letters and Papers of Harme Gansvoort.

57. Robert and Peter Van Brugh Livingston and Company to Henry Van Rensselaer, Jr., June 23, 1735, in Van Rensselaer-Fort Papers; Henry Van Rensselaer, Jr., Account Book, 1734–1742, pp. 15, 62, 108, 118, 123.

58. Philip Livingston to Storke and Gainsborough, July 21, 1735, June 7, June 14, July 14, 1737, July 31, 1738, in Miscellaneous Manuscripts, vol. 5; Philip Livingston to Jacob Wendell, March 28, June 12, 1739, January 15, 1742, December 22,

Although no one else after Livingston could be considered a great fur merchant, another powerful entrepreneur began his rise to prominence in the peltry business at almost the same time that Livingston was relinquishing his leadership. Arriving from Ireland in 1738 for the purpose of developing the lands belonging to his uncle Peter Warren on the Mohawk River, William Johnson, unlike the other fur merchants, concentrated only on the western trade. Within a year, he purchased some land for himself on the Mohawk about forty miles from Albany and built a trading post there in time for dealing with the Indians and traders in the spring of 1739. In this year he also went on a commercial expedition to the cosmopolitan Indian town of Oquaga on the Susquehanna River. Preferring this location to Oswego, which had too many traders—"all a parcell of Meer Bites," Johnson traveled there on his first venture with a battoe or a large canoe full of trading goods and began to establish the excellent relations with the Iroquois that would eventually play a significant role in his rise to fame and fortune.[59] Very few of Johnson's early business records have survived, but his continuing interest in the distant Oquaga indicates that this first expedition was not the last.[60]

Demonstrating the westward shift of the Indian trade away from Albany, Johnson within a decade became a substantial wholesaler of merchandise for the Oswego traders.[61] By 1751 Cadwallader Colden could justly declare, "Coll Johnson is the most considerable trader with the Western Indians and sends more goods to Oswego than any other person . . . ." Describing the results of changing trade patterns over a period of nearly three decades, Colden also stated, "all the six Nations and other Indians to the Westward stopt at his house, and were there

1746, in Livingston Papers; Philip Livingston to Robert Livingston, Jr., and Peter Van Brugh Livingston, March 3 [1740]; Philip Livingston to Robert Livingston, Jr., May 16, 1740, in Livingston Family Papers. For Livingston's involvement in land speculation, see Ruth L. Higgins, *Expansion in New York: With Especial Reference to the Eighteenth Century* (Columbus, Ohio, 1931), pp. 67, 69, 72–73, 76.

59. William Johnson to Peter Warren, May 10, 1739, in *Johnson Papers*, 1: 7; Arthur Pond, *Johnson of the Mohawks* (New York, 1930), pp. 29, 41–47. For the most recent biography of Johnson, see James Thomas Flexner, *Mohawk Baronet: Sir William Johnson of New York* (New York, 1959).

60. Johnson to Goldsbrow Banyar, May 6, 1751; Johnson to the Oneidas and the Tuscaroras, 175[?], in *Johnson Papers*, 1: 921, 3: 187; Johnson to the Board of Trade, September 28, 1757, in *NYCD*, 8: 269–70.

61. Hyde Clarke to Johnson, May 19, 1743; Edward Holland to Johnson, January 15, 1745; John B. Van Eps to Johnson, May 6, 1746; Johnson to Samuel and William Baker, October 28, 1748; Johannes Vander Heyden to Johnson, May 13, 1749; Johnson to [James J.] Ross, May 30, 1749; Albert Van Slyck to Johnson, July 17, 1750, in *Johnson Papers*, 1: 18, 24, 50, 194, 226, 229, 291.

supplied, and from that time few or none were seen in Albany. This touched a people in the most sensible part, who have no other view in life but that of getting money."[62]

By this time the few citizens of Albany who still had large stakes in the peltry business concerned themselves mainly with the Canada trade. King George's War had briefly interrupted the trade both to the north and west, but afterwards it revived rapidly.[63] Both 1749 and 1750 were boom years, and then the trade settled down to about the same pace as before the war.[64] In 1752, however, most New York fur merchants suffered an economic blow that had nothing to do with furs except that it involved exactly the same trade routes.

The problem developed when European merchants involved in the China trade began to offer high prices for ginseng. Greatly valued by the Chinese and others for its medicinal uses, the roots of the ginseng plant were collected by the Indians and sold to the traders. Before 1752 New Yorkers were not interested in the plant, but its sudden popularity caused prices to skyrocket in Europe. In this year, the fur merchants exported large shipments of ginseng, for which they paid high prices knowing that it was selling in England at the extraordinary rate of from twenty to twenty-one shillings per pound.[65] William Johnson became so enthusiastic over the possibilities of making money from native plants that he asked one of his London factors to let him know "whether the flower, or Blossom of the Sassafrass Tree would sell well in London and at what price or any other root, plant &ca which we have here. and let it be a Secret for the first Year to any Body else . . . ."[66]

Fortunately for New Yorkers, the ginseng craze did not develop for sassafras blossoms. "As to Gensing root," William Baker, the great London merchant, explained to Johannes R. Bleecker, "I am very sorry that

62. Cadwallader Colden, "The present state of the Indian affairs . . . ," August 8, 1751, in *The Letters and Papers of Cadwallader Colden*, 10 vols., New-York Historical Society *Collections*, 50–56 (1917–23), 67–69 (1934–35) (New York, 1918–36), 4: 273, 274.

63. John Rutherford to Walter Butler, June 11, 1745; Johnson to Samuel and William Baker, October 28, 1748, in *Johnson Papers*, 1: 32, 194; Lawson, "Extracts from Customs 3."

64. John Lindesay, An account of furs purchased from the Indians at Oswego, August 20, 1749, in *NYCD*, 6: 538; Lawson, "Extracts from Customs 3."

65. *Journal of the Votes and Proceedings of the General Assembly of the Colony of New York [1691–1765]*, 2 vols. (New York, 1764–66), April 19, 1754, 2: 377; Robert Sanders to Storke and Champion, February 15, 1753, in Robert Sanders Letter Book, 1752–1758; William Baker to Johannes R. Bleecker, February 17, 1753, in Johannes R. Bleecker Papers.

66. Johnson to John George Liebenrood, August 4, 1752, in *Johnson Papers*, 1: 373.

you are among the many of my friends that have engaged in the purchase of that commodity, the first that came over was very good and at that time it being a new thing and the quantity not very great, it fetcht a good price . . . ," but by the end of 1752 the bottom had dropped out of the market.[67] In the next year the situation became even worse, and Robert Sanders, an Albany merchant, lamented that the price of the root had fallen "to such a Degree as the like was Never heard or Known of any Commodity."[68] He could speak from bitter experience. One of his several shipments of ginseng, purchased at twelve shillings per pound, amounted to a value of £ 132 4s. sterling, but his factor could sell it at a rate of only 2s. 4d., which left Sanders with £ 23 18s. 4d. or only £ 15 0s. 4d. after expenses.[69] Another of his shipments brought an even greater loss, and most of his fur trading associates suffered in a similar manner.[70]

Mercifully ending almost as soon as it had begun, the ginseng mania apparently had few lasting effects, and the continuing healthy state of the fur trade from 1752 to 1755 allowed the merchants little time to bemoan their losses. With the outbreak of war on the frontier in the late summer of 1755, the fur trade came to an abrupt halt. It would never again be the same.

Up to and including the fateful year 1755, the methods of trading merchandise for peltry had not changed greatly since the late 1720s, when Governor Burnet failed to destroy the Canada trade and when traders began to congregate each spring at the outpost on Lake Ontario. The most significant economic change in this period was the gradual lessening of the fur trade's importance in New York City and later in Albany. With the breaking of their monopoly, the founding of Oswego, and the development of settlements along the Mohawk, the Albany merchants had fewer and fewer contacts with Indian hunters, until by the 1740s they seldom traded directly with the western Indians or with the Iroquois. Inevitably, the economic changes brought about shifts in political alignments.

---

67. William Baker to Bleecker, February 17, 1753, in Johannes R. Bleecker Papers.

68. Sanders to John George Liebenrood, October 9, 1753, in Robert Sanders Letter Book, 1752–1758.

69. Invoice of Peltry, December 2, 1752, and Account of Sales, January 1, 1755, folio 30, in Invoice Book of Robert Sanders, 1748–1756, New-York Historical Society, New York City.

70. Invoice of Peltry, August 19, 1752, and Account of Sales, January 1, 1755, folio 27, ibid.; Cuyler to Champion and Hayley, December 30, 1754, in Cornelius Cuyler Letter Book, 1752–1764.

7

THE FUR MARKET

AT THE BEGINNING of the eighteenth century, many New Yorkers believed that the fur trade had been destroyed. "The beaver trade," reported Governor Bellomont in 1700, "here and at Boston is sunk to little or nothing, and the market is so low for beaver in England that 'tis scarce worth the transporting."[1] Not only had the Iroquois been "mightily diminished," with a consequent reduction in the supply of peltry, but also the demand in England had fallen so much that the price of beaver had decreased from a wartime high of fourteen shillings to five shillings per pound.[2]

In spite of the disastrous blows suffered by the Iroquois and the fur traders during King William's War, the New York fur trade was far from dead. Even as Bellomont made his pessimistic assessment, the trade was beginning to revive. Between June 1699 and June 1700 over fifteen thousand beaver skins had been exported from the colony. Bellomont and others were dissatisfied with what they considered a very low annual production of peltry, but such dissatisfaction involved a comparison of the 1700 figures with those of the spectacularly successful years shortly after the middle of the seventeenth century. In those days, New Yorkers probably exported an average of forty thousand beaver pelts annually. At least once, the total climbed to about sixty-six thousand. The decline in such high production rates had resulted not from the destruction in King William's War, but rather from the decrease in beaver populations within easy reach of the Iroquois homelands. In 1686 New Yorkers had exported only about thirty thousand beaver pelts, and a year later, when the Iroquois renewed their feud with the French, the total fell to less than twelve thousand.[3]

---

1. Bellomont to the Board of Trade, November 28, 1700, in *Documents Relative to the Colonial History of the State of New York*, ed. Edmund B. O'Callaghan and Berthold Fernow, 15 vols. (Albany, 1856–87), 4: 789, hereafter cited as *NYCD*.
2. Ibid.
3. Ibid.; Stephen Van Cortlandt and James Graham to William Blathwayt, 1687,

Although New York traders would never again be able to achieve the successes of earlier years, the amount of furs purchased annually from the Indians or French smugglers cannot be considered insignificant. In the years before New York developed a lucrative trade with the West Indies, the exchange of furs for English manufactured products had constituted the most important element of the colony's economy. In 1687 Stephen Van Cortlandt, the collector of customs and receiver general of New York, and James Graham, the attorney general, had warned "that if the Indian Trade bee disturbed or distroyed it will be Impossible for the Inhabitants of this Province to provide themselfs with Clothinge and other nessisaries from England ther beinge Little else then furrs Sutable to make returnes."[4]

Fortunately, within a few years after 1687 the colony's single-staple economy changed completely because of rapid increases in the production of flour and other foodstuffs, which New Yorkers sold in the West Indies and Honduras for sugar, rum, molasses, cotton, dye-woods, drugs, spices, and specie. Many of these products could be readily exchanged in England for manufactured goods, and by the beginning of the century New York no longer depended exclusively on the fur trade.[5] Nevertheless, the business of exporting peltry continued to be a profitable way of obtaining English goods. In the first two decades of the century, furs and deerskins represented almost all of the colony's native exports to England.[6]

As for total exports from the port of New York to England, furs made up about 20 percent of all shipments in the years from 1700 to 1755. In some years this percentage was much higher. Over a three-year period from 1717 to 1720, total exports came to £63,746 11s. 1d., of which £25,329 2s. 9d.—almost 40 percent—represented the value of furs, not

in William Blathwayt Papers (microfilm), Colonial Williamsburg, Williamsburg, Va.; Thomas Dongan to Captain Palmer, September 8, 1687, in *NYCD*, 3: 476.

4. Stephen Van Cortlandt and James Graham to William Blathwayt, 1687, in William Blathwayt Papers.

5. Virginia D. Harrington, *The New York Merchant on the Eve of the Revolution* (New York, 1935), pp. 165–66; Curtis P. Nettels, *The Money Supply of the American Colonies Before 1720* (Madison, Wis., 1934), p. 81. For information on the trade routes used by New Yorkers and other colonial shippers, see Gary Walton, "New Evidence on Colonial Commerce," *Journal of Economic History* 28 (1968): 363–89.

6. Julius Bloch et al., eds., *An Account of Her Majesty's Revenue in the Province of New York, 1701–1709. The Customs Records of Early Colonial New York* (Ridgewood, N. J., 1966), passim; Naval Office Lists for the Port of New York (microfilm), in C.O. 5/1222, Public Record Office, London; Governor Cornbury to Charles Hedges, July 15, 1705, in *NYCD*, 4: 1150.

including peltry sent to Holland or deerskins.[7] Even as late as 1765, furs accounted for 10 percent of New York's exports to England.[8]

Although Bellomont complained about the small number of furs being exported, New York in 1700 produced 36 percent of England's fur supply, which was more than twice as much as the combined totals from New England and Hudson's Bay. The rest of England's supply came from the other colonies, especially Virginia, Maryland, and Pennsylvania. Even after Hudson's Bay became the largest English producer of furs, New York continued as a significant source of peltry for the mother country. From 1720 to 1755 England received about 25 percent of her total supply from New York. As a result, New York merchants annually received £3000 to £8000 worth of English merchandise in exchange for furs, plus an additional amount for the sale of deerskins.[9] Before the enumeration of furs in 1722, the colony also received many products from Holland, where in the three years from 1719 to 1721, New Yorkers sold about 23 percent of their furs.[10]

In addition to the trade with Europe, the fur merchants of New York sold a large but indeterminable amount of peltry to colonial hatters. In 1732, for instance, Cornelius Cuyler reported that he annually sold more than three thousand pounds of beaver to "our hatters."[11] At a price per pound of five shillings New York currency, Cuyler thus made £750 currency in addition to what he received form the sale of his furs in London. As the size of the colonial hat industry increased, New Yorkers sold a proportionally greater amount of furs within the colonies.

Bellomont's fears about the decline in the fur supply were exaggerated, but his pessimism concerning the market for beaver in 1700 was justified. Along with a temporary change in fashions, a recession at the end of King William's War adversely affected the English hat industry. Within a few years, however, it was again flourishing and growing rapidly. In 1700 only 5,786 dozen hats were exported from England. By 1710 the number stood at 10,501, and by 1750 the hatters produced

7. Harrington, *New York Merchant*, p. 167; An account of imports and exports from and to New York [June 16, 1725], in *NYCD*, 5: 761; An account of furs imported into England from New York, 1717–1723, in *Documentary History of the State of New-York*, ed. Edmund B. O'Callaghan, 4 vols. (Albany, 1850–51), 1: 481.

8. Murray G. Lawson, "Extracts from Customs 3," in the possession of Lawrence A. Harper, University of California, Berkeley; Murray G. Lawson, *Fur: A Study in English Mercantilism, 1700–1775* (Toronto, 1943), p. 135.

9. Lawson, "Extracts from Customs 3."

10. Lawson, *Fur*, p. 35.

11. Cuyler to Samuel Baker, January 6, 1732, in Cornelius Cuyler Letter Book, 1724–1736 (microfilm), American Antiquarian Society, Worcester, Mass.

more than 45,000 dozen for export, which were valued at £263,000, compared to the £44,000 worth of hats exported in the first year of the century.[12] While the fur traders at the end of King William's War waited for the hat industry to recover, they were able to sell much of their surplus as a result of the sizable English export of beaver skins to Russia during the years between 1682 and 1713.[13]

Although beaver hats were a popular item of wearing apparel in New York, only a very limited number of them came from England. In 1740 the English hatters produced nine times as many hats for export as they had in 1700, but in four decades they had only doubled their exports to the thirteen colonies, where the demand was being met by the craftsmen of New York, New England, and Pennsylvania.[14] New York hatters established an industry in the colony as early as 1706. Within ten years they started to export their products to the West Indies, where they competed with English hatters for the slowly but steadily growing market.[15] By 1732 Governor Cosby could report that "the hatt makeing trade here seemed to promise to make the greatest advances to the prejudice of Great Brittain . . ."—but in that year Parliament passed the Hat Act, prohibiting the exportation of hats from any colony.[16] Furthermore, the act provided that colonial hatters could not employ Negroes, and except for members of their families they could only have two apprentices, who had to serve for at least seven years. In practice, the only enforced section of the act dealt with exports.[17]

12. E. E. Rich, *Hudson's Bay Company, 1670–1870*, 3 vols. (New York, 1961), 1: 356–57, 530; Elizabeth B. Schumpeter, *English Overseas Trade Statistics, 1667–1808* (London, 1960), p. 66.

13. E. E. Rich, "Russia and the Colonial Fur Trade," *Economic History Review* 7 (1955): 320–28.

14. Rita Gottesman, comp., *The Arts and Crafts in New York, 1726–1776: Advertisements and News Items from New York City Newspapers* (New York, 1938), pp. 335, 336, 337, 338, 340, 341, 342, 343, 346, 347; Naval Office Lists for the Port of New York, in C. O. 5/1222–1229; Schumpeter, *English Overseas Trade Statistics*, p. 66.

15. Samuel McKee, Jr., *Labor in Colonial New York, 1664–1776* (New York, 1935), p. 30; Schumpeter, *English Overseas Trade Statistics*, p. 66; An account of imports and exports at New York for 1725, December 24, 1725; Archibald Kennedy, Answer to questions from the Board of Trade, January 5, 1745, in *NYCD*, 5: 774, 6: 393; Naval Office Lists for the Port of New York, in C.O. 5/1224.

16. Governor Cosby to the Board of Trade, December 18, 1732, in *NYCD*, 5: 938.

17. Lawrence A. Harper, "The Effect of the Navigation Acts on the Thirteen Colonies," in *The Era of the American Revolution*, ed. Richard B. Morris (New York, 1965), p. 6; Oliver M. Dickerson, *The Navigation Acts and the American Revolution* (Philadelphia, 1951), pp. 19–20.

The Hat Act prevented the rise of any great hat manufacturers in the colony, but the industry continued to flourish by producing hats of a reasonable quality that were less expensive than imported ones. Each spring, hatters and merchants from every northern colony arrived in Albany or Schenectady to buy furs at the lowest possible prices. If they lacked funds to acquire an entire year's supply, they either returned in the fall or made occasional purchases from fur merchants in New York City.[18] The fanciest hats, used by gentlemen on special occasions, were imported from England, but the colonial hatters manufactured a product that compared favorably with most European headgear. "In American cities," Peter Kalm reported in 1749, "one can now get as fine beaver hats made as one ever could in France or England."[19] A decade later, another traveler, Andrew Burnaby, expressed similar sentiments.[20]

Because of its barbed hairs that could be worked into a particularly luxurious, durable felt, beaver was the most important raw material in the felt-making process. The hatters usually mixed it with other furs, including rabbit, muskrat, otter, and raccoon, but their customers judged a hat by the amount of beaver it contained. The cheapest hats contained a mixture of inexpensive fur and wool fibers. Sometimes, the hatters used nothing but wool.[21]

Being well adapted for life in the ponds of North America, the beaver possessed a thick covering of soft fur protected by a layer of guard hairs, which are difficult to remove and of no use in the production of felt. Frequently, the Indians made robes from several skins with the fur on the inside, which resulted in the gradual wearing away of the useless guard hairs. These skins, known as *castor gras* or coat beaver, possessed a greater value than the more common type, called *castor sec* or parchment, which retained all the protective hairs. The French divided each

18. Cuyler to Samuel Baker, January 6, 1732, in Cornelius Cuyler Letter Book, 1724–1736; Philip Livingston to Storke and Gainsborough, July 21, 1735, in Miscellaneous Manuscripts, vol. 5, New York State Library, Albany; Thomas Armstrong to William Johnson, August 31, 1748, in *The Papers of Sir William Johnson*, ed. James Sullivan et al., 14 vols. (Albany, 1921–65), 1: 181, hereafter cited as *Johnson Papers*; Robert Sanders to Robert and Richard Ray, January –, 1756, in Robert Sanders Letter Book, 1752–1758 (microfilm), New-York Historical Society, New York City; Phyn and Ellice to John Thurman, Jr., June 23, 1772, in Phyn and Ellice Letter Book (microfilm), 2: 156, Buffalo and Erie County Historical Society, Buffalo, N.Y.

19. Peter Kalm, *Peter Kalm's Travels in North America*, ed. Adolph B. Benson, 2 vols. (New York, 1937), 2: 535.

20. Andrew Burnaby, *Travels through the Middle Settlements in North America in the Years 1759 and 1760* (London, 1775), p. 82.

21. J. H. Hawkins, *History of the Worshipful Company of the Art or Misery of Feltmakers of London* (London, 1917), pp. 11–18.

of these two categories into numerous grades, but the English merely noted a difference between summer and winter beaver.[22]

Most merchants, whether large or small, did not mind selling a portion of their furs to the colonial hatters. In this way, they could avoid the expenses involved in overseas shipping, but in return they received colonial currency that could not be used as a means of paying debts in England. Notoriously lacking in stability, paper money from the various provinces complicated intercolonial transactions. New York currency, with the exchange rate in relation to sterling ranging from about 130 in the first decades of the century to an average of 177 in the years before the Revolution, remained relatively stable, but in the late 1740s Massachusetts and Connecticut money exchanged at 1100 percent. The situation in Rhode Island was even worse.[23] "On the Emission of the first Paper Money," explained Benjamin Franklin, "a Difference soon arose between that and silver, the latter having a Property the former had not, a property always in Demand in the Colonies, to wit, it being fit for a Remittance."[24] Without specie or currency acceptable in Europe, the businessmen of New York as well as those of other colonies constantly attempted to acquire raw materials which they could exchange in England for manufactured products. Beaver skins were uniquely "fit for a Remittance."

Even though beaver served as a valuable medium of exchange, merchants could not expect to make much of a profit from its sale. The price of New York beaver on the London market was usually only a little higher than its value in the province.[25] In 1750, for example, Robert

22. Louis Armand Lahontan, *New Voyages to North America*, ed. Reuben G. Thwaites, 2 vols. (Chicago, 1905), 1: 173; Harold A. Innis, *The Fur Trade in Canada*, rev. ed. (New Haven, 1962), p. 14; Rich, "Russia and the Colonial Fur Trade," pp. 313–14; Cuyler to Storke and Gainsborough, November 16, 1734, in Cornelius Cuyler Letter Book, 1724–1736.

23. Harrington, *New York Merchant*, p. 108. For more on colonial currency and the shortage of specie, see Bray Hammond, *Banks and Politics in America, from the Revolution to the Civil War* (Princeton, 1957), pp. 3–40. Also see Charles M. Andrews, *The Colonial Period of American History*, 4 vols. (New Haven, 1934–38), vol. 4, *England's Commercial and Colonial Policy*, pp. 350–52; and George Louis Beer, *British Colonial Policy, 1754–1765* (New York, 1907; reprinted, Gloucester, Mass., 1958), pp. 179–88. For a study that demonstrates the relative stability of New York currency, see Roger W. Weiss, "The Issue of Paper Money in the American Colonies, 1720–1774," *Journal of Economic History* 30 (1970): 770–84.

24. Leonard W. Labaree, ed., *The Papers of Benjamin Franklin*, 14 vols. to date (New Haven, 1959–), 14: 84.

25. Cuyler to Joseph Mico, December 8, 1735, in Cornelius Cuyler Letter Book, 1724–1736; Philip Livingston to Storke and Gainsborough, October 31, 1734, August 3, 1738, in Miscellaneous Manuscripts, vol. 5; Samuel and William Baker to Bleecker, March 2, 1738, in Johannes R. Bleecker Papers, New York State Library,

Sanders, who ran a business in Albany and traded extensively with Montreal, sent a shipment of 220 beaver skins, valued at 10s. per pound in New York currency or 5s. 7d. sterling, to John George Liebenrood, who sold them in London for 6s. 6d. This transaction gave Sanders a gross profit of 11d. per pound or 16 percent over what he had paid. It was hardly enough to meet the various shipping charges, including customs duties, commissions, and freight. In New York these skins had been worth £197, and in return, after deduction of expenses, Liebenrood provided Sanders with credit for £205 18s. 2d. currency or £114 13s. 2d. sterling.[26]

The nature of the London fur market caused the small difference between the prices of beaver skins in New York and those in England. Hudson's Bay Company disposed of its beaver at public sales in large lots that often went to such great furriers as Henry Sperling, who exported most of the fur to Amsterdam for shipment to Russia and other parts of Europe. The size of shipments from the Atlantic colonies could substantially affect prices in London, but the price of Hudson's Bay beaver was set at a particular level as a result of the public auctions. New York peltry, considered to be of a lesser quality, then brought prices proportional to the value of the prime northern skins.[27]

If a New York merchant refused to pay a reasonable amount for furs in relation to the London prices, the traders could export their peltry either themselves or through the numerous small merchants who maintained overseas connections. In 1701, for instance, five or six men controlled the major part of the fur exports, but over thirty people exported peltry from the colony.[28] Even when Stephen DeLancey was at the height of his economic power, numerous small merchants continued to ship furs to England. Although many small merchants, after the enumeration of furs in 1722, could no longer effectively take advantage of their contacts in Holland, they now could channel much of their supply into the growing colonial hat industry.[29]

Albany; Invoice to Champion and Hayley, November —, 1754, and Account of Sales, December 20, 1755, in Invoice Book of Robert Sanders, 1748–1756, folio 48, New-York Historical Society, New York City.

26. Invoice to John George Liebenrood, July 15, 1751, and Account of Sales, May —, 1752, in Robert Sanders Invoice Book, 1748–1756.

27. Rich, *Hudson's Bay Company*, 1: 320–21, 395, 658–59; William Baker to Bleecker, February 17, 1753, in Johannes R. Bleecker Papers; Transactions of the Board of Trade, May 12, 1725, in *NYCD*, 5: 753.

28. Bloch et al., eds., *An Account of Her Majesty's Revenues*, pp. 15–16, 26–28, 29, 41.

29. Philip Livingston to Robert Livingston, June 10, 1724, in Livingston Family Papers (microfilm), Franklin D. Roosevelt Library, Hyde Park, N.Y.

Since businessmen could not make substantial profits by selling peltry at levels significantly higher than the purchase price, they made their money through the high mark-up on imported goods. Philip Livingston, however, also attempted to make a profit on the London market by manipulating the price of furs in New York. "I fear," he told his London factor in 1734, "the Little advance in beaver with you will be a means to Raise the price here, but I hope to fix it at 4/ but Suppose shall be oblidged to allow 4/6 per lb. or not buy many."[30] Even if his schemes had succeeded, the profits would not have been much above the average level. On one occasion in 1736 he purchased his beaver for 6s. per pound, which equalled 3s. 9d. sterling at the exchange rate of 160. In London the price of New York beaver stood at 4s. 6d., meaning that if this price held, he would make 9d. per pound, representing a gross profit of 20 percent.[31] Knowing that the price of beaver would not remain at this relatively high level, Livingston did not allow the scarcity of overseas shipping in New York harbor to interfere with his chances of making a profit. He therefore sent his first four hogsheads of beaver to Boston for reshipment to England before the arrival of the fall ships in New York.[32]

Livingston occasionally refused to buy furs at rates that did not allow him a reasonable profit on the London market, and he often lamented about rising prices in New York and about his inability to find "means for preventing of it."[33] In spite of his financial resources and his influence over numerous indebted fur traders, Livingston's attempts to control the price of peltry failed because of the competition from colonial hatters and the inclination on the part of the traders to export their own furs. More often than not, he had to buy beaver at high prices in order to avoid losing customers.[34]

The expense of shipping furs to England and selling them either in Bristol or London presented the greatest obstacle to the possibilities of making significant profits on the sale of peltry. In a typical instance, Hendrick Ten Eyck sent a hogshead containing beaver and an assortment of other furs to Samuel and William Baker, who sold the skins in two different lots and returned an account of the sale in the spring of 1751. The assorted furs, consisting of a wildcat, otters, wolves, foxes,

30. Philip Livingston to Samuel Storke, May —, 1734, in Miscellaneous Manuscripts, vol. 5.

31. Philip Livingston to Storke and Gainsborough, August 24, 1736, ibid.; *New York Journal*, December 22, 1740.

32. Philip Livingston to Storke and Gainsborough, August 6, 1736, Miscellaneous Manuscripts, vol. 5.

33. Philip Livingston to Storke and Gainsborough, October 13, 1735, ibid.

34. Philip Livingston to Storke and Gainsborough, May —, July 16, 1734, November 1, 1736, ibid.

fishers, minks, martens, raccoons, and muskrats or musquashes, as they were called in the colonial period, brought a total of £46 8s. At a rate of 6s. per pound, a fur dealer purchased the 197 beaver skins for £110 8s. In addition to the £4 14s. 4d charged as a 2.5 percent commission and a .5 percent brokerage fee for the handling of the sales, Ten Eyck paid £17 18s. 3d. for customs duties and entry fees, 2s. 1d. for freight, and 5s. 6d. for landwaiters, lighterage, wharfage, porterage, and cooperage. Subtracting the £24 19s. 1d. in expenses from the total sales of £156 16s., his factors credited Ten Eyck's account for £131 16s. 11d.[35] In addition, Ten Eyck had to pay his New York agent a small fee, plus packing and port clearance charges. He also may have taken out insurance which the Baker firm would have arranged for a commission of from 2 to 2.5 percent of the policy's premium,[36] although New Yorkers usually declined to insure fur shipments unless a state of war existed or seemed imminent. As for their return goods from England, they took greater care and often had an arrangement with their factors to insure one-half of the goods and in times of danger to ship them by more than one vessel.[37]

The greatest expense for Ten Eyck and other merchants was the payment of various customs duties and taxes. In the early years of the century, New York, the only northern colony that taxed exports, charged 9d. New York currency per beaver skin, and until 1722 England charged an additional 16d.[38] In a very unusual practice, the royal collector in the colony collected both of these payments.[39] The total assessment of about 2s. per skin was extremely high for an item worth only about 10s., but by 1713 New York eliminated the duty, replacing it in 1715

35. Samuel and William Baker, Account of Sales, April 23, 1751, in Harmanus Bleecker Papers, New York State Library, Albany.

36. [Samuel Baker] to Bleecker, November 18, 1737, in Johannes R. Bleecker Papers; Cuyler to Richard Jeneway, June 10, 1727; Cuyler to Henry and John Cruger, October 13, 1753, in Cornelius Cuyler Letter Books, 1724–1736, 1752–1764.

37. Philip Livingston, Invoice, October 23, 1734, in Miscellaneous Manuscripts, vol. 5; Cuyler to Joseph Mico, July 13, 1734; Cuyler to Storke and Champion, July 9, 1753; Cuyler to Dirk Vander Heyden, November 6, 1755; Cuyler to Isaac Low, May 14, 1761, in Cornelius Cuyler Letter Books, 1724–1736, 1752–1764.

38. Colonial Laws of New York from the Year 1664 to the Revolution, 5 vols. (Albany, 1894–96), May 16, 1691, May 15, 1699, 1: 249, 421–22, hereafter cited as Laws; Bellomont to the Board of Trade, November 28, 1700, in NYCD, 4: 789; Lawson, Fur, p. 18. Since prompt payment reduced the amount of the customs charges, the English duty can also be considered as 15d.; ibid., p. 18n.

39. Laws, May 16, 1699, 1: 404; Thomas C. Barrow, Trade and Empire: The British Customs Service in Colonial America, 1660–1775 (Cambridge, Mass., 1967), p. 66.

with one on flour and bread. With the enumeration of furs in 1722, Parliament reduced the English duty from 16 to 6d. In order to increase their supply of furs, the English hatters in 1764 pressured the government into a further reduction, bringing the charge down to a single penny while eliminating drawbacks and setting an export duty of 7d.[40]

In addition to regular duties and excise taxes on merchandise and rum, New York fur merchants also had to pay a special assessment on goods used in the Indian trade. In earlier years, all trading goods sent up the Hudson River paid 10 percent on the prime costs of the merchandise, which for the purpose of assessment were set by law at such rates as 2s. 4d. per yard of duffels and £8 for each piece of strouds.[41] After King William's War this charge was reduced to 5 percent, and several years later the law was allowed to lapse. For awhile, the fur trade did not contribute directly to the revenue of the province, but in 1726 the assembly enacted a law placing high duties, such as 15s. per piece of strouds, on certain Indian goods transported to the west of Albany. If such goods were carried to the north of Albany, meaning to Canada, the law required all charges to be doubled.[42] Since this new revenue act was connected with Governor Burnet's efforts to prevent the trade with Canada, it fell victim to the general disallowance of these regulations at the end of the decade. In 1731, however, the assembly placed a duty of 10s. on each piece of stroud cloth and 12d. on each gallon of rum carried away from Albany. This law remained in effect for many years, providing the colony with a revenue of a little more than £500 annually.[43]

When furs were enumerated in 1722, the Dutch merchants in Albany, who often had business contacts and relatives in Holland, suffered more than the New York City merchants, who usually had established relationships with English merchants. One of the best examples of the connection between Holland and Albany was the commercial relationship between Anthony Van Schaick and his brother, Levinus Van Schaick, who had once lived in Albany, but had returned to Amsterdam during King William's War.[44]

40. *Laws*, July 1, 1713, July 5, 1715, 1: 779–80, 849; Lawson, *Fur*, p. 18; Harper, "Effect of the Navigation Acts," p. 21.
41. *Laws*, May 16, 1691, 1: 249; Stephen Van Cortlandt and James Graham to William Blathwayt, 1687, in William Blathwayt Papers.
42. *Laws*, May 15, 1699, November 27, 1702, June 17, 1726, 1: 420–21, 517, 2: 281–82.
43. *Journal of the Votes and Proceedings of the General Assembly of the Colony of New York [1691–1765]*, 2 vols. (New York, 1764–66), August 26, 1730, August 27, 1731, 1: 607, 624.
44. Levinus Van Schaick to Anthony Van Schaick (translated from Dutch),

Parliament included furs in the list of enumerated goods because the hatters complained about "an evil practice . . . of carrying very great quantities of beaver-skins from New York, or other plantations to Holland directly . . . ."[45] Although reports that New York sent "twenty or thirty thousand skins annually" to Holland were greatly exaggerated, the colony from 1719 to 1721 did export about 23 percent of its beaver skins to Amsterdam. In other years the total may have gone as high as 40 percent.[46]

The disruption of old commercial patterns between Holland and Albany and a continuing direct, but legal, trade between the two localities opened up the possibility of smuggling beaver to Amsterdam. Such an illicit trade actually did develop, but it never amounted to more than a small percentage of New York's total fur exports. Most of the larger merchants, including Stephen DeLancey, Adolph Philipse, and Philip Livingston, shipped almost all their furs to England after 1722, and during the next several years New York's exports of fur to England increased significantly. Even Cornelius Cuyler, who later developed an illegal overseas trade in furs, made sure that his peltry shipments to Amsterdam were first landed in Great Britain as the law required.[47]

In the 1720s the temptation to smuggle could not have been very great, because beaver skins now required a duty of only 6d., and fur merchants needed a way of paying for the large amount of woolen cloth that they purchased almost entirely from England. In later years, however, as the smuggling of various Dutch goods to New York greatly increased, the colonial merchants occasionally made their remittances in the form of smuggled beaver skins.[48] Consequently, in 1739 a customs official found it necessary to publish an advertisement in the *New York Gazette* stating that he was aware of a "trading with Beaver Skins and other furs, carried on for several Years from this Port directly to Hol-

---

October 29, 1698, in Van Schaick Papers, New York State Library, Albany; David A. Armour, "The Merchants of Albany, New York, 1686–1760" (Ph.D. diss., Northwestern University, 1965), pp. 53–54.

45. "The Hat-Makers Case," December 4, 1721, in *Calendar of State Papers, Colonial Series, America and West Indies,* ed. W. N. Sainsbury et al., 43 vols to date (London, 1860–), 32: 498.

46. *Journal of the Commissioners for Trade and Plantations,* 14 vols. (London, 1920–38), May 12, 1725, 5: 175; Lawson, *Fur,* p. 35; Harper, "Effect of the Navigation Acts," p. 21.

47. Lawson, *Fur,* p. 35; Cuyler to Samuel Baker, June 25, 1729, August 19, 1731, in Cornelius Cuyler Letter Book, 1724–1736. In these two letters, Cuyler instructed Baker to forward peltry to Levinus Clarkson, a merchant in Amsterdam.

48. Harrington, *New York Merchant,* pp. 255–58.

land" without first entering a port in Great Britain. In order to stop this illicit trade, he ordered all merchants to distinguish carefully between enumerated and nonenumerated goods when loading their products aboard ships. He warned them that in the future customs officers would inspect all packages.[49]

Cornelius Cuyler, the most important merchant identifiable as an illegal exporter of furs to Holland, conducted this business with Daniel Crommelin, who owned a large firm in Amsterdam. Although the wily Albany merchant may have been hesitant to mention unlawful transactions in his letter books, his correspondence gives the impression that only a very small portion of his exports went to Crommelin. In one of few notations in his records of any illegal activities, Cuyler instructed Isaac Low, his agent in New York City, to ship a box containing 214 pounds of coat beaver to Crommelin. He noted significantly, "I suppose you know that this must be done Privately / I believe Mr. Charles Crommelin and many Others may inform you."[50] Judging from this statement, Cuyler was not the only merchant engaged in the illegal export of beaver from New York.

One of the other smugglers may have been Cuyler's son, Philip. Before opening a business in New York City, he took his father's advice in 1754 to visit Daniel Crommelin in Holland so that they could "settle a Correspondence" to their "Mutual Advantage."[51] Cuyler also advised his son to make arrangements for illegally sending goods directly from Holland to New York. Warning the young man that such a procedure could be dangerous unless the ship's captain had experience in smuggling, he suggested that Philip talk with a Captain Fletcher. Cornelius soon discovered the validity of his warnings, for in 1756 a shipment of linens from Crommelin was seized in Stamford, which was one of the Connecticut harbors often used as a place to land illegal goods.[52] Another merchant probably engaged in the illicit trade was Hendrick Ten Eyck, who displayed more than casual interest about the price of furs in Amsterdam.[53]

49. *New York Gazette*, October 1, 1739.
50. Cuyler to Isaac Low, November 6, 1762, in Cornelius Cuyler Letter Book, 1752–1764.
51. Cuyler to Daniel Crommelin, May 18, 1752, ibid.
52. Cuyler to Philip Cuyler, June 4, 1754; Cuyler to Daniel Crommelin, September 24, 1756, ibid.; Governor Charles Hardy to the Board of Trade, July 10, 1757, in *NYCD*, 7: 297.
53. Daniel Crommelin, "A price Currant of Goods usually Imported at Amsterdam," June —, 1751; [Hendrick Ten Eyck] to Daniel Crommelin, May 14, 1752, in Harmanus Bleecker Papers.

Although Holland remained a good market for peltry, it produced only gunpowder, firearms, and a few textiles for the Indian trade. Since the Dutch did not manufacture strouds, which over the years became increasingly important to the Indians, New York traders had to use the majority of their furs to make remittances to England in payment for this particular kind of cloth.

Often following specific patterns sent to them by Albany merchants, the English factors ordered strouds in pieces of about twenty-four yards directly from the manufacturers, and the quality varied widely from year to year.[54] In 1750, for instance, the Baker firm explained to William Johnson, "The Strouds we have bought we hope will prove as good as those sent you last Spring, but not at all Cheaper. We cannot be exact as to the quality or price till they come from Dyeing . . . ."[55] If the textiles turned out poorly, the London firms had little choice but to send them to their clients, who often reacted by complaining, as Cornelius Cuyler did to Samuel Baker, that the strouds were "almost good for nothing at all," and that "the 2 pieces of red Stripped Duffils which you sent me Last Fall are Not Worth 40/ a Piece I believe they are made of Dogs hair."[56] Apparently in the following year the quality of Baker's woolens did not improve, because Cuyler again complained, "it seems to Me you are Resolved, to Serve me always Wrong and never observe my orders, the Strouds which you now Sent Me are Course Refuse old musty Strouds good for nothing." For his next order of twenty pieces, he demanded that Baker send him good strouds: "narrow corded, Let the List of both blew and red be Black, you know Very well What is good Strouds."[57]

Not being able to expect high profits from furs, the merchants earned their money from the sale of the imported goods to the traders. For the New York importers, profits were high, but extensive competition kept prices from becoming exorbitant. In dealing with the tribesmen, an Indian trader hoped to acquire an amount of peltry worth considerably more than what he had paid for his rum, strouds, and other goods.

Without accurate statistics concerning the prices that Indian consumers paid for merchandise, it is difficult to judge either the overall

54. Cuyler to Samuel and William Baker, May 27, 1726, June 10, 1731, in Cornelius Cuyler Letter Book, 1724–1736.

55. Samuel and William Baker to William Johnson, January 22, 1750, in *Johnson Papers*, 1: 259.

56. Cuyler to Samuel Baker, June 10, 1731, in Cornelius Cuyler Letter Book, 1724–1736.

57. Cuyler to Samuel Baker, May 20, 1732, ibid.

profits of the trade or the specific amounts made on the sale of particular articles. Usually, prices depended on various factors, including the economic sophistication of a tribe and the degree of the trader's honesty. The demand for goods increased in proportion to the distance of the Indians from European settlements, and even after deductions for high transportation costs, the greatest profits were found in the most distant places.[58] Having no idea that the white men placed such high values on furs, the more remote tribes almost gave away this commodity, of which they seemed to have an unlimited supply. In one instance during the 1680s, a tribe gave some French traders from twenty-four to twenty-six beaver skins for each small keg of rum.[59]

Any attempt to figure the price of goods at Oswego or in the Indian villages can only result in a rough estimate, but at least some degree of accuracy can be obtained by using a list of trading goods drawn up after the Seven Years' War by Sir William Johnson in his role as Superintendent of Indian Affairs. This list enumerated various articles of merchandise along with the prices in furs and deerskins that would have allowed the traders to make an average of 100 percent on the cost of goods after deductions for transportation. According to Johnson's estimates, a thirteen shilling blanket would bring two beaver skins worth approximately twenty-eight shillings. Most other items in the list brought similar profits, but rum was a major exception. When a trader sold a three gallon keg costing no more than twelve shillings, he could expect to receive about eight pounds of beaver worth fifty-six shillings.[60] Although transportation expenses were higher for liquor, few traders could resist making up for this by adding water after the barrels reached their destination.

In 1721 Governor Burnet stated that New York merchants made from 20 to 40 percent on goods that they imported. By this he must have meant the amount of clear profit, since importers usually sold their merchandise for prices ranging from 110 to 200 percent over what they had paid.[61] Large importers of Indian goods had to adjust their prices in

58. William Johnson, Account of goods, October 8, 1764, in *Johnson Papers*, 4: 559.

59. Francois de Crepieul, "Remarks Concerning the Tadoussak Mission . . . ," April 7, 1686, in *Jesuit Relations and Allied Documents: Travels and Explorations of the Jesuit Missionaries in New France, 1619–1791*, ed. Reuben G. Thwaites, 73 vols. (Cleveland, 1896–1901), 63: 255–57.

60. William Johnson, Account of goods, October 8, 1764; Equivalents in barter [1765?], in *Johnson Papers*, 4: 559, 893–95.

61. Governor William Burnet to the Board of Trade, November 3, 1721, in *NYCD*, 5: 643; Harrington, *New York Merchant*, pp. 98, 100.

accordance with the degree of competition from the many Indian traders who were inclined to do their own importing and from the smaller merchants who often attempted to win customers through the technique of severe price-cutting. Philip Livingston often complained of these problems, and in 1734 he learned that some New York City merchants were selling goods to Albany traders at rates as low as 100 to 112 percent over their own cost, which meant that he would not be able to sell his merchandise at what he considered a reasonable profit.[62] At the same time, he found himself being forced to pay higher prices for beaver. In a letter to Storke and Gainsborough, his English correspondents, he lamented, "you may perceive how difficult it is to buy suitable Returns with any advantage, and it is Still more so to sell Merchandise and gett Payment for them."[63] Two years later he expressed anger at a young merchant, who had caused him "a vast deal of Prejudice with the traders" by giving them presents and free battoes. This newcomer's business practices were "astonishing to every body," but Livingston had to resign himself to waiting patiently for his competitor to go bankrupt.[64]

Fortunately for New York traders and merchants, the handful of men in London who handled most of the colony's furs vigorously competed with one another and did not organize for the purpose of controlling prices of fur or merchandise. The possibility of price-fixing always existed, however, because the number of Londoners engaged in this competition seldom, if ever, amounted to more than ten, and in the 1730s to no more than four of five.

Even under circumstances of active competition among the English merchants, Albany businessmen often were dissatisfied with the merchandise received from England, and it is quite possible that the Londoners were earning more on these products than simply the 2.5 percent commission that they charged for making purchases. After the French and Indian War, an acquaintance of Sir William Johnson gave up his business interests in New York in order to establish himself as a London merchant. While doing so, he became curious about how the men trading to the colonies had become rich while supposedly making their profits on the basis of small commissions. He reported to Johnson that after receiving orders from their customers, the merchants engaged the services of the appropriate tradesmen; and upon receiving bills from these men they accounted for payments to them "by debitting a General

62. Philip Livingston to Samuel Storke, August 2, 1734, in Miscellaneous Manuscripts, vol 5.
63. Philip Livingston to Storke and Gainsborough, 1734, ibid.
64. Philip Livingston to Storke and Gainsborough, June 7, 1736, ibid.

account of Merchandize, and then creditted that account by the Sale of these Goods to their Friends, at an advanced price of 10 to 12½ percent on an average; and after that charged a commission of 2½ . . . ."[65] Though probably exaggerated, this accusation may have had some validity since the Londoners were in a position to deceive the colonists through their opportunity of receiving large discounts from the manufacturers for making payments in cash. New York merchants seldom made such accusations; but they did recognize that some London factors charged more for goods than others.[66] In 1756 Cornelius Cuyler complained that a particular merchant, who "Charges his Goods, full as Much as any Merchant in London," demanded a price of seventy-seven shillings per piece of strouds while the Baker firm sold the item for only seventy shillings.[67]

In addition to the danger of price-fixing among English businessmen, another threat to the natural functioning of a free market was the danger of a partnership between one of New York's great merchants and a powerful firm in London. Such a possibility did not exist in the first decades of the century because of the relatively large number of English merchants engaged in the importation of New York furs, but the firm originated by Samuel Storke grew to such an extent that in 1737 it handled from 50 to 60 percent of all furs imported from New York.[68] By this time, Storke and his partner had developed a close connection with Philip Livingston and frequently entered into joint ventures with him involving the fur trade and other business enterprises. In addition, many of the Oswego traders owed the firm of Storke and Gainsborough considerable amounts. Others were in debt to Livingston.[69] Fortunately for the residents of Albany, Samuel and William Baker, who ranked among the greatest merchants in London, had no intentions of giving up their interests in the New York trade. In spite of the powerful competition from Storke and Gainsborough, the Bakers continued to handle

65. William Kelly to Johnson, June 12, 1770, in *Johnson Papers*, 7: 734.

66. Philip Livingston to Storke and Gainsborough, June 7, 1734, in Miscellaneous Manuscripts, vol. 5.

67. Cuyler to Philip Cuyler, January 16, 1756, in Cornelius Cuyler Letter Book, 1752–1764.

68. Philip Livingston to Storke and Gainsborough, September 2, 1737, in Miscellaneous Manuscripts, vol. 5. For an account of this firm, see William I. Roberts, III, "Samuel Storke: An Eighteenth-Century London Merchant Trading to the American Colonies," *Business History Review* 39 (1965): 147–70.

69. Philip Livingston, Invoices, July —, 1735, September 25, 1735, November —, 1735; Livingston to Storke and Gainsborough, June 7, 1736, June 2, 1738, in Miscellaneous Manuscripts, vol. 5.

most of the skins exported by Cornelius Cuyler, Hendrick Ten Eyck, Johannes R. Bleecker, and other independent merchants.[70] Later, they acquired much of the peltry shipped to England by the great trader William Johnson.[71]

The Storke and Baker firms in the 1730s probably imported 80 percent of New York fur shipments to London, but if either of them lost any ground, the aggressive Joseph Mico stood ready to take their place. When Mico began to solicit business in Albany during the early years of the decade he touched off a bitter struggle among the Londoners for New York customers. Both Storke and the Bakers had grown careless in their selection of Indian goods, and Mico, who had relatives in the colony, quickly learned how to acquire merchandise that met with the approval of the fur traders, who were described by Philip Livingston as "fantasticall and Difficult" to please.[72] In an effort to offset the effects of his new competitor, Samuel Storke sent Thomas Gainsborough, who was being groomed for a partnership in the firm, to New York in 1733 with a selection of blankets for inspection.[73] Although Cornelius Cuyler assured Mico that Storke's agent "never Spoke" an ill word against him, Gainsborough must have emphasized the advantages of continuing to do business with a firm that had a reputation for reliability.[74]

Reacting angrily to Gainsborough's trip, Mico sent numerous letters to merchants in New York criticizing Storke's new partner as "a man of pleasure," who "neglected his business."[75] Not to be outdone, the Bakers also entered the fray by writing to the New Yorkers with assurances that the least expensive goods could be obtained from them. In the following year, Mico again unleased a barrage of letters that, in addition to so-liciting business, provided useful information about economic conditions in London, which was a service that the Albany merchants appre-

70. Lieutenant Governor George Clarke to the Board of Trade, August 30, 1739, in *NYCD*, 6: 148. Also see Cornelius Cuyler Letter Books, 1724–1736, 1752–1764; Harmanus Bleecker Papers; and Johannes R. Bleecker Papers.

71. Johnson to Samuel and William Baker, October 28, 1748; Samuel and William Baker to Johnson, October 12, 1749, January 22, 1750, in *Johnson Papers*, 1: 194, 251, 259.

72. Cuyler to Samuel Baker, November 20, 1733, in Cornelius Cuyler Letter Book, 1724–1736; Philip Livingston to Storke and Gainsborough, June 7, 1734, in Miscellaneous Manuscripts, vol. 5; Roberts, "Samuel Storke," pp. 163–64.

73. Cuyler to Storke and Gainsborough, November 5, 1733, June 14, 1734, in Cornelius Cuyler Letter Book, 1724–1736.

74. Cuyler to Joseph Mico, June 10, 1734, ibid.

75. Philip Livingston to Storke and Gainsborough, June 7, 1734; Robert Livingston, Jr., to Storke and Gainsborough, November 12, 1734, in Miscellaneous Manuscripts, vol. 5.

ciated.[76] Continuing to provide better goods than either the Storke or
Baker firms, the newcomer went a step further in 1736 by sending Jasper
Farmer, a ship's captain, to Schenectady for the purpose of asking the
traders to ship their peltry to Mico aboard Farmer's vessel.[77] In the
following years, Mico remained an aggressive competitor, and although
he never became as important as the two older firms in the peltry business, he did establish himself as a substantial merchant and succeeded in
forcing the others to raise the quality of the services they provided for
their clients.[78]

A reliable factor in London represented a valuable asset to the New
York fur merchants. A poor one could mean the loss of money and much
inconvenience. The importance of a good factor was magnified in the
fur trade by the particular care required in the purchase of woolen goods
that would satisfy the meticulous Indian shoppers.[79] For the maintenance of satisfactory relationships between the merchants of New York
and London, a certain amount of mutual trust had to exist. Although the
Londoners extended as little credit as possible, they frequently found it
necessary to do so, because the Albany merchants had to receive the
goods—intended for sale in the early spring—before winter blocked the
Hudson River with ice. Thus, if a client's account did not have enough
of a balance to pay for the goods purchased in the summer, the London
factor had little choice but to carry over the debt until the following
year. Albany merchants expressed particular gratitude to factors who
purchased merchandise promptly so that the shipments would arrive
before the annual freeze of the river.[80] Another situation leading to the
granting of credit developed when a factor could not balance his accounts due to an unexpected drop in the price of peltry after consign-
ments of goods had been shipped to New York.[81]

76. Philip Livingston to Storke and Gainsborough, June 7, 1734, October 27,
1735, ibid.

77. Philip Livingston to Storke and Gainsborough, August 24, 1736, ibid.;
Cuyler to Joseph Mico, June 7, 1735, in Cornelius Cuyler Letter Book, 1724–1736.
On the role of sea captains as merchants see Walton, "New Evidence on Colonial
Commerce," p. 387.

78. Joseph Mico to Peter and Robert Livingston, Jr., May 3, 1740, in Livingston
Family Papers; Harrington, New York Merchant, pp. 306–7.

79. Robert Sanders to Jacob Franks, October 9, 1753, in Robert Sanders Letter
Book, 1752–1758.

80. [Hendrick Ten Eyck] to John Bayeux, June 16, 1721, in Harmanus Bleecker
Papers; Cuyler to Samuel Baker, May 23, 1729, December 29, 1732, in Cornelius
Cuyler Letter Book, 1724–1736; Philip Livingston to Storke and Gainsborough,
June 2, 1738, in Miscellaneous Manuscripts, vol. 5.

81. Robert Sanders to Samuel Storke and Son, June 3, 1743, in Robert Sanders
Letter Book, 1742–1743, New-York Historical Society, New York City.

Before the beginning of the eighteenth century and for a few years afterwards, mutual trust between London and Albany seldom existed, and credit transactions were rare. Consequently, Albany fur dealers usually sold their peltry to their connections in Holland or to large New York City merchants such as Frederick Philipse and Stephen DeLancey. A few of them preferred to do business with Jacob Wendell, a member of a prominent Albany family, who established an import-export business in Boston.[82] Seeking ways of exploiting the New York market, some London merchants sent goods to New Yorkers who acted as factors, but in the fur trade this system, except for a few joint ventures, had completely died out by the 1720s. Almost any of the smaller merchants and traders could now establish overseas connections if he wanted to take the trouble and risk of doing so.[83]

In selecting a London factor, a fur merchant had to place himself in the hands of a stranger, who could have an important influence on the future of his business. Indebtedness to the Londoners, the delays involved in transportation, and the habitual tardiness of the factors in sending accounts for sales to their clients meant that a great deal of damage was likely to be done before a New Yorker could extricate himself from entanglement with an incompetent English businessman. The worst example of this problem occurred after Cornelius Cuyler set up a business in 1723 and began to export furs to Richard Jeneway.

Two years later in 1725 Cuyler became dissatisfied with the quality of Jeneway's service, and the London merchant still had not sent a copy of his accounts detailing the transactions that he had conducted for his client. Since Jeneway had been extending credit to Cuyler, the young man continued to ship furs to him, but increased his demands for an accounting. Jeneway managed to put him off until the end of the trading season in 1726, when Cuyler decided to terminate their business relationship. Finally receiving the accounts from Jeneway more than a year later, Cuyler discovered to his dismay that the Londoner had been selling his skins " Far Below the price then in London" and that the twenty-seven hogsheads had been sold for values bringing £300 under what the market should have brought. Cuyler actually owed £140. Armed

---

82. Jacob Wendell, Invoice of goods sent to Abraham Wendell, October 16, 1710; Jacob Wendell to Abraham Wendell, January 13, 1716, in Wendell Family Papers, New York Public Library, New York City.

83. Lawrence H. Leder, *Robert Livingston, 1654–1728, and the Politics of Colonial New York* (Chapel Hill, 1961), p. 46; Nettels, *Money Supply of the American Colonies,* pp. 73–74; Philip Livingston to Robert Livingston, June 10, 1724, in Livingston Family Papers.

with a power of attorney from the New Yorker, Samuel Baker, his new
factor, investigated the offender's books, but Jeneway proved that he
had done nothing illegal.[84] In a letter to Baker, Cuyler conceded, "Mr.
Richard Jeneway's Distance from here obliges me to desire you to pay
him one hundred and forty pounds Sterling . . . he writes me that the
Reason why he sold my Skins So Cheap was Because he was in advance
for me so that I have paid a Great Interess already, more than 5 per
cent."[85]

Strangely enough, twenty years later Cuyler became embroiled in almost exactly the same kind of situation when Joseph Mico, apparently
in a prolonged fit of anger, stopped doing business with the cantanker-
ous Albany merchant and simply refused for six years to forward a
copy of their account.[86] After finally receiving the desired document,
Cuyler exclaimed, "He has not Sold my Skins but partly Given them
away if he had Sold them as In Justice he ought to have done there
would have been a Ballance in my favor . . . ."[87] Again he had to
make up a balance of well over £100.[88]

Recognizing the risk involved in dealing with distant factors, the fur
merchants were reluctant to make any changes after discovering a reliable London correspondent. Both the Baker and Storke firms established reputations based on the high prices they attained for peltry and
on the solid element of consistency in their services. The latter company,
in particular, took great care to avoid disputes with their clients. Il-
lustrating the extent of Storke's good reputation, Robert Sanders once
told him, "as you Know I always leave it to you to do with Mine as if it
were your own as I have dealt Long with you And never found you
otherways than a fair and Just dealer . . . ."[89]

Under these circumstances of long-established relationships between
Albany and London, new merchants in England ran into numerous
difficulties in attempting to establish connections with colonial fur
dealers. After Storke's demise and shortly before the death of Samuel
Storke, Jr., in 1753, Dirk Vander Heyden left for England with high
hopes of capturing most of the Albany trade due to his many connections

84. Cuyler to Richard Jeneway, May 12, 1725, May 27, 1726, January 13, 1728;
Cuyler to Samuel Baker, October 24, 1728, in Cornelius Cuyler Letter Book, 1724–
1736.
85. Cuyler to Samuel Baker, May 23, 1729, ibid.
86. Cuyler to Joseph Mico, May 18, 1754, ibid.
87. Cuyler to Philip Cuyler, November 2, 1754, ibid.
88. Cuyler to Champion and Hayley, July 12, 1755, ibid.
89. Robert Sanders to Samuel Storke, December 1, 1742, in Robert Sanders
Letter Book, 1742–1743.

among the fur traders.[90] Not only was his father a respected businessman in Albany, but his brother had also established himself as a merchant in New York City. Nevertheless, Alexander Champion, who had become a partner in the Storke firm in the 1740s, and other London factors proved to be strong adversaries, and at least one of them resorted to the old tactic of spreading derogatory rumors about their rivals. Vander Heyden did not enjoy great success.[91] Although Joseph Mico, John George Liebenrood, and Dirk Vander Heyden prevented the great importers from cornering the market in furs from New York, the Baker and Storke firms received the majority of skins shipped from the colony between 1730 and 1755.

To the London merchants, the importance of New York fur imports probably did not change greatly over the years. In general, the volume of furs shipped from the colony to England remained about the same throughout the first half of the century. The fur import figure of £5,709 16s. 1d. in 1750 compared favorably with most other years in the century, and even in the tumultous year 1755 the value came to about £3,870, which was higher than the totals of the early 1730s. In most years after 1720, New York's percentage of England's total supply of furs generally remained consistent.[92]

In the overall economy of New York, the fur trade's importance in the years from 1700 to 1755 greatly decreased. Substantial increases in population and many years of peace had resulted in a complex economy that depended on agricultural production and trade to the West Indies. Export figures and other records indicate that a number of New Yorkers still had an economic stake in the fur trade, but the value of peltry exports at the middle of the century represented only a small fraction of the colony's total income. Even in the relatively limited commerce between England and the province, furs had gradually fallen during the century from about one-third to less than one-sixth of everything shipped from the port of New York.[93] Politically, these changes meant that fur traders by the 1750s no longer possessed the power they had held forty years earlier.

90. Cuyler to Alexander Champion, November 17, 1753, in Cornelius Cuyler Letter Book, 1752–1764; Roberts, "Samuel Storke," pp. 169–70.
91. Philip Cuyler to Dirk Vander Heyden, November 5, 1755, in Philip Cuyler Letter Book, 1755–1760, New York Public Library, New York City.
92. Lawson, "Extracts from Customs 3."
93. Lawson, *Fur*, pp. 106, 135.

8

THE CANADIAN TRADE

ECONOMICALLY, politically, and diplomatically, the trade with Canada constituted one of the most important aspects of life in Albany and, to a lesser extent, within the entire colony. At various times, a large part of New York's furs came down the Lake Champlain route from Montreal, where French merchants eagerly violated the laws of New France in order to obtain inexpensive English strouds and other goods. This trade could hardly have been a more natural economic development. Usually the French had an abundance of furs and a paucity of trading goods. In New York, the situation was at least partially reversed.

While the Canadian government and the French West India Company went through the expense and trouble of establishing relations with distant Indian nations, the French smugglers and New York merchants reaped much of the benefit. The authorities in Canada naturally attempted to disrupt the commerce with New York. The English, on the other hand, suffered no economic disadvantages from the smuggling. Thus, no one opposed the trade until after the outbreak of Queen Anne's War, when New Yorkers continued to carry on the trade by maintaining an unofficial neutrality. This early opposition, coming mostly from Connecticut and Massachusetts, did not have much effect. More serious opposition developed from imperial-minded New York politicians, who believed that by supplying the French with strouds the merchants were helping Canada to maintain friendly relations with the Iroquois and to strengthen alliances with the western tribes.

Usually the Montreal-Albany trade is viewed as an eighteenth-century development, but French authorities were concerned about it as early as the 1670s. Probably the earliest lawbreakers were *coureurs de bois*, who had little difficulty in smuggling their furs to the New Yorkers. As soon as the extent of the profits became known, Canadian officials and merchants hastened to invest in the clandestine trade.[1] Rather than engaging

1. Extract of a memoir from Intendant Duchesneau to Seignelay, November 10, 1679; Anonymous, Extract of a memoir on the prevention of smuggling [1683], in

French employees to take peltry to New York, the Canadian entrepreneurs hired Indian carriers. Thus, they lessened the chances of confiscation since the authorities could not prohibit the Indians from trading with the English. Beginning in the 1670s, many of the Mohawks and other Indians took advantage of this economic opportunity and combined it with a chance to receive religious instruction from the Jesuits by moving to Sault St. Louis near Montreal.[2] Over the years, these "Praying Indians," or Caughnawagas, continued to be the main transporters of peltry from Canada to Albany.

Before King William's War the people of New York displayed only a casual interest in the Canadian trade. Obviously, they would not turn away any Frenchman or Indian porter with a canoe load of inexpensive beaver skins, and occasionally a few Albany traders traveled to Canada. Nevertheless, there is little in the records indicating that the New Yorkers actively pursued this kind of enterprise. Even the comprehensive Albany ordinance of 1686 for the regulation of the fur trade gave no indication of a need to regulate trade from the North.[3]

Until about 1685 the great majority of Albany's beaver skins came from the west, and the traders could see no reason for dealing with French middlemen. By 1686 this situation began to change, as the Iroquois found it difficult to obtain peltry due to the destruction of beaver populations and the increased warfare with the French and their Indian allies. Thereafter, King William's War significantly weakened the Iroquois and further disrupted their traditional methods of obtaining furs. In addition to damaging New York's western trade, the war also acted as a stimulus to the Montreal-Albany trade by making it necessary for New Yorkers to visit Canada at the conclusion of hostilities in order to negotiate various agreements, involving mainly the exchange of

Documents Relative to the Colonial History of the State of New York, ed. Edmund B. O'Callaghan and Berthold Fernow, 15 vols. (Albany, 1856–87), 9: 131, 211–12, hereafter cited as NYCD; William Kingsford, The History of Canada, 10 vols. (London, 1887–98; reprinted, New York, 1969), 2: 7–9, 15–21, 30–35; Allen W. Trelease, Indian Affairs in Colonial New York: The Seventeenth Century (Ithaca, N.Y., 1960), pp. 250–51. On the coureurs de bois, see W. J. Eccles, The Canadian Frontier, 1534–1760 (New York, 1969), pp. 109–11.

2. Frontenac to Louis XIV, November 2, 1681, in NYCD, 9: 145–46. For an account of the Albany-Montreal trade from the French viewpoint, see Jean Lunn, "The Illegal Fur Trade Out of New France, 1713–1760," Canadian Historical Association Report, 1939 (1939), pp. 61–76.

3. Philip Schuyler to Governor Thomas Dongan, September 2, 1681; Examination of Jean Rosie, September 25, 1688, in NYCD, 3: 478–79, 563; Joel Munsell, ed., Annals of Albany, 10 vols. (Albany, 1850–59), 8: 205–14.

prisoners. On December 29, 1697, Abraham Schuyler, Jean Rosie, and a member of the Vroman family left for Canada to announce that the Treaty of Ryswick had been signed. In the following spring the first two of New York's official negotiators, Peter Schuyler and Godfrey Dellius, both of whom had grandiose plans concerning the fur trade, used their visit as an opportunity to establish connections with French merchants. On their way back, they encouraged several Canadian Indians to travel to Albany with over four hundred beaver skins. With Jean Rosie as an interpreter, John Schuyler also went on an official trip to Canada during the summer of 1698, accompanied by John Livingston, David Schuyler, and Dirk Vander Heyden, who apparently acted as his assistants.[4]

In the next two years New Yorkers continued to make inordinately frequent journeys to the French province on official or semiofficial business. Others went without any such pretext.[5] By 1700 the most persistent of these traders, David Schuyler, had developed a close friendship with a Montreal merchant named Bondour and had made contacts with other businessmen and governmental officials.[6] In later years some New Yorkers even set up their own businesses in Canada, causing Intendant Charles Thomas Dupuy to complain in 1727 that there was a "great number of English artizans, merchants, and others established at Montreal."[7]

Except in the 1720s and during intercolonial wars, Albany's businessmen did not violate New York law in carrying on the Canadian trade, but when they continued to deal with French Indians in time of war, the harassed citizens of neighboring colonies criticized them severely. Even during peacetime, the imperial-minded politicians in New York made every effort to have it outlawed. Consequently, the Albany traders

---

4. Memorandum by Peter Schuyler and Dirk Wessels, April 21, 1698; A report on negotiations in Canada by Peter Schuyler and Godfrey Dellius, July 2, 1698; A report on a journey to Canada by John Schuyler, 1698, in *NYCD*, 4: 338, 351, 404–6; Minutes of a meeting of the New York Council, October 7, 1698, New-York Historical Society *Collections*, 1869 (New York, 1870), p. 422; William Smith, Jr., *The History of the Late Province of New-York from Its Discovery to the Appointment of Governor Colden in 1762*, 2 vols. (New York, 1829–30), 1: 125; David A. Armour, "The Merchants of Albany, New York, 1686–1760" (Ph.D. diss., Northwestern University, 1965), pp. 65–67.

5. Council and Assembly of New York to John Schuyler and John Bleeker, [April 7, 1699]; John Nanfan to Governor Callières, July 3, 1699; Bellomont to the Board of Trade, May 25, 1700, in *NYCD*, 4: 498–500, 577, 644; *Calendar of Council Minutes, 1668–1783*, New York State Library bull. 58 (Albany, 1902), p. 136.

6. David Schuyler to Bellomont, August 17, 1700, in *NYCD*, 4: 747; Munsell, ed., *Annals of Albany*, 4: 129–30.

7. Intendant Charles Thomas Dupuy, Abstract of a memoir about the English, November 1, 1727, in *NYCD*, 9: 985.

maintained a defensive attitude and usually carried on the trade clandestinely. Cornelius Cuyler, for example, obtained almost all of his furs from Canada, but in his extensive correspondence he seldom gave any indication of his peltry sources and never flatly stated that he traded with Montreal merchants. This secrecy, combined with incomplete statistics on the total annual production of furs in New York, makes it impossible to accurately estimate the amount of peltry that annually came from Canada. Yet the number of skins remained consistent enough in the first half of the century to provide a good living for several Albany merchants.

Fortunately, a letter book kept by Robert Sanders and various documents containing official complaints about the trade provide a considerable amount of information concerning the methods used to carry on this commerce. Sanders, who was mayor of Albany during the peak of his career as a Canada trader in the early 1750s, suffered no embarrassment as a result of his involvement in the controversial trade. "I do assure you Sir," he told his London factor, "that you had not a beaver skin from me last year but what I had from Canada."[8] His boldness may have been due to his political power, which included a friendship with William Johnson—a prominent member of the imperial faction that opposed the Montreal-Albany trade.[9]

Unlike other Albany citizens trading to Canada, Sanders kept copies of the letters carried by Indian porters to his Montreal correspondents, who were extremely cautious about the possibility of being discovered by Canadian authorities. In order to avoid danger to his customers through interception of the letters, Sanders addressed them in a code that was understood by other Montreal and Albany merchants.[10] Identifying most of the Canadians by Roman numerals, Sanders also used symbols such as a tobacco pipe complete with smoke and the image of a chicken for the man who happened to be his most timid customer. Montreal smugglers demanded such great secrecy that for more than nine months even Sanders did not know the identity of one frequent correspondent.[11] By using the letter book, two of his secret contacts can

8. Sanders to John George Liebenrood, August 11, 1752, in Robert Sanders Letter Book, 1752–1758 (microfilm), New-York Historical Society, New York City.

9. Robert Sanders to Johnson, June 19, 1745, October 23, 1758, in The Papers of Sir William Johnson, ed. James Sullivan et al., 14 vols. (Albany, 1921–65), 1: 36, 3: 9.

10. Sanders to Monsieur A., October 19, 1752, in Robert Sanders Letter Book, 1752–1758. On Sanders' code, see chapter 6, note 33.

11. Sanders to Monsieur G (chicken), May 16, 1753; Sanders to Monsieur B, October 27, 1752, June 23, 1753, ibid.

be identified. In a letter to a Monsieur Meriers, he agreed to establish a business relationship and told him that in the future he would use an appropriate code name.[12] On another occasion in a memorandum for his own use, Sanders noted that he had written to "Monsieur Revair or III the 19th October 1752" to acknowledge a shipment of beaver skins.[13]

Caution on the part of the Canadians was completely justified. Facing the danger of prosecution, they also accepted all the risks involved in both the shipment of their furs and the return of their goods from Albany. French military patrols on Lake Champlain in the spring and summer presented such a serious threat that Montreal merchants seldom sent large shipments of beaver with a single group of Indians. Partly because of these patrols, the Albany merchants sometimes shipped goods to Montreal over the ice of Lake Champlain in the winter.[14]

Canadians could often avoid the risk of confiscation by dealing with foreigners living in Montreal or with frequent foreign visitors, who, as King Louis XV complained, were "never at a loss for a pretext to visit Montreal and the other towns of the Colony."[15] The frequency of visits by Albany merchants indicated that they made the journey not only to establish business contacts but also to purchase furs. On an official trip to Canada in 1751, for example, Cornelius Cuyler brought along his brother John, whose activities resulted in a protest from Governor La Jonquière to Governor George Clinton: "It has been reported to me that this John Cuyler, who is a merchant, was trading with the French, and even with the Indians, and was constantly conferring with them in the house in which he lodged in this town, all which is highly improper."[16]

Frequent seizures of peltry and trade goods cut into the profits of the French smugglers by an average of approximately 10 percent, but the profits of the trade could absorb this loss. In spite of efforts by the Canadian government to raise the price of beaver artificially, the smugglers found that on occasion skins sold for twice as much in Albany as in Montreal, and the English could provide better and less expensive goods

12. Sanders to Monsieur Meriers, July 21, 1753, ibid.
13. Sanders, Memorandum, October [19], 1752, ibid.
14. Sanders to Monsieurs E and F, May 5, 1753; Sanders to Monsieur B, August 30, 1753; Sanders to Monsieur G, May 16, 1753, ibid.; Lunn, "Illegal Fur Trade," p. 69; Governor Bellomont to the Board of Trade, August 24, 1699, in NYCD, 4: 556; Cuyler to Samuel Baker, January 4, 1731, in Cornelius Cuyler Letter Book, 1724–1736 (microfilm), American Antiquarian Society, Worcester, Mass.
15. Louis XV, Memoir serving as instructions for Governor Beauharnois, May 7, 1726, in NYCD, 9: 957.
16. Governor La Jonquière to Governor George Clinton, August 10, 1751, ibid., 6: 734.

than those available in Canada.[17] By the middle years of the eighteenth century, the French succeeded in bringing the prices of Canadian furs more in line with those of New York. Still, Montreal businessmen could not resist the English merchandise.[18] Although French smugglers made their largest profit from English strouds, they also utilized the illegal trade to secure much-needed wampum, which was not manufactured in Canada. Both Philip Livingston and Cornelius Cuyler handled large amounts of wampum, and Robert Sanders sold more of it than any other commodity in his trade with the French. Of the other common trading goods, rum and gunpowder did not play an important part in the Canadian trade.[19]

At times, Lake Champlain and the other waterways between Albany and Montreal must have been crowded with canoes passing back and forth filled nearly to the gunwales with peltry or merchandise. As early as 1699 an Iroquois spokesman told the New York Indian Commissioners, "there is an open road from this place to Canada of late, yea, a beeten path knee deep, soe bare you have trod it of late."[20] Fortunately for the smugglers, French officials could not make indiscriminate seizures without antagonizing the Caughnawagas, who were valuable military allies due to the location of their village a few miles south of Montreal.

To a great extent the livelihood of the Caughnawagas depended on the money that many of them earned as porters in the illegal trade. Without this incentive most members of the tribe would have returned to their homelands in New York, where they maintained close contacts with their Iroquois relatives. In one instance, a group of them succeeded in obtaining passes from the French governor by telling him that if he did not give them permission to take a large quantity of furs to

17. Lunn, "Illegal Fur Trade," p. 62; Intendant Duchesneau, Extract of a memoir, November 13, 1681, in *NYCD*, 9: 160; Pontchartrain to Denis Riverin, June 3, 1708, in *Supplement to Dr. Brymner's Report on Canadian Archives, 1899*, ed. Edouard Richard (Ottawa, 1901), p. 414; New York Executive Council Minutes [October 18, 1751], vol. 23, New York State Library, Albany, hereafter cited as Council Minutes.

18. Philip Livingston to [Storke and Gainsborough], November 25, 1738, in Miscellaneous Manuscripts, vol. 5, New York State Library, Albany; Sanders to Monsieur B, October 27, 1752, in Robert Sanders Letter Book, 1752–1758.

19. Philip Livingston to [Storke and Gainsborough], November 25, 1735, in Miscellaneous Manuscripts, vol. 5; Cuyler to William Darlington, January 20, 1753, in Cornelius Cuyler Letter Book, 1752–1764 (microfilm), American Antiquarian Society, Worcester, Mass.; Robert Sanders Letter Book, 1752–1758, passim.

20. Indian Conference, June 13, 1699, in *NYCD*, 4: 569.

Albany, they would no longer remain in Canada.[21] As the imperial rivalry between France and Great Britain increased, the Caughnawagas, who understood their value as French allies, became bolder, and in 1741 Governor Beauharnois could justly complain, "Sault Saint Louis ... has become a sort of Republic and it is only there that foreign trade is carried on at present."[22]

In selecting porters, New York and French merchants were mainly concerned with the qualities of reliability and discretion. In all his business transactions over a three-year period, Robert Sanders dealt with only five or six Indians, who had apparently established good reputations. Frequently, their names—Joseph Harris, Agness, and Marie Magdelain—indicated the location of their homes in the Catholic village of Sault St. Louis or Caughnawaga. Judging from the large size of the cargoes often assigned to them, it would seem that each of the Indians mentioned by Sanders acted as an agent for a small group of canoemen.[23]

The Caughnawagas were not the only inhabitants of the village engaged in smuggling. In 1741 Governor Beauharnois explained to the Minister of Marine, "Almost all the people of the Sault, My Lord, have English hearts, as the Indians express it. For this I can blame only their Missionaries and the Misses Desauniers, who make them trade with New-York."[24] The two Desaunier sisters had moved to Caughnawaga in 1727, where they enjoyed a long career of smuggling furs for themselves and for merchants in Montreal. Undoubtedly, they could not have succeeded without the approval of the Jesuit missionaries, who may not have personally profited from the trade but knew that the economic well-being of their Indian parishioners depended on it. Although a disgruntled fur trader in 1730 accused Father Lauzon of promoting the illicit trade at Caughnawaga, the authorities refused even to consider such a "frivolous accusation." Thus, for many more years this Jesuit missionary continued at his post in the midst of the largest smuggling operation in Canada.[25] Apparently the Desaunier business prospered without interference until 1741, when officials of the French West India Company realized "that these Ladies have not brought a single Beaver

21. Indian Conference, June 20, 1700; David Schuyler to Bellomont, August 17, 1700; George Clinton to the Board of Trade, July 17, 1751, ibid., 4: 692–93, 747, 5: 714.

22. Governor Beauharnois to Maurepas, September 21, 1741, ibid., 9: 1071.

23. Sanders to Monsieur B, October 27, 1752, August 30, May 16, 1753; Sanders to Monsieurs E and F, May 5, 1753, in Robert Sanders Letter Book, 1752–1758.

24. Beauharnois to Maurepas, September 21, 1741, in NYCD, 9: 1071.

25. Lunn, "Illegal Fur Trade," p. 61; Beauharnois and Hocquart to Maurepas, October 15, 1730, in NYCD, 9: 1020.

to the Company's office in fifteen years."[26] The government soon forced them to close their store, but the sisters demonstrated the strength of the smuggling establishment in Canada by continuing their illicit operations at Caughnawaga until ordered to leave the village in 1752.[27]

The most serious threat to the Montreal-Albany trade was military conflict between France and Britain. From 1689 to 1697 King William's War completely interrupted the commerce between the two cities, and New York's western trade was nearly obliterated. Within five years Queen Anne's War threatened to disrupt the fur trade for another decade. In the meantime, however, Iroquois and French diplomats had been at work to establish the neutrality agreement that greatly lessened the likelihood of war on the New York frontier. Even before the formal signing of the treaty between the French and the Iroquois in the summer of 1701, New Yorkers discovered that in case of war Governor Callières of Canada would be willing to avoid any hostilities that might endanger his agreement with the Indians. While preparing for the great peace conference, French officials decided to sound out New Yorkers on the subject of a neutrality agreement.

Ironically, the most notorious of the Albany traders to Canada, David Schuyler, found himself sitting down to dinner with the governor of Montreal and engaging in a conversation of such momentuous importance that even the wily Dutchman must have had difficulty in keeping his composure. The French official casually stated that he remembered "the Cruell and Barbarous murders committed by the heathens in shedding of Innocent Christian Blood in the late warr, and that it would be much better for these parts in America, in case a warr break out between the two crownes . . . for us to sett still, since wee only injured one another by such skulking parties."[28] Schuyler told the Montreal governor that he did not expect a war, but he agreed that it was a shame to see Christian Blood so spilt by heathens . . . ." The Frenchman responded that, if a war did occur, Canada "would not be the first to send out such partyes against" the people of New York. Whereupon, Schuyler promised that "in case there came no skulking partyes" from Canada "there would be none sent from" New York.[29] Clearly, this conversation represented more than just a momentary whim on the part of this particular

26. Beauharnois to Maurepas, September 21, 1741, in *NYCD*, 9: 1071.
27. Lunn, "Illegal Fur Trade," p. 75.
28. Munsell, ed., *Annals of Albany*, 4: 129. The governor of New France looked after the direct administration of the Quebec region. Two other districts—Montreal and Three Rivers—each had a local governor. Gustave Lanctot, *A History of Canada*, 3 vols. (Cambridge, Mass., 1964), 2: 211.
29. Munsell, ed., *Annals of Albany*, 4: 129–30.

French official. Within a few days, the mayor of Montreal also expressed a desire for peace to Schuyler and several other Albany traders.[30]

Not long after the outbreak of Queen Anne's War the effectiveness of these conversations became apparent when raiding parties of French and Indians terrorized New England while completely ignoring the exposed farms along the Mohawk and the Hudson. During much of the war, one prominent Albany official, possibly Kiliaen Van Rensselaer, who owned Rensselaerswyck and served on the New York Council, kept up a secret correspondence with Governor Vaudreuil, assuring him of the colony's desire to remain at peace. During his administration in New York from 1701 to 1708, Governor Cornbury sent letters to England indicating a desire to attack Canada, but within the colony he displayed much less belligerence. In the early years of the war no other prominent figure in the province even hinted publicly at a desire to break the neutrality.[31]

As more and more frontier families in New England fell victim to the tomahawks of French allies, the Yankees became increasingly resentful of the New Yorkers, who, according to one Bostonian, maintained "a correspondence and trade with and afford supplies to the French Indians of Canada and the Eastern parts, who have often made bloody incursions upon us . . . ."[32] The charges that the people of Albany continued to trade with the French Indians were completely true, although business relations with Montreal must have suffered to some extent since English citizens could not freely travel to Canada. New Englanders, who attempted to establish a neutrality for themselves in 1706, appeared to have been angered not so much by the existence of peace on the New York frontier but by the profits which Albany secured thereby.[33] New Yorkers, on the other hand, did not feel much sympathy for neighbors who, during King William's War, had taken advantage of the destruction along the

30. Ibid., p. 130. For another account of these meetings, see Armour, "Merchants of Albany," pp. 71–72.

31. Beauharnois to Maurepas, October 10, 1734; Cornbury to the Board of Trade, September 29, 1702, June 30, 1703, August 20, 1708, in *NYCD*, 9: 1039–40, 4: 977, 1061, 5: 65; Smith, *History*, 1: 153; G. M. Waller, "New York's Role in Queen Anne's War, 1702–1713," *New York History* 33 (1952): 45.

32. Anonymous, Memorial from Boston complaining about the neutrality of the Five Nations, May 31, 1708, in *NYCD*, 5: 42. For an account of the frustrations of the people on the New England frontier, see Douglas Edward Leach, *The Northern Colonial Frontier, 1607–1763* (New York, 1966), pp. 118–25.

33. Evert Wendell, Jr., Account Book, 1695–1726, New-York Historical Society, New York City; Governor Vaudreuil to Pontchartrain, April 28, 1706; Vaudreuil, Proposed treaty between Canada and New England, October —, 1705, in *NYCD*, 9: 775–76, 770–72.

Mohawk to attract more of the fur trade to themselves.[34] Nor had the New Yorkers forgotten that in the previous war the other colonies had refused an order from England to send soldiers to New York's assistance, and that Massachusetts had disregarded a royal command to vote funds for the building of forts on the New York frontier.[35]

Under the circumstances, New Yorkers chose to look out for themselves first. No evidence exists, however, to indicate that they relished the idea of profiting from the agonies of their neighbors. In fact, Peter Schuyler, who took charge of the colony's frontier defenses, worked diligently to have New England included within the neutrality agreement. In 1704 he indirectly informed Governor Vaudreuil that he would consider negotiating a more formal arrangement with Canada if New England could be added. After this effort failed and after Governor Joseph Dudley of Massachusetts experienced a similar futile correspondence with Vaudreuil in 1706, Schuyler asked the Caughnawaga Indians to stop their raids against the New England frontier. In a letter explaining this unneutral action to Vaudreuil, Schuyler wrote, "You will pardon me if I tell you that I am disgusted when I think that a war which is carried on by christian Princes . . . should degenerate into savage and reckless barbarity."[36] Schuyler and other Albany officials also pleaded for good treatment of English prisoners and aided the New Englanders by gathering intelligence for them about French military movements.[37]

Despite Albany's efforts on their behalf, New Englanders understandably continued to stress the accusation that their neighbors remained neutral for the purpose of reaping the benefits of the fur trade. During the postwar years, as the fur trade became less important to Manhattan merchants, the New York City political opponents of Albany pointed to

34. Governor Benjamin Fletcher to William Blathwayt, February 14, 1963, in NYCD, 4: 2.

35. Queen Mary to William Phips, October 11, 1692; William Phips to Benjamin Fletcher, September 18, 1693, ibid., 3: 855–56, 4: 67–68; Board of Trade to the King, January 10, 1701; William Stoughton to the Board of Trade, June 3, 1701; Extract from the journal of the House of Burgesses, August 19, 1701, in Calendar of State Papers, Colonial Series, America and West Indies, ed. W. N. Sainsbury et al., 43 vols. to date (London, 1860–), 19: 22, 276, 424, hereafter cited as Calendar of State Papers; Herbert L. Osgood, The American Colonies in the Eighteenth Century, 4 vols. (New York, 1924–25; reprinted, Gloucester, Mass., 1958), 1: 98–108.

36. Vaudreuil to Pontchartrain, November 16, 1704; Peter Schuyler to Vaudreuil, September 26, 1708, in NYCD, 9: 761, 818.

37. Lawrence H. Leder, ed., The Livingston Indian Records, 1666–1723 (Gettysburg, Pa., 1956), pp. 190, 191–92, 194, 195, 198–99, 202; Peter Schuyler to Colonel Samuel Partridge, October –, 170[8], in Emmet Collection, vol. 3, no. 8175, New York Public Library, New York City.

Queen Anne's War to demonstrate the disloyalty and avarice of the Albany Dutch. The polemicists, however, conveniently forgot that in the first decades of the century the men who controlled the fur trade lived in New York City, not in Albany. Three of these fur merchants—John Barberie, Adolph Philipse, and Rip Van Dam—held seats on the New York Council. In matters concerning frontier security, the Manhattan businessmen had far less reason than Albany to fear the military consequences of fighting an Indian war. Whatever their motives, the furs traders of Albany, the fur merchants of Manhattan, and many other inhabitants of the colony favored neutrality, and except for brief expeditions in 1709 and 1711, they succeeded in resisting the pressures for opening hostilities against Canada.[38]

In early 1709 Samuel Vetch, a Scottish adventurer, who had made numerous contacts in the colonies and had married a daughter of Robert Livingston, convinced the British government to support a major attack on Canada during the summer and fall. The plan called for a naval assault against Quebec in conjunction with a land expedition over the Lake Champlain route to Montreal. With this commitment from Great Britain in his pocket and with the assistance of Francis Nicholson, former governor of Virginia, Vetch whipped up support in all of the northern colonies. Appearing before the New York assembly, Nicholson and the persuasive Vetch assured the legislators that the plan would succeed. The province then found itself entrapped in the web that it had so carefully avoided for seven years, and even a number of Iroquois warriors were persuaded to lend their services.[39] Despite this auspicious beginning, the entire plan was on the brink of failure by the middle of summer. In July the British ministry decided not to send the fleet to Quebec. Around the city of Albany, opposition to the expedition quickly developed after the residents had an opportunity to view the incompetent attempts to establish supply lines between the city and Wood Creek, a stream that flowed into Lake Champlain.[40]

38. Smith, *History*, 1: 177, 211. For evidence of their participation in the fur trade, see Julius Bloch et al., eds., *An Account of Her Maestey's Revenue in the Province of New York, 1701–1709. The Custom's Records of Early Colonial New York* (Ridgewood, N.J., 1966), passim. Barberie served from 1705 to 1726, Van Dam from 1703 to 1735, and Philipse from 1705 to 1721. Patricia W. Bonomi, *A Factious People: Politics and Society in Colonial New York* (New York, 1971), p. 314.

39. Bruce T. McCully, "Catastrophe in the Wilderness: New Light on the Canada Expedition of 1709," *William and Mary Quarterly* 11 (1954): 442; Osgood, *American Colonies in the Eighteenth Century*, 1: 429–32.

40 Robert Livingston, "The Camp at the Wood Creek Reviewed, with an Account of the Forts Built between Albany and the Said Camp, and of the Forces

Reacting to the scalping of two children near Schenectady, the leading citizens of Albany sent a memorial to the provincial authorities asking them to look after frontier defenses before giving further support to offensive movements.[41] Critics of Albany interpreted this opposition as an attempt to prevent the disruption of trade with Canada.[42] In at least this case, however, the attribution of economic motives to the people of Albany had little validity. Everyone connected with the expedition realized by the end of July that nothing would result from the overland plan. Although the military leaders were reluctant to admit their impending failure, Robert Livingston, a leading opponent of the Canada traders, wrote, "It is observed there is not that Genious Zeal forwardness or Contrivance to promote the present Expedition, even in those that are or ought to be the Principal managers thereof yet the Provisions and other Necessaries are Sent up from hence and so forwarded daily from Stage to Stage till they arrive at the Camp at the Wood Creek." Before the first snowfall, the ragtail army at Wood Creek made a disorganized and unauthorized retreat to less dangerous localities.[43]

Upon arriving at his post as New York governor in 1710, Robert Hunter found an empty treasury and completely inadequate defenses. Adding to these problems, the Iroquois, who had recently received severe threats from Canada, demonstrated no desire to again violate the neutrality.[44] Regretting the necessity of suppressing his martial spirit, Hunter had little choice but to accept the advice of the Indian Commissioners to avoid "any Extraordinary Measures that may draw an Inevitable Expence upon this province."[45] In the following year the indefatig-

Posted there in Order for the Expedition against Canada and how they Subsisted &c.," August 16, 1709, in Livingston Family Papers (microfilm), Franklin D. Roosevelt Library, Hyde Park, N.Y. For a printed copy of this document, see McCully, "Catastrophe in the Wilderness," pp. 447–55.

41. Robert Livingston, "Camp at the Wood Creek," August 16, 1709, in Livingston Family Papers.

42. Thomas Cockerill to William Popple, July 2, 1709, in NYCD, 5: 81.

43. Robert Livingston, "Camp at the Wood Creek," August 16, 1709, in Livingston Family Papers; McCully, "Catastrophe in the Wilderness," p. 443.

44. Journal of the Votes and Proceedings of the General Assembly of the Colony of New York [1691–1765], 2 vols. (New York, 1764–66), September 1, 1710, 1; 172, hereafter cited as Assembly Journal; Peter Wraxall, An Abridgment of the Indian Affairs Contained in Four Folio Volumes, Transacted in the Colony of New York, from the Year 1678 to the Year 1751, ed. Charles H. McIlwain (Cambridge, Mass., 1915), July 2, August 19, 1710, pp. 75, 78.

45. Minutes of the Indian Commissioners, August 20, 1710, in NYCD, 5: 229; Assembly Journal, September 1, 1710, 1: 172. For a strong defense of New York's refusal to conduct further offensive actions, see Smith, History, 1: 178–79.

able Francis Nicholson arrived from England with a plan very similar to the one of 1709. New Englanders immediately gave him their complete support. In New York the people demonstrated less enthusiasm, but Hunter changed his earlier position and personally directed the overland part of the invasion. Hunter's expedition came to an abrupt halt before reaching Lake Champlain when the participants learned that much of the British fleet had gone to the bottom of the treacherous St. Lawrence.[46]

This new failure solidified opposition in New York toward any further military action. Even Governor Hunter appeared to be considerably sobered by his experiences in the forests of North America. In the fall of 1711 he received requests from Connecticut and Massachusetts to use his influence to force the Iroquois into breaking their treaty with Canada and joining the British in the war. Hunter explained to Governor Gurdon Saltonstall of Connecticut that he could not act upon the "neutrality entered into by our Indians with the French" without the "advice of the Council; and the Concurrence of the assembly who have the purse to prosecute the rupture that would thereupon ensue . . . ."[47] A week later Hunter wrote to Governor Dudley of Massachusetts, telling him that the Council had unanimously voted to oppose any such plans. Before long, the New York assembly also expressed opposition to the New England proposals.[48]

As the war drew to a close, the trade between Montreal and Albany returned to the same pattern that had developed in the years after King William's War. In 1712 the Caughnawaga Indians traveled to Albany on an official visit to repair any diplomatic damages resulting from the few clashes between them and New Yorkers during the expeditions of 1709 and 1711. A spokesman for the Caughnawagas asked to make peace or, as he put it, "to take the hatchet out of the heads of those that were kild, and to Burry the Same that it may be forgotten and forgiven." As for the role of the Praying Indians in the fur trade, he requested "that the path may be open and free for us as formerly."[49] In the following year, experienced traders including David Schuyler once again began making trips to Canada, and they were joined by new, energetic men such as

46. Osgood, *American Colonies in the Eighteenth Century*, 1: 441–50; Wraxall, *Abridgment*, ed. McIlwain, August 17, 18, 20, September 8, 1711, pp. 91, 92.

47. Robert Hunter to Gurdon Saltonstall, October 15, 1711, in New York Colonial Manuscripts, 56: 126, New York State Library, Albany.

48. Robert Hunter to Joseph Dudley, October 22, 1711; Opinion of the New York Assembly, November 23, 1711, ibid., pp. 134, 137; Council Minutes, October 18, 1711, vol. 11; Smith, *History*, 1: 188.

49. "Propositions made by Sarachdowne . . . to the Commissioners of Indian Affairs in Albany," May 19, 1712, in New York Colonial Manuscripts, 57: 152.

Myndert Schuyler and Philip Livingston.[50] About the only notable difference in the postwar trade was its development as a political issue within the colony.

After his arrival in the province, Governor Hunter had almost immediately allied himself with Robert Livingston, who had long opposed the cooperation between English and French subjects. Hunter had to spend most of his administration attempting to rebuild the economy and to stabilize the domestic politics that had been in disarray since Leisler's Rebellion in 1689. As for the fur trade, he recognized that the people of Albany would not be content to rely on the few furs obtained by the Iroquois. Thus, he began an effort to undermine the commerce with Canada by developing an alternate source of peltry through a trade with the Indians of the western Great Lakes. The Five Nations displayed some hesitation at first over Hunter's request that they allow ancient enemies to pass freely through their territory and thereby eliminate their chances of becoming middlemen between these tribes and the Europeans. Nevertheless, within a few years Hunter had convinced them to allow distant tribes to travel through Iroquois country.[51]

One reason for Iroquois acquiescence was their interest in developing alliances with western tribes. They also realized that they could benefit from a weakening of the Canada trade, which they had opposed since the 1680s. New York opponents of the Albany-Montreal commerce attempted to show that Iroquois opposition to the Canada trade developed because of a desire to help the British imperialists in the overall struggle against France. In actuality, the Iroquois had vehemently opposed this commerce, on the grounds that it drew away members of their tribes to Caughnawaga, long before anyone in the colony made any significant statements against it.[52]

Among New Yorkers, the Canadian trade did not become a burning

50. Myndert Schuyler to George Clarke, April 2, 1712; Minutes of the Indian Commissioners, August 13, 1712, ibid., 57: 128, 60: 122; Philip Livingston to Robert Livingston, April 13, 1713, in Livingston Family Papers.

51. Lawrence H. Leder, *Robert Livingston, 1654-1728, and the Politics of Colonial New York* (Chapel Hill, 1961), pp. 211-15; Wraxall, *Abridgment*, ed. McIlwain, August 19, 1710, p. 77. On Hunter's western policies, see chapter 9.

52. Deposition from a Mohawk sachem, April 5, 1687, in Cadwallader Colden Papers, New-York Historical Society, New York City; Cadwallader Colden, "Continuation of Colden's *History of the Five Indian Nations*, for the years 1707 through 1720," in *The Letters and Papers of Cadwallader Colden*, 10 vols., New-York Historical Society *Collections*, 50-56 (1917-23), 67-69 (1934-35) (New York, 1918-36), 9: 425, 430; Minutes of the Commissioners of Indian Affairs (microfilm), November 12, 1724, 1: 107, Public Archives of Canada, Ottawa, hereafter cited as Minutes of the Indian Commissioners.

issue during Hunter's administration (1710–19), but opposition to it was gradually increasing. One of the reasons for the developing opposition was the renewal of trade with the western Indians. Everyone in the colony approved of luring these tribes to New York, but Albany merchants expected the trade to be carried on within the walls of the city, according to the monopoly provisions of their charter. On the other hand, the Schenectady traders, who illegally pursued a trade with the western Indians, knew that their businesses would improve if French traders were unable to supply these same tribesmen with strouds from Albany. As many Schenectady residents became more dependent on the developing western trade, their old resentments against the privileged classes in Albany greatly increased. Playing upon these antagonisms, the Livingston-Hunter faction quietly helped the residents of Schenectady in their efforts to undermine the Albany monopoly. If the imperialists could establish a substantial trade with the western Indians, they would have a case for arguing that the Albany-Montreal commerce worked against the interests of the colony.[53]

At the same time that opposition to the Albany-Montreal trade increased among Schenectady traders and provincial officials, support for it lessened among New York City merchants, whose interests had been increasingly diverted toward the rapidly expanding West Indies trade. Coincidently, but significantly for New York fur traders, Stephen De-Lancey, the leading exporter of furs acquired from Canada, lost his assembly seat in 1716 and did not regain it until well after the legal assault against the Canada trade had been launched.[54]

By 1717 Governor Hunter decided that New York would eventually have to outlaw the trade with Canada. In a private conference with Dekannissora and other principal sachems of the Five Nations, he explained, "It is an Evil which must be prevented, and I shall forthwith use my Endeavour to put a final End to that pernicious trade which I am sure is hurtful to both of us and only serves to put money in the Pocketts of a few Traders."[55] Realizing that his administration would soon be over, Hunter did not make a public issue of the subject during the remainder of his stay in the colony.

After his return to England in 1719, however, he lobbied for a continuation and expansion of his policies. In addition to condemning the traffic in Canadian furs during testimony before the Board of Trade, he used his considerable influence in England to select William Burnet as

53. See chapters 4 and 9.
54. *Assembly Journal*, December 14, 1714, June 5, 1716, September 13, 1725,
55. Wraxall, *Abridgment*, ed. McIlwain, June 13, 1717, p. 120.
1: 367, 381, 516; Osgood, *American Colonies in the Eighteenth Century*, 2: 412.

his successor. Then he carefully schooled this energetic son of Bishop Burnet in the art of colonial politics. During his administration, Hunter had cultivated an assembly that generally agreed with his policies. He therefore acted quickly in 1719 to head off a possible attempt by Peter Schuyler, senior councilor and head of the government, to call for new elections. Responding to Hunter's request, the secretary of state sent a letter to Schuyler ordering him not to dissolve the assembly.[56]

When Burnet's ship sailed into New York harbor in September 1720, the new governor stepped ashore with full confidence that the trans-formation of the fur trade would be the major accomplishment of his administration. After his first meeting with Robert Livingston, Burnet found that his ideas were in complete harmony with those of the New Yorker, who went away delighted by the prospects of finally using the fur trade to challenge French expansion in the backwoods of North America.[57] The plan favored by Burnet and Livingston seemed rela-tively simple. After the passage of a law to abolish the Canada trade, the French would no longer be able to obtain strouds. The western Indians would then be forced to deal with British traders, who would be encouraged to establish themselves on the shores of Lake Ontario. Before presenting these proposals to the assembly, Burnet spent the first six weeks of his administration consolidating his support and un-dermining the strength of potential opponents.

Moving with disarming swiftness, the governor immediately an-nounced that he would break with tradition by not dissolving the assembly upon the arrival of a new chief executive. Thus, the supporters of Robert Hunter remained in office, owing a debt of gratitude to Burnet for protection from numerous opponents, who had been anxiously awaiting an opportunity to challenge them at the polls. The assembly-men quickly rewarded their protector by passing a tax bill to support his administration for five years. Bitterly resenting Burnet's highhanded political maneuver, Peter Schuyler and Adolph Philipse demanded that he dissolve the assembly. When he refused, they angrily asked permis-sion to be temporarily relieved of their duties on the Council. Burnet complied and then wrote to London asking that Schuyler and Philipse be removed permanently. After the home government acted on his re-quest in 1722, he replaced the two offenders with James Alexander and Cadwallader Colden.[58]

56. Minutes of a meeting of the Board of Trade, July 20, 1720, in NYCD, 5: 552; Leder, Robert Livingston, p. 250; Smith, History, 1: 202, 212, 225; Secretary Craggs to Peter Schuyler, December 26, 1719, in Calendar of State Papers, 32: 289.
57. Leder, Robert Livingston, pp. 252–53.
58. Burnet to the Board of Trade, September 24, November 26, 1720; Burnet

In addition to subduing the opposition within the provincial government, Burnet made an effort to blunt the effects of opposition in Albany
by removing those Indian Commissioners who might prove uncooperative. In explaining his actions to Philip Livingston, the governor accused
these commissioners of having "misrepresented the true Cause of the
French Success with the Indians, tho your Father had prepared Clauses
for that purpose in a Memorial delivered to them, these I find they have
changed so as to Shelter the Profit some of them had and concealed the
Mischief the Country received from their Pernicious Trade with the
French."[59] The removal of these men did not amount to a full-scale
purge. Many of the old commissioners, including Peter Schuyler, remained in office, but no elected officials of Albany served on the new
board. Although Robert Livingston retired from the board, Philip Livingston became both a commissioner and Indian Secretary. Two of the
other new members, John Collins and Henry Holland, were allies of the
Livingston family and proved to be staunch supporters of the new trade
policies.[60]

With the cooperation of the Indian Commissioners secured, Burnet
persuaded the assembly to pass an act in November 1720 making it unlawful for any New York citizen to sell Indian goods, including strouds,
duffels, guns, kettles, lead, and gunpowder "to any Subject of the
French Kings or to any Person or Persons whatsoever for or on behalf of
any Such Subject." No one could have in his possession any Indian
goods "to the Northward of a line Extending from the North Limits
and boundaries of the City of Albany due East and West by the Naturall
possition unto the utmost limits and boundaries" of the province.[61]

To facilitate the enforcement of the restrictive regulations, the Albany
sheriff—Henry Holland—or his deputies were given the right to search

---

to William Popple, October 17, 1720; Board of Trade to Burnet, June 6, 1722, in
NYCD, 5: 573, 578–79, 574, 647; *Assembly Journal*, November 18, 1720, 1: 448;
Bonomi, *A Factious People*, pp. 89–90; Osgood, *American Colonies in the Eigh-
teenth Century*, 2: 417.

59. Wraxall, *Abridgment*, ed. McIlwain, October 20, 1720, p. 132.

60. Ibid.; Council Minutes, November 12, 1720, vol. 13; John Collins to Robert
Livingston, February 17, 1721, in Livingston Family Papers; Leder, ed., *Livingston Indian Records*, p. 229. Charles H. McIlwain maintained that the commissioners supported Burnet, "probably because they were small rather than large traders
. . . ." Wraxall, *Abridgment*, ed. McIlwain, p. lxxiv. Actually, none of the board
members were small traders, but the Livingstons were more closely tied to the
western trade than to the commerce with Canada. On the other hand, some of
Burnet's commissioners were Canada traders. See chapter 5.

61. *Colonial Laws of New York from the Year 1664 to the Revolution*, 5 vols.
(Albany, 1894–96), November 19, 1720, 2: 8, 9, hereafter cited as *Laws*.

"all houses Outhouses, Barnes, Stables, Barracks, Ricks, or Stacks of hay or Corne, Boats, Sloops, Canoes Carts, Waggons, Sleads, or other Land or Water Carriage, and in all other places" to the northward of the line. They even had the power to "breake open the door of any House or Chamber" that might contain contraband. The penalty for violating the law was a fine of £100 and the confiscation of the illegal goods, which were given to the informer or discoverer, along with one-half of the fine. According to the preamble of the act, these severe penalties and enforcement procedures were necessary because the French had been using English merchandise to win friends among the Iroquois, and if the Canada trade was not abolished, they would "alltogether Alienate the minds of the Said Indians, which will prove of the most dangerous Consequence to the English Interest in America." [62]

Stony silence was the only reaction of Albany to the new law. The city residents made no immediate public outcry, and their surviving correspondence provides no clues to their feeling on the subject. They and their New York City associates must have resented the act of 1720, but their distress was soon eased by the ineffectiveness of the law, made readily evident during 1721 and 1722.

Even before the beginning of the trading season in 1721, Henry Holland and Philip Livingston expressed serious doubts about the feasibility of the plans for restricting the northern trade. In the fall Burnet told the Board of Trade that he had found it necessary to build a blockhouse on "the carrying place to Canada" in an effort to stop the illegal commerce. [63] This measure did more harm than good, because in the following year the Indian Commissioners discovered that this new fort at Saratoga had become a center of the smuggling operations. Apparently the officer in charge was corrupt and involved in the trade himself. On another occasion in 1722, the commissioners told Burnet that the law against the Canadian trade had proven to be ineffectual. [64]

One of the main weaknesses in the act of 1720 was its failure to prohibit the trade in goods intended for consumption by French Canadians. A trader, therefore, could import all the furs that he wanted from Montreal as long as he paid for them with goods not ordinarily used in the Indian trade. Either through naivete or duplicity, Burnet contributed to this problem by granting numerous passes for Albany residents

62. Ibid., pp. 8–11.

63. Philip Livingston to Robert Livingston, February 20, 1721, in Livingston Family Papers; Burnet to the Board of Trade, October 16, 1721, in NYCD, 5: 633.

64. Wraxall, Abridgment, ed. McIlwain, June 4, 1722, July–August, 1722, pp. 140, 141. For more information on the ineffectiveness of the trade law in 1721 and 1722, see Armour, "Merchants of Albany," pp. 149–50, 154–56.

to journey across the border. In one instance, he sent a letter to Governor Vaudreuil through a Mr. Cuyler, "who requests my passport to go to Canada on his private affairs, and who is highly deserving of whatever favor I may have in my power to grant him."[65] The Cuylers were notorious traders with Montreal.

Rather than breaking off the Albany-Montreal commerce too abruptly and thus irritating the Caughnawagas, Burnet may have looked the other way when potential political supporters in Albany engaged in the illegal commerce. Almost assuredly, Burnet attempted to divide the Canada traders by winning some of them over to his side. Early in his administration, he appointed Myndert Schuyler as Albany's mayor, and later in 1725 Johannes Cuyler, another Canada trader, received the same honor.[66] In a letter to his father, Philip Livingston provided the strongest evidence against Burnet: "If no amendments be made to the act for preventing uncle John's [Schuyler] trade so[o]n he getts it now alone . . . and is able to Supply . . . as many pieces as the french have occasion for, and it seems he is much in favour of his Excellency."[67] Since Robert Livingston acted as Burnet's chief adviser, the governor would have had little difficulty in discovering the nature of Schuyler's commercial relations with Canada. Whether or not Burnet fully understood his own role in the circumvention of the law, he shared at least part of the responsibility for its initial failure.

An inadequate police force combined with Albany deceptiveness presented another major obstacle to the successful abolition of the Canada trade. Albany businessmen had been engaged in smuggling for nearly two generations, and the techniques that they had perfected against the French were equally effective when applied to a handful of deputies and Sheriff Henry Holland, who refused to venture away from his comfortable lodgings during the nasty weather of early spring in central New York. On some occasions in late winter, the traders smuggled their goods to hiding places either in or near the village of Saratoga, which provided a convenient base for dealing with the Caughnawagas.[68]

If a trader wanted to avoid almost all risk, he hired a few Mohawks to take the merchandise to their villages, where the Caughnawagas

---

65. Burnet to Vaudreuil, July 11, 1721, in *NYCD*, 9: 899.

66. Beverly McAnear, "Politics in Provincial New York, 1689–1761" (Ph.D. diss., Stanford University, 1935), p. 320; Cuyler Reynolds, ed., *Albany Chronicles* (Albany, 1906), pp. 190, 195.

67. Philip Livingston to Robert Livingston, February 15, 1721, in Livingston Family Papers.

68. Philip Livingston to Robert Livingston, February 20, 1721, ibid.; Wraxall, *Abridgment*, ed., McIlwain, July–August, 1722, p. 141.

could come to trade "out of the power of Any officer" to interfere.[69] At an Indian conference in the fall of 1722, Burnet told the Iroquois that if they helped in the conviction of illicit traders, they would receive all of the confiscated goods and the fine of £100. The Iroquois, being "peaceable People," refused to become policemen for the governor. They said it would create "a great many enemies" for them. Coming from the tactful Iroquois diplomats, this blunt refusal represented a stinging rebuke, and Burnet angrily replied, "If you don't stop the Path to Canada as I advised you it is your own faults that Goods are not cheaper for if that Trade be stopped there will be more goods to be sold to you and at more reasonable Rates."[70] His argument had little effect. As in all disputes among white men, the Iroquois could not afford to be on the losing side, and at this moment Burnet appeared to be the loser.

Even before the beginning of the trading season in 1721, the governor's supporters in Albany had become convinced that "there can hardly a Law be made to bridle the people of these parts in matter of trade with the Indians unless every person is obliged to purge himselfe on oath."[71] Though frequently asked to recommend a law requiring oaths, Burnet hesitated to present such a recommendation to the assembly probably due to his fear that such a drastic step would arouse opposition among those British officials who opposed oath-taking as a device for discovering law violators. As it became obvious in the spring of 1722 that the fur traders were paying almost no attention to the law, Burnet could either admit defeat or recommend new regulations. He chose the latter alternative, and the assembly passed a law allowing most officials in Albany, including the sheriff and the Indian Commissioners, to administer an oath to any person suspected of trading with the French or the Caughnawagas. If a trader refused to take the oath, he would "Ipso facto be adjudged" guilty and fined £100. Providing for elaborate procedures to prevent corruption, the act threatened dishonest officials with fines of £200 and banishment from office. Since it did not become effective until August 16, the new law did not affect the traders during 1722. In the following year smuggling became a much more hazardous way of life.[72]

69. Leder, ed., *Livingston Indian Records*, p. 229.
70. Indian Conferences, September 13, 14, 1722, in *NYCD*, 5: 666, 668–69.
71. Philip Livingston to Robert Livingston, February 20, 1721, in Livingston Family Papers.
72. Burnet to the Board of Trade, December 12, 1722, in *NYCD*, 5: 682; *Laws*, July 7, 1722, 2: 98–101. For a discussion of how the requirement of oath-taking may have been in conflict with English law, see Wraxall, *Abridgment*, ed. McIlwain, p. lxxi.

During the rest of the years that the Canadian trade remained prohibited, the Indian Commissioners called dozens of traders before them to take the oath. In 1723 several traders including John Schuyler and Cornelius Cuyler refused to do so and received fines of £100. Schuyler's conviction caused a number of raised eyebrows in the province. Unfortunately no one recorded the governor's reaction.[73] The great majority of traders used the oath to acquit themselves, causing the Indian Commissioners to wonder "how People can take the said Oath . . . who received large Quantities of Bever."[74] Many prominent Albany merchants eased their consciences by not directly engaging in the trade. Instead, they sent their sons to meet the Caughnawagas. Several of the traders openly disobeyed the law on the assumption that it eventually would be disallowed and their fines returned. In 1724, for example, Cornelius Cuyler hid from the sheriff during the trading season and later went before the commissioners, again refusing to commit perjury.[75]

The act of 1722 made business less pleasant and more expensive for the illegal traders, but it did not have much effect on the quantity of strouds that New Yorkers smuggled to Canada. As in the past, Caughnawaga Indians, straining under the weight of strouds and furs, crowded the portages on the route between Montreal and Albany. During one season, Cornelius Cuyler received about three hundred packs of beaver from Canada, and others did nearly as well.[76] Feeling more than a little frustrated, Philip Livingston complained, "I hear Strowds is plentyfully Conveyed to Canada and I am the only person that dare not medle for fear of disoblidging the Governor which I think a hard Case but must have patience it seems."[77] The smugglers could not be stopped, he argued, unless they were threatened by confiscation of their estates and banishment from the county.[78] Expressing a similar sentiment, the Indian Commissioners told Burnet, "How to prevent this

73. Minutes of the Indian Commissioners, June 19, 1723, 1: 43; Isaac Bobin to George Clarke, July 2, 1723, in *Letters of Isaac Bobin, Esq., Private Secretary of Hon. George Clarke, Secretary of the Province of New York, 1718–1730*, ed. Edmund B. O'Callaghan (Albany, 1872), p. 132.

74. Wraxall, *Abridgment*, ed. McIlwain, October 12, 1724, p. 156.

75. Minutes of the Indian Commissioners, October 2, 1724, June 11, 1725, 1: 101, 103; *Journal of the Commissioners for Trade and Plantations*, 14 vols. (London, 1920–38), May 12, 1725, 5: 165; Wraxall, *Abridgment*, ed. McIlwain, October 12, 1724, p. 156.

76. Philip Livingston to Robert Livingston, September 6, 1725, in Livingston Family Papers; Minutes of the Indian Commissioners, October 2, 1724, 1: 104.

77. Philip Livingston to Robert Livingston, August 25, 1725, in Livingston Family Papers.

78. Philip Livingston to Robert Livingston, September 6, 1725, ibid.

Pernicious Trade is a great Mystery to us . . . since a few Men break thro the severest Laws that can be invested for the Good and Prosperity of this Province in general, tho we shall resolve to tender the said Oath to whole Families among whom any may be suspected . . . ."[79] Even this tactic probably would not have worked, because many traders by 1725 no longer had any qualms about taking a false oath, if it dealt with the fur trade.[80]

Although the trade to Canada had not been seriously interrupted, the heavy fines and constant need for secrecy after 1722 reduced the profits of those men involved in the illicit commerce. Consequently, they now asked their correspondents in London to petition the Board of Trade for a disallowance of Burnet's restrictive laws. With strong support from Albany, Stephen DeLancey and Adolph Philipse became the colony's leading proponents of disallowance.[81] In July 1724 twenty London merchants, including Samuel Storke, Richard Jeneway, Samuel Baker, Joseph Bayeux, and Robert Hackshaw, responded to the pleas from New York and told the Board of Trade that Burnet's laws had proved "Very Pernicious to the *British Trade* in general and to the Interest of *New York* in particular."[82]

The main argument of the merchants centered around the danger that Candians would be able to obtain an adequate supply of strouds from other sources, with the result that New York would no longer have any way of competing with them. The merchants claimed that the French were already manufacturing adequate imitations as well as getting strouds from England, Holland, and New England. The result, it was alleged, had been fewer fur exports to England from New York, a rise in fur prices, and a reduction in the amount of goods being exported to the colony. Combined with these premature assessments of how Burnet's policies were working, the petitioners demonstrate considerable ignorance about the geography of North America. Being justifiably "doubtful of some of the facts alleged by the merchants," the

79. Wraxall, *Abridgment*, ed. McIlwain, October 12, 1724, p. 156.

80. Ibid.; Minutes of the Indian Commissioners, June 11, 1725, 1: 136.

81. Cuyler to Richard Jeneway, October 31, 1724, in Cornelius Cuyler Letter Book, 1724–1736; Cadwallader Colden, *The History of the Five Indian Nations of Canada, Which are Dependent on the Province of New York in America, And Are a Barrier Between the English and French in That Part of the World*, 2 vols. (New York, 1902), 1: 104–5; Smith, *History*, 1: 215, 232.

82. Cadwallader Colden, ed., *Papers Relating to An Act of the Assembly of the Province of New York, For Encouragement of the Indian Trade &c. and for Prohibiting the selling of Indian Goods to the French, viz. of Canada* (New York, 1724), pp. 2, 4.

Board of Trade recommended to the king that he take no action until Burnet could reply to the charges.[83]

When he learned of the petition, Burnet told the Indian Commissioners to draft a memorial defending his policies.[84] The arguments that they formulated provided the main store of ammunition used by the government in its efforts to refute the position taken by the Canada traders. Cadwallader Colden sent this document to England under the title of a report from the New York Council, and he used much of the information to produce his own famous memorial on the subject. Following Burnet's instructions, Colden combined the relevant documents, including the petition of the London merchants, into a pamphlet that was published before the end of 1724. Realizing that Burnet intended to emphasize the inaccuracies in the petition of the London merchants, his Albany opponents sent John Groesbeek, Jr., and Dirk Schuyler to England for the purpose of lobbying against the acts and giving more accurate information to their supporters.[85]

In May 1725 the Board of Trade held hearings to discuss the arguments for and against the policies of the New York government. John Sharpe, the attorney acting for the merchants, argued that the New York laws had reduced the fur exports from the colony and had actually helped French officials by undermining the Montreal smugglers. On the other hand, the colonial agent, Peter Leheup, maintained that the French would soon lose all their trade with the western Indians, because they were unable either to manufacture strouds or to import the cloth inexpensively from England. Although admitting that the fur trade might have been "lessened upon the first alteration of its channel," he correctly pointed out that New York fur exports were "now gradually increasing." At Leheup's suggestion the board summoned Robert Hunter, who strongly endorsed the New York acts. In their decision the board members agreed with Burnet's supporters that the restrictive laws

83. Ibid., p. 2; Memorial of the Board of Trade to the King, 1724, in *NYCD*, 5: 709.

84. Minutes of the Indian Commissioners, November 12, 1724, 1: 106a. A draft of this document was probably in Burnet's hands by November 6; see "The Draft of the Commissioners of Indian Affairs Report to the gov about the act Prohibiting Indian goods going to Canada," received November 6, 1724, in Livingston Family Papers.

85. Burnet to the Board of Trade, November 7, 1724; Affidavit of John Groesbeek, Jr., and Dirk Schuyler, February 15, 1725, in *NYCD*, 5: 712, 743–44; Colden, ed., *Papers Relating to An Act of the Assembly*; Armour, "Merchants of Albany," pp. 168–70. The papers compiled by Colden contain the New York Council's report, which can also be found in Smith, *History*, 1: 217–30.

had not damaged the fur trade and were actually beneficial to British interests in North America.[86] Nevertheless, they recommended disallowance of the acts because of the oath-taking provisions and suggested that New York could replace the offensive laws with a new act "whereby proper encouragements" could be given to the Oswego trade. Although the Privy Council took no action on these recommendations, Burnet began to consider a change in his policies.[87]

By the middle years of the decade the governor's opposition in New York was gaining strength while his supporters had become disorganized and less enthusiastic. Not surprisingly, the trend began in Albany, when the death of Hendrick Hansen, a Burnet supporter, necessitated an election in the spring of 1724 to fill his place in the assembly. The Canada traders selected Myndert Schuyler to run against Robert Livingston, Jr., the nephew of his namesake and former guardian. Instead of supporting the nominee of the Livingston faction, Burnet split the vote of his friends in Albany by endorsing a third candidate in order to repay a political debt. Philip Livingston might have prevented the governor's thoughtless defection by running for the office himself, but he explained, "'while the Assembly Sitts its comonly the best trade here which must be attended as well as a farmer his plow."[88] No statement could better illustrate Livingston's lifelong belief that business came first, politics second. Myndert Schuyler easily won the election and immediately began to seek out allies in southern New York. During the campaign, Philip Livingston privately admitted to his father that his former misgivings about the restrictions on the Canada trade had turned into complete disillusionment, because the law was only hurting the honest merchants. In addition, he feared that the French would be able to shake off their dependence on English strouds and thus capture almost the entire trade.[89]

A year later in 1725 Burnet's opponents found new and better opportunities to flex their muscles. When the assembly met in the fall, it replaced the ailing Robert Livingston with Adolph Philipse as speaker of the house. Philipse not only opposed the restrictions on trade with

86. *Journal of the Commissioners for Trade and Plantations*, May 5, 12, 13, 1725, 5: 163–67, 168–78.

87. Representation of the Board of Trade on the New York Indian trade acts, June 16, 1725, in *NYCD*, 5: 760–63.

88. Leder, *Robert Livingston*, pp. 277–79; Philip Livingston to Robert Livingston, March 25, 1724, in Livingston Family Papers.

89. Bonomi, *A Factious People*, pp. 92–93; Isaac Bobin to George Clarke, June 18, 1724, in *Letters of Isaac Bobin*, ed. O'Callaghan, p. 185; Philip Livingston to Robert Livingston, March 25, May 15, May 30, 1724, in Livingston Family Papers.

Canada, but also carried a grudge against the governor for having brought about his removal from the Council. Stung by this act of defiance, Burnet turned his wrath against Stephen DeLancey, who had been recently elected to fill a vacancy in the assembly. When DeLancey appeared before the governor to be given the oath of office, Burnet rebuffed him on the grounds that he had never been properly naturalized as an English citizen.[90] Even DeLancey's worst enemies refused to support this attempt to abrogate the assembly's traditional right of judging the qualifications of its members. "The refusing the oath to Mr. DLancey," declared Philip Livingston in Albany, "is a great Surprise to Maney here as well as at N: York . . . . There can be no good expected from it."[91] Within a few days the intensity of the opposition forced Burnet to retreat, and on September 24 he administered the oath to his political enemy.[92]

By electing Adolph Philipse as speaker and standing firm in the dispute concerning the qualifications of its members, the assembly declared its independence. No longer could Burnet expect automatic approval of the acts introduced by his supporters, and the change could not have occurred at a worse time. During this session his supporters had to introduce bills for new tax laws and for an extension of the act against trading with Canada. After initial defeats of attempts to modify the trade regulations, the assembly postponed further debate on the subject by extending the prohibition of the Canada trade until the end of the spring session in 1726.[93] In a lengthier debate the assembly argued over the duration of the revenue act for the support of the government. Burnet desired a law to last for five years; his opponents would allow only a two-year support. Hoping that the legislators would be more agreeable at a future date, the governor prorogued the assembly until the following spring. In a letter to the Board of Trade, he complained that since the merchants had not been able to prevent the continuation of the fur trade laws, they had "exerted themselves to the utmost

90. *Assembly Journal*, April 31, September 13, 1725, 1: 513, 514–15; Smith, *History*, 1: 232–33. For a full account of political developments in 1725, see Leder, *Robert Livingston*, pp. 282–88.

91. Philip Livingston to Robert Livingston, September 23, 1725, in Livingston Family Papers.

92. *Assembly Journal*, September 21, 1725, 1: 520. The opposition to Burnet among the merchants was based on more than just the issue of the Canadian trade. See Bonomi, *A Factious People*, pp. 93–95; and McAnear, "Politics in Provincial New York," p. 344.

93. *Assembly Journal*, October 22, 1725, 1: 526; *Laws*, November 10, 1725, 2: 248–50.

in opposing the continuance of the support of Government for five years . . . ."[94]

When the assembly met again in April, Burnet decided to blunt the attack of his opponents by agreeing to modifications in the trade acts. "I wish," he told the assemblymen, "I could say the Laws for promoting a Trade with the far *Indians*, and prohibiting it with *Canada*, had been as duly executed as they were well intended; and I leave it to your Consideration, whether a Method less severe may not be more effectual."[95] The resulting legislation indicated that Burnet's supporters had not entirely lost their influence in the assembly. The new act placed duties on all Indian goods, but merchandise taken to the north of Albany had to pay double the rate of similar articles sold at Oswego. Every piece of strouds, for instance, required a payment of either fifteen or thirty shillings. The only exceptions were small pieces of merchandise sold to Indians within the city. To provide "for the better collecting" of the duties, the assembly decided to farm out this responsibility to the highest bidders, who would naturally see that the law was enforced so that they could make a profit. To detect violators the tax farmers could require anyone with beaver skins in his possession to take an oath stating where he had obtained the peltry. Either deliberately or through an oversight, the new trade law failed to place any effective controls on the farmers of the duties. As a result, the new system quickly became discredited due to corruption and unfair enforcement.[96]

Recognizing the advantages of being a collector of the duties, Philip Livingston, Stephanus Groesbeek, Dirk Ten Broeck, John DePeyster, Hans Hansen, and Cornelius Cuyler paid far more for the privilege than the assembly had anticipated.[97] Thus, the enforcement of the law hindering the Canada trade came to rest in the hands of the more energetic participants in this commerce. By November the assembly had to pass a bill to close loopholes in the new regulations and to control the farmers of the duties, who were vigorously enforcing the law against everyone except themselves. To solve the problem, the assembly now required each of the farmers to produce sworn accounts of all the Indian trading goods that they had sold in the past year and to pay the required duties.[98]

Although the legislation to control the tax collectors probably stopped corruption from getting completely out of hand, it apparently had no

94. Burnet to the Board of Trade, November 24, 1725, in *NYCD*, 5: 766.
95. *Assembly Journal*, April 6, 1726, 1: 530.
96. *Laws*, June 17, 1726, 2: 281–94.
97. Ibid., November 11, 1726, p. 350.
98. Ibid. pp. 351–53.

effect on the rising tide of opposition in Albany. When the sheriff attempted to serve suspects with summonses ordering them to take the oath, he usually met with locked gates and barred doors. The tax farmers continued to enforce the law to their own advantage, and by the end of 1727 nearly everyone in the city was disgusted with the situation. Fortunately for the merchants, Burnet was transferred to the governorship of Massachusetts, and the New York fur dealers sensed victory when they sent new protests to London in January 1728.[99]

Seeking to bring about political harmony, the new governor, John Montgomerie, made no effort to oppose the efforts of the merchants. In November 1729 the Board of Trade recommended disallowance of all New York acts affecting the Canada trade. Although agreeing that the intent of the acts was not objectionable, the board refused, as it had also done in 1725, to condone the enforcement of the laws through the use of oaths and random searches. Within a short time, the Privy Council accepted the recommendations and disallowed all fur trade acts passed in New York during the 1720s.[100]

Thus, in the end, it was British officials who abolished the restrictions on the trade to Canada. For all practical purposes, however, the issue had already been decided in New York, where Burnet had failed to achieve a substantial reduction in the number of beaver skins arriving from Montreal. The main reasons for the failure were Burnet's political ineptness and the tenacity of the resistance in Albany. Relying almost entirely on the advice of Livingston and Hunter, Burnet had plunged into the difficult project without first appraising the situation for himself. At the beginning, his confidence far outweighed his caution, and he apparently had no concept of the difficulties that stood in his way. When he began to meet the inevitable frustrations, he failed to rally his supporters and even inadvertently aided his enemies by engaging in unwise political maneuvers.

Once Burnet left the colony, the political faction that had been the center of his support soon fell into disarray. Robert Livingston, who had retired, died before the end of 1728. His son therefore felt no further obligation to refrain from participating in the commerce with Canada. In the general election held after the arrival of Governor Montgomerie,

99. Wraxall, *Abridgment,* ed. McIlwain, pp. lxxviii–lxxixn; *Laws,* September 20, 1728, 2: 485; Cuyler to Richard Jeneway, January 13, 1728, in Cornelius Cuyler Letter Book, 1724–1736.

100. Cadwallader Colden, "Letters on Smith's *History of New York,*" New-York Historical Society *Collections,* 1868 (New York, 1869), pp. 220–21; Smith, *History,* 1: 240; Board of Trade to the Privy Council, November 19, 1729, in *NYCD,* 5: 898; *Assembly Journal,* August 26, 1730, 1: 606; W. L. Grant and James Munro, eds., *Acts of the Privy Council, Colonial Series,* 6 vols. (London, 1908–12), 3: 209–14.

Lewis Morris, an energetic politician who had been an ally of Hunter and Burnet, failed to regain his seat in the assembly. While the Burnet supporters dwindled in numbers, the Philipse-DeLancey faction greatly increased their strength by winning favor with Montgomerie, who promptly received a five-year support from the new assembly. In return, he nominated James DeLancey, the son of Stephen DeLancey, to the Council.[101]

After the election in 1728, the disapproving attitude of the assembly toward the restrictions on the Canada trade soon became apparent. Several of the convicted smugglers applied to the legislators for mercy and received reductions of their fines. All others owing penalties of £100 were allowed to settle for £60. In 1730, after officially being informed of the action taken by the Crown against the trade acts, the assembly and the Council demonstrated their new attitude by writing a letter to the Board of Trade that implicitly congratulated the members for having recommended the repeal of the laws. Almost quoting the words used by the petitioners against the restrictive laws, the letter contended that the interference with the trade may have actually helped the French to become independent of New York by forcing them to obtain their strouds either through imitations or through trade with England.[102]

Upon receiving the news about disallowance of the trade laws, the Albany merchants reacted with feelings of exuberance and vindication. "I was Very glad," wrote Cornelius Cuyler to Samuel Baker, "to here that the act Imposeing Dutyes fines etc. was Repealed—the Making of those unjest acts was Done out of Envy and Malice with Self Interest by Some ill Designing persons here."[103]

Although envisioning an era of increased profits, Cuyler and his fellow Canada traders immediately ran into unexpected difficulties. Ironically, the disallowance of the trade acts and the success of the British traders at Oswego caused the French to increase their own efforts to prevent furs from reaching New York. In the summer of 1731 several Albany citizens started out on a journey to Canada, but French authorities turned most of them back even though Governor Montgomerie had

---

101. *Assembly Journal*, March 25, July 22, August 7, 1728, 1: 573, 574, 580; Colden, "Letters on Smith's *History of New York*," pp. 220–21; Smith, *History*, 1: 240–41; Montgomerie to the Board of Trade, November 22, 1729, in *NYCD*, 5: 856; Nicholas Varga, "New York Politics and Government during the Mid-Eighteenth Century" (Ph.D. diss., Fordham University, 1960), pp. 31–32, 34.

102. Attorney-General Bradley to the Board of Trade, November 22, 1729, in *NYCD*, 5: 899–900; *Laws*, July 12, 1729, 2: 538–40; *Assembly Journal*, October 29, 1730, May 4, 1734, 1: 621, 657.

103. Cuyler to Samuel Baker, April 11, 1730, in Cornelius Cuyler Letter Book, 1724–1736.

given them passes. Montgomerie then wrote to Canada complaining that Governor Beauharnois was intentionally helping Montreal merchants to avoid paying old debts. During the same summer, the French built a fort at Crown Point on Lake Champlain mainly for the purpose of interrupting the illegal trade. They had also started a campaign to prevent the western Indians from trading with the British at Oswego.[104]

The new vigor on the part of the French authorities and a serious economic depression in the American colonies caused a drastic decline in the New York fur trade during the early 1730s. Shipments of furs to England fell from £6,952 11s. 7d. in 1725 to £2,610 15s. 4d. in 1730 and remained at approximately this level for five more years.[105] Both the trade to the west and the north of Albany suffered during this period. "We have this Summer," reported Cornelius Cuyler in 1733, "a Very Poor Trade at oswego and also no Trade from Canada so that skins amongst us are Very much in demand . . . ."[106] In 1734 exports of furs slowly began to improve and reached a value of £4,268 17s. 3d. in 1740. After another successful year in 1741, the value of fur exports declined moderately and did not rise again until after King George's War.[107]

During these years, the Montreal-Albany trade fell into a very irregular pattern, with the size of the commerce depending on the vigilance of the Canadian government. The amount of furs coming from Montreal began to increase in 1736, and in the following year Philip Livingston told his London correspondents that "it seems as if the French at Canada have opened the trade between them and this place for a larger quantity do come hither than heretofore . . . ."[108] Yet, only a year later, he had to

104. *Assembly Journal*, October 29, 1730, 1: 621; Beauharnois and Hocquart to Maurepas, October 31, 1731, in *NYCD*, 9: 1029; Minutes of the Indian Commissioners, February 11, 1731, July 29, 1731, 1: 332a, 346; Wraxall, *Abridgment*, ed. McIlwain, October 24, November 23, 1730, September 25, 1731, pp. 180–81, 184; Kingsford, *History of Canada*, 3: 286–87; Lanctot, *History of Canada*, 3: 34–35; Lunn, "Illegal Fur Trade," pp. 68–70.

105. Murray G. Lawson, "Extracts from Customs 3," in the possession of Lawrence A. Harper, University of California, Berkeley; Naval Office Lists for the Port of New York (microfilm), in C.O. 5/1225–1226, Public Record Office, London. For a full discussion of the economic depression that lasted from 1728 to 1740, see McAnear, "Politics in Provincial New York," pp. 356–76.

106. Cuyler to Samuel Baker, July 4, 1733, in Cornelius Cuyler Letter Book, 1724–1736.

107. Lawson, "Extracts from Customs 3"; Naval Office Lists for the Port of New York, in C.O. 5/1225–1227; Robert Sanders to [Samuel Storke] [1742], in Robert Sanders Letter Book, 1742–1743, New-York Historical Society, New York City.

108. Philip Livingston to Storke and Gainsborough, November 1, 1736, September 25, 1737, in Miscellaneous Manuscripts, vol. 5.

report that the French governor had been working to "the uttmost of his power" to stop the commerce. As a result, "We have had no trade from Canada which is a vast disappointment to me."[109]

In addition to the general economic depression and the effective interference from French officials, Livingston and his competitors began running into difficulties caused by the law of supply and demand. Decreasing quantities of beaver and other factors had caused prices to rise in Canada to such an extent that on at least one occasion they were higher in Montreal than in Albany.[110] On the other hand, the demand for strouds in Canada decreased due to a great surplus of this commodity in New York. So many small traders had started importing their own merchandise and selling it to the French and Indians at such low prices that, according to Livingston, "European goods Seem to be a drugg even to the Remotest part of the Continent."[111] Because of these economic changes, the Albany merchants doing business with Montreal sometimes had to pay for their furs with one-half merchandise and one-half specie.[112]

Facing reduced profits from his investments in both the Canada and Oswego trade routes, Livingston lost interest in the peltry business and concentrated on his other commercial enterprises. Well before he made this move, other Albany merchants had gradually allowed the fur trade to take second place to their commercial relations with the West Indies, where they sold the agricultural surpluses of the Hudson and Mohawk Valleys. Even many of those merchants who continued to depend primarily on the Canadian trade sold flour and other products to customers in the Caribbean area.[113] Two decades earlier at the beginning of Burnet's administration, the trade with Montreal had been of such economic importance that the restrictive laws had resulted in vigorous opposition. By 1740 an attempt to restrict the northern commerce would have produced far less protest, because the Canadian trade had diminished in relative importance.

The refusal of most Albany residents to accept Burnet's prohibition of trade with Canada was often cited by their critics as an example of Albany's lack of concern for British interests. To be convincing, however,

109. Philip Livingston to Storke and Gainsborough, July 4, September 29, 1738, ibid.

110. Philip Livingston to Jacob Wendell, August 3, 1738, in Livingston Papers, Museum of the City of New York.

111. Philip Livingston to Storke and Gainsborough, September 6, 1737, in Miscellaneous Manuscripts, vol. 5.

112. Philip Livingston to Storke and Gainsborough, November 1, 1736, September 6, 1737, ibid.

113. See chapter 6.

the critics would first have had to prove that Burnet's policies actually were beneficial. Although the Albany merchants, in this instance, were mainly motivated by economic considerations, Burnet's supporters were unable to demonstrate to either Albany or to the British government that it was necessary to interfere with the Canadian trade. Some observers, including Philip Livingston, believed that the restrictive laws might actually work to the advantage of the French. In any case, the opposition of the Albany Dutch to Burnet should not be construed as part of their Indian policy, because the Canadian trade mainly involved economic relations between Europeans, and no one, except Colden, stressed the effects of this commerce on relations with the Iroquois.

Governor Burnet would have been pleased by the changes that had taken place in the fur trade by 1740. His immediate attempts to abolish the commerce with Canada had failed. Yet, in the long run he had contributed to its economic decline by establishing Oswego as a center of trade with the western Indians. Changing economic conditions and greater vigilance on the part of French authorities were, however, probably more influential than Burnet's policies.

Since the second decade of the century, the trade with Montreal had been a significant political issue in the province. Its decline in economic importance did little to reduce the intensity of the political controversies that had surrounded it over the years. After Burnet's departure from New York, politicians who viewed the trade as a detriment to imperial expansion had to lower their battle flags, but in the 1740s they again found opportunities to use the issue of the Canadian trade as a rallying point to advance their political goals. In these final years of struggle with France for empire, they were destined to achieve success.

9

WESTERN INDIANS AND

NEW YORK POLICY

THE ATTEMPT by Governor Burnet and his supporters to abolish the Canadian trade was only part of the overall program to reduce French influence among the tribes living around the Great Lakes. Little purpose would have been served by destroying the Montreal-Albany commerce without substituting another method for obtaining the peltry of the western Indians, since the French would then have been in a position to acquire nearly all of the furs of the Great Lakes as well as to strengthen their relations with dozens of tribes, including the Miami, the Potawatomi, the Chippewa, and even some members of the Iroquois Confederacy. New York therefore not only had to counter French influence with the western tribes; it also had to establish economic relations with these tribes by building a trading post somewhere on or near Lake Ontario.

When Burnet arrived in New York in the fall of 1720, the idea of challenging the French in the west was far from new. It had been a dream of some New Yorkers since the 1680s, when Governor Thomas Dongan suggested the construction of several forts stretching from Albany to Niagara.[1] In order to test the reaction of the French to English commer-

1. Arthur H. Buffinton, "The Policy of Albany and English Westward Expansion," *Mississippi Valley Historical Review* 8 (1922): 344–45. For the best account of Dongan's relations with the Indians, see Allen W. Trelease, *Indian Affairs in Colonial New York: The Seventeenth Century* (Ithaca, N.Y., 1960), pp. 176–77, passim. Also see David A. Armour, "The Merchants of Albany, New York, 1686–1760" (Ph.D. diss., Northwestern University, 1965), pp. 3–21; John Romeyn Brodhead, *History of the State of New York*, 2 vols. (New York, 1859–71), 2: chaps. 8, 9; Peter Wraxall, *An Abridgment of the Indian Affairs Contained in Four Folio Volumes, Transacted in the Colony of New York, from the Year 1678 to the Year 1751*, ed. Charles H. McIlwain (Cambridge, Mass., 1915), pp. lx–lxii; and William Smith, Jr., *The History of the Late Province of New-York from Its Discovery to the Appointment of Governor Colden in 1762*, 2 vols. (New York, 1829–39), 1: 61–62, 71–79.

cial activities in the Great Lakes region, Dongan sent trading expeditions deep into the interior.

In 1685 he gave a license to an Albany citizen, Johannes Roseboom, who took a party with ten canoes as far west as Lake Huron and enjoyed a very successful trading season.[2] Knowing that the traders from Albany could undersell them, the French were alarmed by this expedition. In a letter to his superiors, Denonville, the governor of Canada, declared, "Missilimakinac is theirs. They . . . have been to trade there with our Outawas and Huron Indians, who received them cordially on account of the bargains they gave . . . ."[3]

Ignoring official complaints from Canada, Dongan sent out another expedition under Roseboom in the fall of 1686.[4] The governor ordered these fifty traders "to show all Civility and kind usage to the Indians att Ottowaas and to use the best Ways and Methods to Influence them to trade and Correspond with the Inhabitants of the Citty of Albany . . . ."[5] In the following spring Major Patrick Macgregory, who was one of Dongan's confidants, took command of another expedition.[6] The two trading parties, composed mostly of Dutchmen from upper New York, soon ran afoul of French military forces and were arrested.[7]

In pursuing his plans for the west, Dongan found considerable support in Albany and little, if any, opposition.[8] Part of this support was due to

2. Helen Broshar, "The First Push Westward of the Albany Traders," *Mississippi Valley Historical Review* 7 (1920): 233–34.

3. Denonville to Seignelay, November 8, 1686, in *Documents Relative to the Colonial History of New York*, ed. Edmund B. O'Callaghan and Berthold Fernow, 15 vols. (Albany, 1856–87), 9: 297, hereafter cited as *NYCD*. On French activities as far south as Oswego in the seventeenth century, see Frederick W. Barnes, "The Fur Traders of Early Oswego," New York State Historical Assiciation *Proceedings* 13 (1914): 128–29.

4. Broshar, "First Push Westward," pp. 234–35; Brodhead, *History of New York*, 2: 443–44.

5. Lawrence H. Leder, ed., *The Livingston Indian Records, 1666–1723* (Gettysburg, Pa., 1956), p. 107.

6. Broshar, "First Push Westward," pp. 234–35; Trelease, *Indian Affairs*, p. 270.

7. Leder, ed., *Livingston Indian Records*, pp. 106–7n, 111n; Father Beschefer to Cabart de Villermont, September 19, 1687, in *Jesuit Relations and Allied Documents: Travels and Explorations of the Jesuit Missionaries in New France, 1619–1791*, ed. Reuben G. Thwaites, 73 vols. (Cleveland, 1896–1901), 63: 281, 282; W. J. Eccles, *The Canadian Frontier, 1534–1760* (New York, 1969), p. 119; Wraxall, *Abridgment*, ed. McIlwain, p. lxii.

8. Buffinton, "Policy of Albany," pp. 345–47; Broshar, "First Push Westward," pp. 228–41; Douglas Edward Leach, *The Northern Colonial Frontier, 1607–1763* (New York, 1966), p. 150. Two historians have noted that in expanding the trade

the great popularity that the governor had won in 1686, when he granted the city a monopoly over the fur trade. The licenses issued to the western expeditions protected this economic privilege by firmly prohibiting any commercial relations with members of the Iroquois Confederacy.[9] Leading residents of Albany not only supported Dongan's expeditions, but also went along on these dangerous ventures. Hendrick Hansen, Abraham Schuyler, Jacob Lokermans, and other prominent Dutchmen took the risk because of the recent reduction in the number of skins reaching Albany.[10] Declining beaver populations and renewed warfare with the French had cost the Iroquois their ability to obtain an adequate supply of furs.[11] Economic survival for Albany required another source of peltry.

With the successes of the French against Roseboom and Macgregory and with the outbreak of King William's War, most people stayed close to home. A few, however, could not resist the lure of the western profits. Shortly after the beginning of the war, one John Mashe traveled to the westernmost Great Lakes.[12] Between 1692 and 1694 Arnout Viele, who had lost his job as official interpreter by his support of the rebellious Leisler, went on an expedition down the Ohio River as far as the Wabash, where he traded with the Shawnees and the Miamis.[13] Despite Viele's successes, no one followed his example while war still raged along the frontier.

When hostilities ended, Albany merchants again began looking for new sources of furs. They could see that the devastated Iroquois would not be able to acquire an adequate number of skins, and the likelihood of renewed warfare with the French discouraged them from again supporting any plans to send commercial expeditions into the wilderness. Thus, their economic future required rapid development of trade with Canada. By the end of the trading season in 1700, they had succeeded. As for trade with western tribes, the Albany merchants either hired Iroquois agents to sell their goods on Lake Ontario or encouraged the western Indians to bring their furs to Albany.[14]

to the west Dongan may have been acting at the request of Albany. See Trelease, *Indian Affairs*, p. 269; and Armour, "Merchants of Albany," p. 11.

9. Leder, ed. *Livingston Indian Records*, pp. 106, 111.

10. Ibid., pp. 106–7n; Armour, "Merchants of Albany," pp. 13–14.

11. See chapter 2.

12. John Mashe to the King or his Queen or Council, September 15, 1692, in William Blathwayt Papers, Miscellaneous Manuscripts, New-York Historical Society, New York City.

13. Broshar, "First Push Westward," p. 239; Leach, *Northern Colonial Frontier*, p. 150.

14. See chapter 8.

The new governor, Lord Bellomont, advocated the building of a fort in Iroquois country, but he could find little support in Albany. The French had been able to turn back English expeditions in the 1680s, when the Iroquois Confederacy possessed great power. Now that the Iroquois had been severely chastised and were coming to terms with their enemies, the Albany leaders must have scoffed at any new proposals for challenging Frenchmen in the west. In 1700 the probability still existed that a new war with France would shut off the Montreal trade, but after Albany traders met with French officials in the spring of 1701, it appeared likely that the city could protect itself by arranging to remain neutral. The protection of a neutrality agreement meant more to the city residents than simply economic advantage. With the horrors of frontier warfare still fresh in their minds, they were sincere when they told Bellomont that he should not build forts in the wilderness until he first improved the inadequate fortifications around Albany and Schenectady.[15]

When Bellomont first arrived in the colony he knew almost nothing about Indian affairs, but he soon received an education on the subject from his political ally, Robert Livingston, who had already spent a quarter-century as New York's Indian Secretary. More than any other individual, Livingston was responsible for developing and keeping alive the idea that the English should challenge Canada for commercial control of the region around the Great Lakes. Livingston had probably worked out his thoughts on the subject while conferring with Governor Dongan, and by 1699 he had reached certain conclusions that he consistently advocated throughout the next twenty-five years. During this first quarter of the eighteenth century, he exerted considerable influence over the western policies of Governors Bellomont, Hunter, and Burnet.

In 1699 Livingston set forth most of his ideas on western expansion in a memorial to Bellomont, who sent a copy of it to the Board of Trade.[16] Within the next two years, Livingston further elaborated on his plans in a letter to the Board of Trade and in a report on his visit to Onondaga in the spring of 1700. The most important part of his plan concerned the construction of forts deep in the interior. Always ambitious, he recommended a strongly fortified post as far west as Detroit, to be linked with Albany by a series of other forts. French traders already at

15. Address of the citizens of Albany to Bellomont, August 24, 1700, in *NYCD*, 4: 752–53.

16. Memorial of Robert Livingston to Bellomont, April 12, 1699; Bellomont to the Board of Trade, April 13, 1699, ibid., pp. 500–501, 488; Lawrence H. Leder, *Robert Livingston, 1654–1728, and the Politics of Colonial New York* (Chapel Hill, 1961), pp. 138–39.

Detroit were to be expelled. In addition, he called for the encouragement of peace between the Iroquois and the western Indians, the development of a class of "bushlopers" to be the equivalent of the French
coureurs de bois, and the building of towns on the frontier. Recognizing
that these last two proposals would upset the economic structure of
Albany, he emphatically stated that no one should worry about a monopoly possessed by the selfish traders of this Dutch city. Although
Livingston later opposed the Montreal-Albany trade, he did not make
an issue of it at this time, because he still hoped to participate in the
northern commerce himself. In his recommendations he did agree with
the general Albany sentiment that the other colonies should share in
the expenses of establishing and maintaining frontier forts.[17]

Being in a position of responsibility, Governor Bellomont was less
inclined than Livingston to antagonize both the French and Albany at
the same time. He therefore announced plans to build a fort only as far
west as Onondaga country and indicated that it would not be used for
commercial purposes. In New York he never publicly divulged where
he intended to build the fort, but by the fall of 1700 he had selected a
site at the mouth of the Oswego River. Ambiguity about the location
and purpose of the fort was necessary in order to avoid intensifying the
opposition expressed by both the Iroquois and Albany to his plans.[18]

Meanwhile, the Board of Trade had been listening with sympathy
to the complaints of Albany residents about the inadequacy of their
defenses. In December 1700 the board advised Bellomont to give his
attention to rebuilding fortifications at Albany and Schenectady before
becoming involved in plans for westward expansion. Shortly after this
remonstrance from the board, King William revived the governor's
spirits by giving his total approval to the Oswego project and by donat-
ing £500 toward it, as well as £200 for work on the defenses around
the settlement.[19] Apparently, the king had been persuaded by Bellomont's arguments about the importance of establishing a trade with the
western Indians. Once New York had secured the friendship of these

17. Robert Livingston, Report on a journey to Onondaga in April 1700; Robert
Livingston to the Board of Trade, May 13, 1701, in *NYCD*, 4: 650–51, 872–74;
Leder, *Robert Livingston*, p. 126.

18. Indian Conference, August 28, 1700; Bellomont to the Board of Trade,
October 17, 1700, in *NYCD*, 4: 732, 717; *Journal of the Votes and Proceedings
of the General Assembly of the Colony of New York [1691–1765]*, 2 vols. (New
York, 1764–66), April 14, 1701, 1: 109, hereafter cited as *Assembly Journal*;
Wraxall, *Abridgment*, ed. McIlwain, p. lxiii.

19. Board of Trade to Bellomont, December 20, 1700; King William to Bellomont, January 19, 1701, in *NYCD*, 4: 819–20, 838.

Indians, the English, according to the governor, would be able to "laugh at all" the French efforts to outflank them in North America. To spread the word of inexpensive English merchandise, he sent agents to Ottawa country and beyond.[20]

For more than a decade after Bellomont's death in 1701, New York officials were concerned mainly with the problems presented by Queen Anne's War. In most of these years, New Yorkers displayed little desire to upset the neutrality between themselves and Canada, and even Robert Livingston remained quiet. In addition to financial difficulties, he did not enjoy good relations with Governor Cornbury. Livingston's influence on western policy did not again become apparent until after the arrival of Governor Robert Hunter in 1710 and the conclusion of peace with France in 1713.

During his first three years in New York, Hunter concerned himself with matters relating to the war. Afterwards, he expended most of his energies in a successful effort to end the senseless political strife that had been going on since Leisler's Rebellion. Nevertheless, he did not ignore the threat presented by the French in Canada. Like his predecessors, Dongan and Bellomont, he believed that the best method for assuring the eventual defeat of the French was to win away their Indian allies. Because of the emphasis on domestic affairs during his administration, his role in Indian policy is sometimes overlooked, but he did much to lay the foundation for the successful establishment of a trade with the western tribes.[21]

Undaunted by instructions from London to the contrary, Hunter made preparations soon after his arrival for establishing two forts among the Iroquois. By 1712 the nearest outpost, named Fort Hunter, had been completed and garrisoned with twenty soldiers. The more distant project at Onondaga had to be abandoned because of insufficient financial resources and opposition from the Iroquois.[22] In spite of this setback, Hunter continued to advocate the construction of wilderness forts

20. Bellomont to the Board of Trade, January 16, 1701, in *Calendar of State Papers, Colonial Series, America and West Indies*, ed. W. N. Sainsbury et al., 43 vols. to date (London, 1860–), 19: 34; New York Executive Council Minutes, April 18, 1701, vol. 8, New York State Library, Albany, hereafter cited as Council Minutes; Allen W. Trelease, "The Iroquois and the Western Fur Trade: A Problem in Interpretation," *Mississippi Valley Historical Review* 49 (1962): 44.

21. Two of the more knowledgeable historians on the subject of New York Indian relations did not give Governor Hunter the credit due him. See Buffinton, "Policy of Albany," pp. 352–66; and Trelease, *Indian Affairs*, p. 356.

22. Draft of Instructions for Robert Hunter, December 27, 1709; A contract, October 11, 1711; Hunter to the Board of Trade, October 31, 1712, in *NYCD*, 5: 140, 279, 380; Leach, *Northern Colonial Frontier*, pp. 128–29.

in order to prevent the "natural enemies" of the British from "extending their limits."[23]

Although he failed to establish a military post as far west as Onondaga country, Hunter did succeed in bringing a similar French project to an abrupt halt. While he had been considering his plans for the construction of a fort somewhere near the Onondaga village, the Canadians were making the first move.[24] In April 1710 a force of thirty-four Frenchmen arrived at Onondaga, and with permission of the Indian residents they completed a small blockhouse by early May. The Onondagas had given their approval in return for a present worth £600. They also seem to have recognized that they could use the existence of this French threat in their frequent attempts to persuade the British to lower the prices of merchandise.[25]

After hearing of the French project, the Commissioners of Indian Affairs immediately complained to Hunter and asked that some "effectual means" be taken to defeat the French designs. Following the governor's instructions, Peter Schuyler and a small group of frontiersmen proceeded to the Onondaga village, where they reminded the Indians of their promise not to "permit any armed men, Priest or Emissarys" from the French to live among them. In his negotiations with the Onondagas, Schuyler asked them for permission to tear down the blockhouse. Not daring to give official permission, the Iroquois told Schuyler that they would do nothing to interfere with a British effort to destroy the offending structure. Schuyler then proceeded to the blockhouse, where the French had left a small garrison. Apparently, the Canadians had been merely testing New York's reaction, because the troops departed as soon as they spotted the small party of New Yorkers. Schuyler's party then destroyed the blockhouse, along with some boards that had been cut for a chapel. In the territory directly to the south of Lake Ontario, the French never again seriously attempted to build fortifications.[26]

Several years after his successful confrontation with the French at Onondaga, Hunter became the first New York governor since Dongan to encourage actual trading expeditions to the Great Lakes. In the spring of 1716 six traders applied for and received a license to spend the summer at Irondequoit on Lake Ontario about halfway between Oswego

23. Hunter to the Board of Trade, November 12, 1715, in *NYCD*, 5: 459.

24. Indian Conference, August 9, 1710, ibid., p. 218.

25. Wraxall, *Abridgment*, ed. McIlwain, April 21, May 7, 11, 1711, pp. 81, 82, 86; Report of Lawrence Claessen, May 7, 1711, in *NYCD*, 5: 244.

26. Leder, ed., *Livingston Indian Records*, pp. 219–20; Indian Commissioners to Hunter, May 4, 1711; Journal of Peter Schuyler's negotiations with the Onondagas [May 15, 1711], in *NYCD*, 5: 242, 248.

and Niagara. After reaching Irondequoit, these traders received permission from the Senecas to build the traditional bark house in the vicinity of a similar French establishment.[27] In December Hunter initiated the policy of sending official agents deep into Iroquois country to stay for lengthy periods of time. Agreeing to remain until the following October, the five agents took with them instructions to keep the Iroquois "firm to their Allegience and to watch the Motions and defeat the Intrigues of the French."[28]

A year later in 1717 Hunter presented a license to Robert Livingston, Jr., Johannes Cuyler, and Hendrick Hansen, giving them permission to open a trade with the far Indians at a location west of the Senecas. Significantly, all three of the licensees were prominent Canada traders. Like most of their associates in the Montreal-Albany commerce, they had no objections to receiving furs from the west as well as from the north.[29] New York records do not mention any other trading expeditions during the last two years of Hunter's administration, but in 1720 the French complained that New Yorkers had been trading near Niagara for several years.[30]

In his western policies Hunter's greatest success resulted from his efforts to bring about good relations between the Iroquois and the western Indians. This step was necessary before the distant tribes would dare to venture into Iroquois country for the purpose of trading with the New Yorkers along the southern side of Lake Ontario. When Hunter first came to New York, almost no direct commercial contact existed between the British and the western Indians. Albany traders were not traveling to the west, and the Iroquois were not allowing many of their former enemies to pass through their lands to Albany. The Ottawas were probably the only major group with permission to travel in Iroquois country. In the first decade of the century, Governor Cornbury had urged the granting of this privilege to other tribes, but the Iroquois made only a few concessions. At his first meeting with Iroquois sachems, Hunter began to change their minds, and within a few years they had granted travel rights to numerous tribes of the interior.[31]

27. Wraxall, *Abridgment*, ed. McIlwain, April 30, July 17, 1716, pp. 112, 113; Buffinton, "Policy of Albany," pp. 347–58.

28. Wraxall, *Abridgment*, ed. McIlwain, December 12, 1716, p. 117.

29. Robert Hunter, A license, September 9, 1717, in New York Colonial Manuscripts, 60: 174, New York State Library, Albany.

30. Vaudreuil and Begon, Abstract of their report on Niagara, October 26, 1720, in *NYCD*, 9: 897. Also see Barnes, "Fur Traders of Early Oswego," p. 130.

31. Philip Livingston to Robert Livingston, June 17, 1714, in Livingston Family Papers (microfilm), Franklin D. Roosevelt Library, Hyde Park, N.Y.; Trelease, "The Iroquois and the Western Fur Trade," pp. 45–46.

Although preoccupied with pressing military and domestic problems, Hunter succeeded in clearing the way for a vigorous British push to the Great Lakes and did much to put Robert Livingston's proposals into effect. By the end of his administration, he became convinced that New York would not succeed in opening a trade with the west until after the prohibition of the commerce between Albany and Montreal that provided the French with the goods demanded by their Indian customers. Even after his departure from the New York scene, Hunter continued to advocate the building of western forts and the suppression of the Canadian trade.[32] The continuity between his programs and those advocated by his handpicked successor should not be overlooked.

When William Burnet boarded his ship for the voyage to America in 1720, he was not unprepared for the task ahead of him. In the drawing rooms and fashionable clubs of London, he and Robert Hunter had found ample time to discuss the problems of a governor in New York.[33] Apparently Hunter had stressed in these conversations the difficulties of establishing a fort in the wilds of America, because Burnet displayed far more caution in this matter than he did in attempting to prohibit the trade between Montreal and Albany. Making preparations with great care, he waited for more than six years before building a fort at Oswego. Most of these preparations involved the continuation and expansion of Hunter's programs.

In the interval of more than a year between Hunter's departure and Burnet's arrival, the French had increased their efforts to win Indian allies. By the end of 1720 they completed a fort at Niagara, where they had abandoned a blockhouse during their wars with the Iroquois. They hoped that the presence of both French traders and soldiers at this strategic location would prevent the western Indians from bringing their furs to Albany. For once, New Yorkers were unified on a question of frontier policy. In May Peter Schuyler, as temporary head of government, dispatched Lawrence Claessen to Niagara, where he told the French that the Iroquois had not given anyone permission to build fortifications on their lands. In answer to Claessen's demands that they abandon the project, the French told him that they had received permission from the young Seneca warriors and that only the governor of New France could order them to leave. Schuyler then unsuccessfully at-

---

32. See chapter 8.
33. Wraxall, *Abridgment*, ed. McIlwain, pp. lxv–lxvi; Herbert L. Osgood, *The American Colonies in the Eighteenth Century*, 4 vols. (New York, 1924–25; reprinted, Gloucester, Mass., 1958), 2: 416; Smith, *History*, 1: 212.

tempted to persuade the Iroquois to destroy the French establishment.[34]

At this point in the early fall of 1720, William Burnet arrived in the colony. He, too, urged the destruction of Niagara, but the Iroquois refused to disrupt the peace and tranquility that had now existed for two decades. Unable to do anything about Niagara, Burnet immediately ordered the Indian Commissioners to post a blacksmith and three others in Seneca country to promote British interests. Although each of the three men living with the smith received a payment of £20, they refused to obey orders not to trade with the Indians. This inability of official agents to resist the temptation of quick profits continued to be a problem for the rest of the colonial period. In 1721 Burnet again stationed a smith and another man in Seneca country, but by this time he had decided that British traders would do more to win the allegiance of the western Indians than any number of diplomats.[35]

Early in 1721 the governor gave about ten young men licenses to trade to the west of Albany as long as they did not begin selling goods before reaching the Senecas. Realizing that these private traders might not be effective or reliable, Burnet also sent out an official party of traders to live among the Senecas for a year. Under the command of Peter Schuyler, Jr., they were to establish a trading house at Irondequoit, where they would trade with the Indians and the *coureurs de bois*, while attempting to maintain British influence among the Senecas.[36] "This my Lords," Burnet exclaimed in a letter to the Board of Trade, "is the beginning of a great Trade that may be maintained with all the Indians upon the Lakes and the cheapness of all our goods . . . will by degrees draw all that Trade to us . . . ."[37] When this first expedition returned to Albany in the fall of 1722, Burnet sent out another group under Abraham Schuyler with orders to live at Irondequoit or some other convenient location and to "use all lawfull means to draw the farr trade" to New York.[38]

Even while planning the establishment of a British trading post on

34. Journal of Lawrence Claessen's visit to Niagara, May 22, 1720, in *NYCD*, 5: 550–51; Wraxall, *Abridgment*, ed. McIlwain, August 31, 1720, pp. 128–30.

35. Wraxall, *Abridgment*, ed. McIlwain, October 20, December 22, 1720, pp. 132–33; Council Minutes, September 11, 1721, vol. 13; Eccles, *Canadian Frontier*, p. 143.

36. Philip Livingston to Robert Livingston, February 1, 1721, in Livingston Family Papers; Burnet to Peter Schuyler, Jr., September 11, 1721, in *NYCD*, 5: 641.

37. Burnet to the Board of Trade, October 16, 1721, in *NYCD*, 5: 633.

38. Council Minutes, September 4, 1722, vol. 13; Leder, ed., *Livingston Indian Records*, pp. 233–35.

the southern side of Lake Ontario, Burnet continued the policy of encouraging the Iroquois to allow the more distant Indians to pass through their territory to Albany. Both of the official expeditions sent out in 1721 and 1722 received instructions to tell the western Indians that the Iroquois had given the governor their absolute "promise and Engagement . . . that they will not only Suffer them to passe freely and Peaceably" through their country, but would also "Sweep and keep the Path open and Clean."[39] In the fall of 1724, Burnet personally thanked the Iroquois for allowing so many of the western tribes to enjoy the "happy correspondence" with Albany.[40] Burnet realized, of course, that this trade would eventually fall into the hands of any British trading post established on Lake Ontario. In the meantime, an increase in the number of Indians arriving in Albany with cargoes of beaver would help to undermine Dutch opposition to his attack on the Canadian trade.

Although most Albany merchants naturally had nothing good to say about William Burnet, they did not leave any record of opposition to his plans for the construction of a fort on Lake Ontario. In fact, they would have encouraged such a project if Burnet had intended it only for military purposes and not for commercial activities as well. The construction of a French fort at Niagara greatly disturbed the leaders of Albany, who now feared that French influence among the Indians had reached a critical point. Shortly before the arrival of Burnet in the colony, Albany city officials wrote to Peter Schuyler with a recommendation for the construction of two forts on Lake Ontario. This had to be done, they declared, "to defeat the intreagues of the French and secure and preserve the Five nations to the British interest and likewise to keep the path open and patent for all the Far Indians to come hither and trade . . . ." Recognizing that such forts might threaten their monopoly, they made clear their desire that the Indian trade be wholy and solely confined within the walls of the City of Albany pursuant to the Charter of this City . . . and that a law be made to inflict severe penalties on those that shall transgress."[41]

In spite of these strong sentiments, the residents of Albany must have realized by 1723 or 1724 that their monopoly rights were doomed. Fortunately, the increased security, resulting from a fort among the Iroquois, helped to alleviate their distress. The Albany merchants, therefore, di-

39. Leder, ed., *Livingston Indian Records*, pp. 233–34.
40. Indian Conference, September 15, 1724, in *NYCD*, 5: 715–16.
41. Officials of Albany to Peter Schuyler, September 14, 1720, ibid., pp. 570–72, 572.

rected most of their energies toward protecting the Canadian trade from the onslaught of the governor and his supporters.

Before proceeding with plans to build a trading post, Burnet was apparently waiting to see if trade could be successfully established with the far Indians from a base on Lake Ontario at either Irondequoit or Oswego. The results of the first three trading seasons were inconclusive, but the year 1724 represented a significant turning point. British customs records for the early 1720s are not reliable indicators, because the enumeration of furs in 1722 meant an automatic increase in the quantity of peltry arriving in London from New York. Nevertheless, the testimony of Philip Livingston indicates that the moderate rise in export figures in 1724 can be traced to the success of the trade from the west. In March he complained to his father that Burnet's policies were failing and that "a few boys" on Lake Ontario could not have much effect, but by the end of May he reported that these western traders were enjoying a successful season. Several weeks later he noted that his store rooms now contained "£600 worth" of furs acquired on Lake Ontario.[42] Also during 1724, the Indian Commissioners noted that the number of far Indians arriving in Albany had decreased, because they were "stopped in their way hither by our People that go up to trade."[43]

Encouraged by the success of the trading season, Burnet met with the Iroquois in the fall of 1724 for the purpose of receiving their permission to build "a good Block House at the mouth" of the Oswego River. This trading post, he promised, would "bring the great Beaver Trade into your own country," which would result in an abundance of trading goods and a lowering of prices. To demonstrate the seriousness of his desire to obtain more beaver skins from the west, Burnet had come to the conference "cloathed . . . in Cloth made of Beaver."[44] Although apparently preferring a fort at a location that would be more suitable for the protection of the Onondaga village, the Iroquois gave their approval to the governor's plan.[45] Shortly before this meeting with the Iroquois, the confident governor spent £150 of the province's money to improve the route between Schenectady and Oswego. Workmen dragged trees out of the waterways, constructed a road over the main

42. Philip Livingston to Robert Livingston, March 25, May 25, June 16, 1724, in Livingston Family Papers.
43. Minutes of the Commissioners of Indian Affairs (microfilm), July 6, 1724, 1: 82, Public Archives of Canada, Ottawa, hereafter cited as Minutes of the Indian Commissioners.
44. Indian Conference, September 15, 1724, in NYCD, 5: 716.
45. Indian Conference, September 17, 1724, ibid., pp. 717–18.

portage from the Mohawk to Wood Creek, and even built a bridge.[46]

By the end of the trading season in 1725, Burnet had obtained convincing evidence to demonstrate that his western policies were now producing significant results. In the spring he had ordered the Indian Commissioners to keep a careful record of the furs brought to Albany by the western traders, who now seem to have been conducting nearly all of their business at Oswego. On September 2 the commissioners sent him a letter with an enclosed list showing that the Oswego traders had obtained 738 packs of peltry including deerskins. Since compiling the list, fifty more packs had arrived, and several companies of traders had not yet reported to the commissioners. In addition, the far Indians had carried two hundred packs of skins directly to Schenectady or Albany.[47] Philip Livingston estimated that the western trade for the year would account for nearly 1,200 packs, and export figures confirm that 1725 was a boom year for the New York trade.[48] With great but understandable exaggeration, Burnet reported, "in fact never more Beaver went home in a year from this place to England than this present year, nor were ever more goods imported hither from thence which has been occasioned by the great trade carried on by our people with the Indians upon this side of Lake Ontario."[49]

Before completing plans for a fort at Oswego, the governor had to find some way of financing it. In 1720 and 1724 the assembly had enacted legislation to encourage the western trade by putting a 2 percent duty on all European goods imported into the colony. Since such duties ran counter to British mercantile philosophy, the king disallowed both of the laws. In the earlier years of Burnet's administration, the assembly would have found some other method to finance the government's pet project; but, by the time he made a request for funds in 1726, his enemies had greatly increased their strength in the lower house. They were not in a generous mood.[50]

46. Minutes of the Indian Commissioners, September 19, 1724, 1: 99; Council Minutes, October 8, 15, 1724, vol. 15.

47. Minutes of the Indian Commissioners, September 2, 1725, 1: 142–43; *Assembly Journal*, September 22, 1725, 1: 520; Wraxall, *Abridgment*, ed. McIlwain, p. lxix.

48. Philip Livingston to Robert Livingston, September 6, 1725, in Livingston Family Papers; Naval Office Lists for the Port of New York (microfilm), in C.O. 5/1223, Public Record Office, London; Murray G. Lawson, "Extracts from Customs 3," in the possession of Lawrence A. Harper, University of California, Berkeley; Smith, *History*, 1: 233.

49. Burnet to the Board of Trade, November 24, 1725, in *NYCD*, 5: 766.

50. Burnet to the Board of Trade, November 26, 1720; Board of Trade to Burnet, June 6, 1722; Order in Council, April 30, 1724, ibid., pp. 576–77, 647, 706.

Impressed by the success of the trade on Lake Ontario, no official in the colony spoke out publicly against the project. In fact, many former opponents now favored it. Philip Livingston dropped all of his reservations, and in the spring of 1726 the Indian Commissioners reported that "even those who were at first against it" now supported the western trade.[51] Thus, the governor's financial problems resulted not from opposition to Oswego, but from the anger aroused over his efforts to abolish the Canadian trade and from the usual parsimonious attitude of colonial assemblies.

After listening to Burnet's appeal concerning the importance of maintaining a trade with the western Indians, the assembly in the fall appropriated £300 for the construction of a blockhouse. Since this sum was far below what was needed, Burnet agreed to loan the colony enough money to make up the difference.[52] He then immediately dispatched Captain Evert Bancker to Seneca country, where he was to spend the winter in an effort to prevent French agents from convincing the Iroquois that a British trading post would not be to their advantage. During his stay among the Senecas, Bancker also attempted to stir up resentment against the French, who had recently completed a stone fort at Niagara to replace the log blockhouse built in 1720. In the spring of 1727 Bancker traveled back to the Oswego River to select the exact site for the fortified trading post.[53]

Following Robert Livingston's advice, Burnet had originally planned to construct the fort as far west as the Niagara region. Like previous governors, however, Burnet soon discovered that, on this subject, Livingston uncharacteristically allowed his optimism to outweigh his caution. In addition to presenting considerable logistics problems, Niagara was completely surrounded by the Senecas, whose loyalty to the British was often in question. By now, Burnet also realized that a fort could not be built at Niagara "without an open Breach with the French."[54] Another possible location would have been Irondequoit near the mouth of the Genesee River. In the early 1720s this had been a popular location

---

51. Philip Livingston to Robert Livingston, July 3, 1725, in *Livingston Family Papers*; Wraxall, *Abridgment*, ed. McIlwain, April 27, 1726, p. 163.

52. *Assembly Journal*, September 27, 1726, 1: 546; *Colonial Laws of New York from the Year 1664 to the Revolution*, 5 vols. (Albany, 1894–96), November 11, 1726, 2: 369, hereafter cited as *Laws*; Burnet to the Board of Trade, May 9, 1727, in *Documentary History of the State of New-York*, ed. Edmund B. O'Callaghan, 4 vols. (Albany, 1850–51), 1: 291, hereafter cited as *New York Documentary History*.

53. Minutes of the Indian Commissioners, September 14, 15, 1726, February 4, April 6, May 2, 1727, 1: 170–71, 174, 179a–80, 183.

54. Burnet to the Board of Trade, November 21, 1724, in *NYCD*, 5: 739.

for British traders, but it, also, was in territory controlled by the Senecas. Burnet therefore decided to build at the mouth of the Oswego River, where the garrison would stand a reasonable chance of protecting its supply lines in case of war.[55]

In the early spring of 1727 the Indian Commissioners began putting together a crew of masons, carpenters, and laborers to construct a fort at Oswego. Perhaps hearing rumors that the French were planning to attack, most laborers in Albany demanded exorbitant wages, and as a result the commissioners rented "Servants" belonging to Jeremy Schuyler, John Beekman, Jr., and Nicholas Wyngaert. Under the supervision of Evert Bancker and Isaac Boguert, the workers spent several months at their labors, and by August they had completed a fort of "good large stone" with walls four feet thick. Believing that the French could not transport sizable cannons to Oswego from Montreal, Burnet considered his fort to be impregnable.[56]

Although they were not surprised by the British activities, the French reacted angrily. Economically and diplomatically, the fur trade with the western Indians had always been essential for the Canadians, who knew that cheap liquor and inexpensive English strouds threatened to lure away their customers. With the completion of Oswego, it appeared that the long-awaited disaster had finally struck. For several years, the French had been contemplating a fort of their own at Oswego to block British expansion, but they had not moved quickly enough. They could only hope that threats of military conflict would undo the damage caused by their procrastination.

In July Governor Beauharnois of New France sent a Major Begon to Oswego with an order telling the British commander to abandon the fort. While Begon was in route, Beauharnois wrote to Burnet complaining that a "Redoubt with Galleries and full of Loop holes" was a violation of the Treaty of Utrecht, which prohibited British or French encroachments in this area until a commission had decided on the boundaries.[57] "The Court of France," he concluded, "will have Room to

55. Burnet to the Board of Trade, November 26, 1720, November 7, 1724, ibid., pp. 576–80, 712; Cadwallader Colden, ed., *Papers Relating to An Act of the Assembly of the Province of New York, For Encouragement of the Indian Trade &c. and for Prohibiting the selling of Indian Goods to the French, viz. of Canada* (New York, 1724), p. 11; Leach, *Northern Colonial Frontier*, p. 153.

56. Minutes of the Indian Commissioners, April 3, 4, 1727, 1: 178a–79; Burnet to the Board of Trade, August 24, 1727, in *New York Documentary History*, 1: 297–98. For a full description of Oswego's development as a military outpost, see Johnson Gaylord Cooper, "Oswego in the French-English Struggle in North America 1720–1760" (Ph.D. diss., Syracuse University, 1961).

57. Beauharnois to Burnet, July 20, 1727, in *New York Documentary History*, 1: 292; Eccles, *Canadian Frontier*, p. 143.

look upon this undertaking as an act of hostility on your part, and I dont doubt but you will give attention to the justice of my Demand."[58]

By mentioning the Treaty of Utrecht, the French governor had simply reopened an old debate about the meaning of the ambiguous Article 15, which had settled nothing except to state that France should "give no Hindrance or Molestation to the five Nations or Cantons of *Indians,* subject to the Dominion of *Great Britain,* nor to the other Natives of *America,* who are Friends to the same." The British agreed to act in a similar manner toward French Indians. Except in the case of the Iroquois, the question of which tribes could be claimed by either side was left to the future decision of a special commission, which never met. As for the question of forts in the disputed territory, Beauharnois based his argument on the statement in Article 15 guaranteeing that "the Natives of those Countrys shall . . . resort, as they please, to the *British* and *French* Colonys, for promoting Trade on one side and the other, without any Molestation or Hindrance, either on the part of the *British* Subjects, or of the *French.*"[59]

In reply to Beauharnois, Governor Burnet used basically the same arguments that he had stated in 1721 and again in 1726 to protest the building of fortifications at Niagara.[60] Since the military outpost at Oswego could not be used to block anyone's trade with the Indians, it did not conflict with the agreement made at Utrecht in 1713. On the other hand, the French fort violated the treaty by restricting trade and by its presence in the territory of the Iroquois, who had been recognized as subjects of Great Britain. Burnet further stated that any future commission, established according to the treaty, would have no jurisdiction to decide which European nation owned the lands around Lake Ontario. This question, he claimed, had already been decided in favor of Great Britain, when France agreed that the Iroquois Confederacy was subordinate to the British Crown. Thus, the British subjects in New York had every right to build a fortified post at Oswego, but their counterparts in Canada could not legally do the same at Niagara.[61]

In the meantime, Major Begon had arrived at Oswego, where he

58. Beauharnois to Burnet, July 20, 1727, in *New York Documentary History,* 1: 293.

59. Fred L. Israel, ed., *Major Peace Treaties of Modern History, 1648–1967,* 4 vols. (New York, 1967), 1: 210.

60. Burnet to Vaudreuil, July 11, 1721; Burnet to Longueil, July 5, 1726; Burnet to Newcastle, December 4, 1726, in *NYCD,* 9: 899–903, 5: 802, 803–4; Gustave Lanctot, *A History of Canada,* 3 vols. (Cambridge, Mass., 1964), 3: 16; Smith, *History,* 1: 236–37.

61. Burnet to Beauharnois, August 8, 1727, in *New York Documentary History,* 1: 295–96.

delivered an order from Beauharnois, telling Evert Bancker to remove the garrison and to demolish the fort within fifteen days.[62] The order, drawn up in the form of a legal document, declared that the British must "leave the mouth of this river free, as it has always been, to the French, failing which his Lordship the Marquis of Beauharnois will take measures against you and against your unjust usurpation as he will think fit."[63] Though containing strong language, this order did not indicate that Begon had authorization to take immediate action. In response, Bancker told him that the New Yorkers were well within their rights, and he refused to abandon the fort.[64]

Having made his point, Governor Beauharnois decided to let the home governments decide the issue. The Paris diplomats refused to accept Burnet's argument that Indian claims to hunting grounds could be considered ownership according to the European understanding of the word. Under European law, they argued, the Iroquois owned only their villages and agricultural lands. As for the rest of the territory around Lake Ontario, they maintained that France had established solid claims long before the first Englishman had ever entered the area. While making these protests, the French diplomats also presented other complaints about British observance of the Treaty of Utrecht, but none of the issues were resolved.[65]

Since France was reluctant to use force, Oswego remained unmolested for the time being. Through patience and careful planning, Burnet had succeeded in culminating the long struggle to establish a trading post on the Great Lakes. Now retired, Robert Livingston lived just long enough to see the achievement of the program that he had advocated for more than forty years.

At this moment of his greatest success, Burnet was transferred from New York to the governorship of Massachusetts, and his enemies soon gained control of politics in New York. Except in the Albany area, most New Yorkers during the next fifteen years displayed little concern for either military security or for the fur trade. In spite of this apathy, the colonial government continued to recognize the fort at Oswego as essential to British interests. Although there were disputes over who

62. Begon, Report on a conference at Oswego, August 1, 1727, ibid., p. 294.
63. A summons from Beauharnois to the English commander at Oswego, ibid.
64. Begon, Report on a conference at Oswego, August 1, 1727, ibid.
65. Osgood, *American Colonies in the Eighteenth Century*, 3: 373–74. For a discussion of the controversy over Oswego in the context of European events, see William Kingsford, *The History of Canada*, 10 vols. (London, 1887–98; reprinted, New York, 1969), 3: 251–56.

should pay to support the garrison, few people advocated a reduction in either commercial or military activities at Oswego.[66]

After the general disallowance of the Indian trade acts in late 1729, the assembly engaged in a heated dispute over how to raise funds for the maintenance of Oswego. Governor John Montgomerie, with strong support from the frontier areas, favored a general land tax. The majority in the assembly, being from the lower counties, advocated either a direct tax on the trade or the formation of a private company to monopolize the western commerce and to pay the expenses. They pointed out that only nine members out of twenty-six in the assembly came from sections of the colony that benefited from fur trading.[67] In part, the strong support for a direct tax was an indication that the great merchants in New York City had lost much of their interest in the fur business. The handful of influential Albany residents who now had nearly complete control of the Canadian trade apparently made no effort to weaken the British position at Oswego. In fact, when Montgomerie warned that the Oswego post might have to be abandoned, the representatives from the Albany area took the lead in trying to reach a satisfactory solution to the problem. Thus, the controversy within the assembly appears to have been based on sectional motives, rather than on purely economic ones.[68]

In the fall of 1730 the assembly reached a temporary compromise for the support of Oswego in the following year, but the legislators told Montgomerie that the burden thereafter would have to fall entirely on the shoulders of the fur traders. Realizing that in the future the assembly might refuse to appropriate money for Oswego, Montgomerie urged the Board of Trade to allow a tax on the fur traders, even though such a provision would run counter to mercantilistic scruples against restrictions on trade in staples. While expressing displeasure at the reluctance of New Yorkers to support a general tax for the security of the frontier, the Board of Trade indicated that it would not complain about how

---

66. *Assembly Journal*, October 29, 1730, 1: 622.

67. Montgomerie to the Board of Trade, December 21, 1730, in *NYCD*, 5: 906–7; *Assembly Journal*, October 29, 1730, 1: 622.

68. Montgomerie to the Board of Trade, December 21, 1730, in *NYCD*, 5: 906–7. For a detailed account of how money was raised for the support of Oswego, see Cooper, "Oswego in the French-English Struggle," pp. 62–76. Cooper assumes that the Canada traders worked against support measures for Oswego but offers no evidence to prove the contention. For a different interpretation, maintaining that the controversy centered on sectional differences, see Osgood, *The American Colonies in the Eighteenth Century*, 3: 374–75. Also see Wraxall, *Abridgment*, ed. McIlwain, p. lxxxi.

the colony decided to raise the necessary funds.[69] The assembly then passed an act in 1731 providing for duties of ten shillings on every piece of strouds carried to the westward or northward of Albany and twelve pence on every gallon of rum intended for sale in the wilderness. In each year from then on, the province received a revenue from this tax of about £500 currency.[70]

Out of these funds the province had to pay for the provisions consumed by the garrison and for the salaries of a doctor, who lived at the fort throughout the year, and for a commissary, who stayed there during the trading season to regulate the trade. In 1726 Governor Burnet had recommended the appointment of a law officer at Oswego in order "to prevent the frauds usually committed in trade with the Indians." In response, the assembly passed an act establishing rules for the conduct of the trade and providing for a commissary with the power of a justice of the peace. Under this law, anyone wishing to trade in the west had to conduct his business within five hundred yards of the fort at Oswego. Having "full power and Authority" to watch over the trade, the commissary could make the final settlement in disputes between traders and Indians.[71] In return for these services, the commissaries, who usually served for only one season, received a salary of £50.[72]

In providing for a fair regulation of the trade, the Oswego commissaries achieved only a partial success. Possessing considerable power, they seem to have kept acts of violence between the Indians and the traders at a minimum. On the other hand, they did not succeed in preventing the high rate of fraud that caused great bitterness among western tribes.[73] Even if a commissary had compassion for the Indians, he could not watch over the multitude of transactions going on day and night in a rough collection of bark huts, housing a hundred or more

69. *Assembly Journal*, August 26, October 29, 1730, 1: 610, 623; Osgood, *American Colonies in the Eighteenth Century*, 3: 375.

70. *Assembly Journal*, August 27, 1731, August 11, 1732, October 22, 1735, September 19, 1739, 1: 624, 633, 682, 760; William Smith to [Hendrick] Ten Eyck and Robert Roseboom, July 10, 1732, in Harmanus Bleecker Papers, New York State Library, Albany.

71. *Assembly Journal*, September 14, 1732, 1: 642; Burnet to the Board of Trade, December 20, 1726, in *NYCD*, 5: 812; *Laws*, November 11, 1726, 2: 370–71.

72. Minutes of the Indian Commissioners, August 7, 1732, March 31, 1735, 1: 361, 2: 60; *Assembly Journal*, September 14, 1732, 1: 642.

73. Minutes of the Indian Commissioners, June 24, 1730, September 20, 1735, 1: 320, 2: 74; Wraxall, *Abridgment*, ed. McIlwain, September 8, 1733, pp. 187–88; Cadwallader Colden to John Mitchell, August 17, 1751, in *The Letters and Papers of Cadwallader Colden*, 10 vols., New-York Historical Society *Collections*, 50–56 (1917–23), 67–69 (1934–35) (New York, 1918–36), 9: 103–4.

traders.[74] Away from the watchful eyes of the Albany sheriff, his deputies, and the city magistrates, these traders must have given the Indians far worse treatment than they had ever received when the trade was confined within the walls of Albany.

In spite of widespread fraud, the Indians continued to be attracted by rum and inexpensive woolens. As a result, the Oswego traders prospered, and by the 1740s these relatively small businessmen probably were acquiring the major part of New York's annual supply of furs. During the 1730s the size of the trade with Canada had been reduced by increased French vigilance and by the tendency of large Albany merchants such as Philip Livingston to give up their commerce with Canada in favor of the lucrative trade in foodstuffs with the West Indies.[75] Nevertheless, the remaining Canada traders still accounted for a sizable percentage of the colony's peltry supply. Each of them handled far greater quantities than any of the western traders except William Johnson. Unfortunately, a scarcity of business records for the 1740s and 1750s permits only a rough estimate of the proportion of furs obtained from Canada and Oswego.[76]

In each of three years from 1751 to 1753, Robert Sanders, a leading Canada trader, exported peltry worth an average of about £650 sterling, and during this period Cornelius Cuyler conducted a business of a

74. In the colonial period, estimates concerning the number of traders at Oswego varied greatly. Cadwallader Colden claimed that as many as three hundred traded there each year, but the average was probably closer to one hundred. William Johnson estimated that before the French and Indian War the number was around eighty. A list kept by the Indian Commissioners for the prosperous trading season of 1725 indicates that approximately ninety men had participated in the trade. Cadwallader Colden, *The History of the Five Indian Nations of Canada, Which are Dependent on the Province of New York in America, and Are a Barrier Between the English and French in That Part of the World*, 2 vols. (New York, 1902), 1: 105; Johnson, "A State of the Indian Trade . . . ," October 8, 1764, in *The Papers of Sir William Johnson*, ed. James Sullivan et al., 14 vols. (Albany, 1921–65), 4: 556, hereafter cited as *Johnson Papers*; Minutes of the Indian Commissioners [September 2, 1725], 1: 142a–43.

75. See chapter 6.

76. In the boom year of 1749 the commissary at Oswego estimated that peltry worth £21,406 (probably New York currency) had been purchased from the Indians at this outpost. For the years from the late 1720s until after the French and Indian War, this estimate is the only figure concerning the size of the trade at Oswego. As the first trading season after King George's War, which had hindered the Indian trade and had prevented France from sending supplies to Canada, the spring of 1749 does not serve as a typical example of business activities at Oswego. John Lindesay, An account of transactions with the far Indians, August 20, 1749, in *NYCD*, 6: 538.

similar size. Between the two of them, they were handling about 20 percent of New York's total fur exports. The identities of other merchants trading with Montreal in the 1750s cannot be determined with certainty, but Cuyler and Sanders did have some significant competition. It does not seem likely, however, that their few competitors could have obtained more skins than the total exported by the two largest Canada traders. Thus, the trade with Montreal was probably accounting for no more than 40 percent of all furs shipped from the port of New York, and with colonial hatters consuming a large quantity of skins, the totals shown in the customs records represent much less than the complete supply of peltry. Furthermore, skins from Canada were more likely to be shipped to England than poorer quality ones from Oswego, because exported furs had to compete on the London market with Hudson's Bay beaver. The Oswego traders, therefore, often had to sell their less desirable peltry to colonial hatters, and these skins are not accounted for in the customs records. Probably, then, Oswego by the middle of the century had surpassed Montreal as New York's major source of peltry.[77]

One indication of Oswego's success was the continuing hatred expressed against it by the French, who spared no effort in waging economic warfare to counter the effects of the Oswego traders. Even before the completion of the British fort, the Canadians built two sailing vessels designed to patrol the southern shores of Lake Ontario to intercept *coureurs de bois* headed for Oswego and to persuade Indian convoys to turn back. In 1727 French traders began selling brandy at Niagara in spite of threats from the religious leaders of the colony.[78] Over the years, French agents attempted to stop the western Indians from going to Oswego by using a wide variety of arguments ranging from threats of violence to false stories of smallpox among the British.[79]

Although the French were unable to stop the Indians from traveling to Oswego, their increased watchfulness did have an effect. Even as

77. Invoice Book of Robert Sanders, 1748–1756, passim, New-York Historical Society, New York City; Cornelius Cuyler Letter Book, 1752–1764 (microfilm), passim, American Antiquarian Society, Worcester, Mass.; Sanders to Monsieur G, May 16, 1753, in Robert Sanders Letter Book, 1752–1758, New-York Historical Society, New York City; George Clinton to William Johnson, February 6, 1749, in *Johnson Papers*, 1: 211–12; Clinton to the Board of Trade, July 17, 1751, in *NYCD*, 6: 714.

78. Louis XI to Beauharnois and Dupuy, May 14, 1726, in *NYCD*, 9: 957–58; Minutes of the Indian Commissioners, June 10, 1727, 1: 186; Kingsford, *History of Canada*, 3: 282–83.

79. Minutes of the Indian Commissioners, June 18, 1727, May 10, 1739, 1: 188–88a, 2: 165–65a; Philip Livingston to Storke and Gainsborough, June 18, 1735, in Miscellaneous Manuscripts, vol. 5; Wraxall, *Abridgment*, ed. McIlwain, February 8, 1731, July 30, 1736, pp. 182, 197.

early as 1727, disappointed traders reported that French activities had prevented the trade from reaching the levels of the previous two years. In 1729 Louis XV personally went over the figures concerning the fur trade and convinced himself that Oswego had done no damage to Canada's economy. Actually, no one could have reached an accurate assessment of Oswego's effect, because in the middle 1720s Canada expanded its trade into the area north of the Great Lakes, which resulted in a doubling of fur exports.[80]

In the 1730s the trade at Niagara and at Fort Frontenac on the eastern end of Lake Ontario greatly declined, but this may have been the result of the vigorous commercial activities deeper in the interior. Officials both in France and Canada, however, believed that Oswego was at fault. They continued to consider the British trading post as a threat to their commercial relations with the Indians around the Great Lakes and thus a threat to lure these tribes away from their alliances with the French. Upon his return to France in 1750 after a two-year assignment as governor of Canada, the Marquis de La Gallissonnière expressed the view of most French officials of his generation when he declared that Oswego was "capable of causing the entire ruin of Canada" and had "already inflicted on it the greatest injury." "Nothing, then," he concluded, "must be left undone to destroy this dangerous post . . . ."[81]

Despite constant French hostility, Oswego continued to be a commercial success until the outbreak of the French and Indian War, but due to its easterly location and other factors, it did not prove as successful as some had hoped in spreading British influence among the western tribes. It had therefore partially, but not entirely, fulfilled the desires of such New York leaders as governors Dongan, Bellomont, Hunter, Burnet, and their adviser Robert Livingston. Nevertheless, Oswego existed for more than a quarter-century as Canada's only significant competitor for the peltry and the allegiance of those tribes who were considered by both sides as indispensable French allies in time of war.

80. Minutes of the Indian Commissioners, July 14, October 11, 1727, 1: 191a, 206; Beauharnois and Hocquart to Maurepas, October 12, 1736, in *NYCD*, 9: 1049; Philip Livingston to Storke and Gainsborough, November 1, 1736, in Miscellaneous Manuscripts, vol. 5; Lanctot, *History of Canada*, 3: 118.

81. La Gallissonnière, Memoir on the French colonies in North America, December —, 1750," *NYCD*, 10: 228–29. For an account of La Gallissonnière's administration, see Kingsford, *History of Canada*, 3: 387–95. For more information on French opinion concerning Oswego and for a description of Montcalm's destruction of the fort in 1756, see Cooper, "Oswego in the French-English Struggle," pp. 51–53, 57–58, 114–15, 212–70. Another account of the attack on Oswego can be found in Osgood, *American Colonies in the Eighteenth Century*, 4: 376–84.

10

FUR TRADERS, POLITICS, AND

THE ROAD TO EMPIRE

IN THE YEARS after Governor Burnet's administration, the men who had lent him support continued to maintain a relationship that in many ways resembled a modern political party. Under the leadership of the Morrises, James Alexander, William Smith, Sr., Cadwallader Colden, and later William Johnson, these politicians remained united on the principle of challenging the French for control of the area around the Great Lakes. While lacking some characteristics of modern political organizers, they displayed remarkable unity on issues involving Anglo-French relations. Since most residents of the Albany area favored a defensive policy rather than one of imperial expansion, the New York imperialists consistently denounced the Dutch for not showing enough patriotism.[1]

During Queen Anne's War New Englanders had frequently accused

1. Those historians who deny the early existence of political parties in New York maintain that before 1765 provincial politics had little to do with principles or party loyalty. Instead, they argue that New York leaders changed sides whenever they saw the possibility of establishing a favorable connection with the governor or someone else in a position to dispense patronage. See Carl L. Becker, *The History of Political Parties in the Province of New York, 1760–1776* (Madison, Wis., 1909), pp. 7–22; Becker, "Nominations in Colonial New York," *American Historical Review* 6 (1901–2): 260–75; Becker, "Growth of Revolutionary Parties and Methods in New York, 1765–1774," ibid., 7 (1901–2): 56–76; Nicholas Varga, "New York Politics and Government during the Mid-Eighteenth Century" (Ph.D. diss., Fordham University, 1960), pp. 25n, 48; and Stanley Nider Katz, *Newcastle's New York: Anglo-American Politics, 1732–1753* (Cambridge, Mass., 1968), pp. 44–49. For studies that question the Becker thesis, see Patricia W. Bonomi, *A Factious People: Politics and Society in Colonial New York* (New York, 1971), pp. 14–15; and Milton W. Klein, "Democracy and Politics in Colonial New York," *New York History* 60 (1959): 221–46. Also see Klein, "Politics and Personalities in Colonial New York," *New York History* 47 (1966): 3–16; and Beverley McAnear, "Politics

Albany of opposing military action against the French in order to protect the neutrality that allowed the continuance of trade with Montreal.
During Burnet's administration the imperialists revived this old argument and used it vigorously, and often irresponsibly, against their political enemies. Since the Dutch had little to say in their defense, future
generations accepted the word of such polemicists as Cadwallader
Colden and Peter Wraxall. In the colonial period, however, Albany
often found strong support in other parts of the colony. After Burnet
left the scene early in 1728, the imperialists found themselves in a defensive position when Governor John Montgomerie chose to side with
the Philipse-DeLancey faction, which had grown greatly in strength
since the middle of the decade.[2] Montgomerie managed to keep the
political controversies to a minimum; but when Governor William
Cosby came to New York in 1732, the imperial party entered into a four-
year struggle with the governor and his supporters, the Philipse-
DeLancey faction. The imperialists suffered several defeats at the hands
of Cosby and his successor, Lieutenant Governor George Clarke, and
from 1737 until 1746 they remained in relative obscurity.[3]

In the 1730s and early 1740s, the political aggregation opposing the
imperialists was not well organized. It maintained no particular philosophical position and was composed of several separate factions that
were sometimes at odds with one another. Two of the factions had come
together in Burnet's administration, when Adolph Philipse and Stephen
DeLancey joined forces with their fellow fur merchants in Albany to
oppose Burnet's restrictions on the Canada trade. In the 1730s, however,
this alliance was a tenuous one at best, because the DeLancey-Philipse
faction believed that the residents of Albany County, who had now
taken the fur trade almost completely into their own hands, should bear
the full cost of maintaining Oswego.[4] Also in these years, some of the

---

in Provincial New York, 1689–1761" (Ph.D. diss., Stanford University, 1935), pp.
1–2, 954–55.

2. See chapters 5 and 8.

3. William Smith, Jr., *The History of the Late Province of New-York from Its
Discovery to the Appointment of Governor Colden in 1762*, 2 vols. (New York,
1829–30), 1: 240. For a brief summary of political developments in this era, see
Klein, "Democracy and Politics in Colonial New York," pp. 223–40. For greater detail, see Herbert L. Osgood, *The American Colonies in the Eighteenth Century*, 4 vols.
(New York, 1924–25; reprinted, Gloucester, Mass., 1958), 2: 443–81, 4: 174–200;
and Katz, *Newcastle's New York*.

4. Adolph Philipse to Peter Leheup, December 25, 1730, in *Calendar of State
Papers, Colonial Series, America and West Indies*, ed. W. N. Sainsbury et al., 43
vols. to date (London, 1860–), 37: 420, hereafter cited as *Calendar of State Papers*;
also see chapter 6.

wealthier citizens of Albany switched sides and opposed Governor Cosby when he began to question the validity of land grants in the Mohawk Valley and elsewhere. Usually the anti-imperialists could count on the support of assemblymen from the middle counties of the province and Long Island. These apathetic individuals could not see how imperial politics directly affected them, and their lack of concern for such affairs usually worked to the advantage of those politicians who opposed the imperialists. On purely domestic issues, of course, these county representatives could select whatever side they preferred.[5]

Later, after the outbreak of King George's War, the anti-imperialists united under the strong leadership of Chief Justice James DeLancey, the son of Stephen DeLancey. This alliance, however, was not held together by a mutual interest in the fur trade. By the early 1730s New York City merchants no longer had a vital interest in the trade; and before the end of the decade, most large Albany merchants had also turned to more profitable commerce with the West Indies.[6]

Of all the political groups in New York, only two consistently displayed any great concern about the French threat from Canada. Paradoxically, the two were the imperialists and the political leaders of Albany County, who were usually at one another's throats over questions concerning frontier security. Both groups favored strong defenses on the frontier, but Albany opposed any activities that might trigger a war with France. In fact, some Albany residents in the 1730s and 1740s

5. Alice P. Kenny, "Dutch Patricians in Colonial Albany," *New York History* 49 (1968): 269; Katz, *Newcastle's New York*, pp. 81–85; Cadwallader Colden, *History of Governor William Cosby's Administration and of Lieutenant-Governor George Clarke's Administration through 1737*, in *The Letters and Papers of Cadwallader Colden*, 10 vols., New-York Historical Society *Collections*, 50–56 (1917–23), 67–69 (1934–35) (New York, 1918–36), 9: 304–6, 354–55, hereafter cited as *Colden Papers*; Philip Livingston to Jacob Wendell, January 14, June 2, 1746, in Livingston Papers, Museum of the City of New York; George Clarke to the Board of Trade, June 19, 1743, in *Documents Relative to the Colonial History of the State of New York*, ed. Edmund B. O'Callaghan and Berthold Fernow, 15 vols. (Albany, 1856–87), 6: 225, hereafter cited as *NYCD*; George Clinton to the Duke of Newcastle, July 23, 1747, in C.O. 5/1095 (microfilm), Public Record Office, London.

6. Adolph Philipse to Peter Leheup, December 25, 1730, in *Calendar of State Papers*, 37: 420; Minutes of the Commissioners of Indian Affairs (microfilm), November 27, 1746, 2: 405–5a, Public Archives of Canada, Ottawa, hereafter cited as Minutes of the Indian Commissioners. For a full discussion of the economic changes in Albany, see David A. Armour, "The Merchants of Albany, New York, 1686–1760" (Ph.D. diss., Northwestern University, 1965), pp. 181–217. Also see Kenny, "Dutch Patricians in Colonial Albany," pp. 268–69; and William I. Roberts, III, "Samuel Storke: An Eighteenth-Century London Merchant Trading to the American Colonies," *Business History Review* 39 (1965): 166–67; and chapter 6.

wanted to arrange a neutrality agreement between New York and Canada if a general war broke out.[7]

The imperialists, dominated largely by Scotsmen who often displayed an ethnic bias against the Dutch, denounced the Albany policy as disloyal, pro-French, and financially self-interested.[8] In actuality, none of these factors accurately explain Dutch motives. Certainly, the Dutchmen of Albany were not pro-French. With increasing intensity after King William's War, the people of Albany expressed anxiety over the threat of French military and commercial activities both to the north and west of their city. Knowing that there was little standing between them and a French assault from Lake Champlain, they usually took the lead in warning the rest of the colony about French encroachments. A few merchants may have been motivated by a desire to protect the Canada trade, but they were only a handful among a populace whose older members could well remember the disastrous effects of frontier warfare.[9] As events indicated in the 1730s and 1740s, the Albany leaders were mainly concerned with security for the inhabitants of the region and with protection of the investments that their families had painstakingly developed along the Hudson and the Mohawk rivers.

After 1730 the people of the New York frontier had good reason to be concerned for their safety. Resentful over the construction of the fort at Oswego, Canadian officials believed that war was inevitable, and they began to make appropriate preparations. In addition to their vigorous efforts at hindering the trade to Albany and Oswego, they built a fort in 1731 at Crown Point on Lake Champlain. From here, it was only 150 miles to Albany. Throughout the rest of the decade, the French continued to strengthen the fortifications at Crown Point and also fre-

7. Beauharnois to Maurepas, October 10, 1734, in *NYCD*, 9: 1039–40.

8. For examples of the anti-Dutch attitude, see Witham Marsh to William Johnson, February 28, 1763, in *The Papers of Sir William Johnson*, ed. James Sullivan et al., 14 vols. (Albany, 1921–65), 13: 284, hereafter cited as *Johnson Papers*; and Wraxall, *An Abridgment of the Indian Affairs Contained in Four Folio Volumes, Transacted in the Colony of New York, from the Year 1678 to the Year 1751*, ed. Charles H. McIlwain (Cambridge, Mass., 1915), p. 135n. For further examples and evaluations of this bias, see Kenny, "Dutch Patricians in Colonial Albany," pp. 272–73; Armour, "Merchants of Albany," chaps. 4, 5; Berne A. Pyrke, "The Dutch Fur Traders of Fort Orange and Albany," *Yearbook of the Dutch Settlers Society of Albany* 18–19 (1942–44): 5–19; and chapter 5.

9. For a map indicating the scarcity of population above Albany, see Douglas Edward Leach, *The Northern Colonial Frontier, 1607–1763* (New York, 1966), p. 130. On the psychological effects of King William's War upon Albany residents, see Sung Bok Kim, "A New Look at the Great Landlords of Eighteenth-Century New York," *William and Mary Quarterly* 27 (1970): 589–92.

quently alarmed the residents of Albany by indicating that they were interested in building forts even closer to British territory. Canadians not only sought permission from the Iroquois to build at Irondequoit, but in the late 1730s also considered establishing a settlement near the lower end of Lake George, only a few miles from Saratoga.[10]

During Governor Cosby's administration from 1732 to 1736, the Albany Dutch were the only people in the colony to express any real concern over the activities of the French. Everyone else in the province was involved in several heated political controversies, including Cosby's prosecution of the publisher John Peter Zenger, who was supported by the imperialists. The governor's support in this dispute came from the Philipse-DeLancey faction, which controlled the assembly and achieved a major victory in 1733, when Cosby replaced Chief Justice Lewis Morris, Sr., with James DeLancey.[11] No one paid much attention to the frequent reports from the Commissioners of Indian Affairs and other Albany County residents complaining that New York's frontier fortifications were falling apart while the French improved their forts and relentlessly strove to destroy New York's commerce with the western Indians.[12] In 1734, for example, the commissioners warned that the French might be able to win the allegiance of the Iroquois Confederacy —an event that would result in the "utter ruin of many Flourishing Families." Even if nothing else were done, they pleaded for a strengthening of the fort at Albany. Two years later, Philip Livingston, who was not nearly as imperialistic as his father had been, told his London correspondents that the New York government would "Tamely Suffer the French to make what incroachments" they pleased.[13]

10. Gustave Lanctot, *A History of Canada*, 3 vols. (Cambridge, Mass., 1964), 3: 35; William Kingsford, *The History of Canada*, 10 vols. (London, 1887–98; reprinted, New York, 1969), 3: 286–87; Commissioners of Indian Affairs to Abraham Wendell and Co., November 23, 1730, in *Calendar of State Papers*, 37: 402–3; Commissioners of Indian Affairs to George Clarke, August 30, 1738, in *NYCD*, 6: 131; Minutes of the Indian Commissioners, March 4, 1734, April 28, 1735, June 29, August 7, 1739, 2: 50–50a, 60a, 168a, 171.

11. Katz, *Newcastle's New York*, pp. 63–90; Smith, *History*, pp. 1–26; Colden, *History of Governor William Cosby's Administration*, in *Colden Papers*, 9: 317–43.

12. George Clarke to the commander at Oswego, November 1, 1736, in *Documentary History of the State of New York*, ed. Edmund B. O'Callaghan, 4 vols. (Albany, 1850–51), 1: 300, hereafter cited as *New York Documentary History*; Minutes of the Indian Commissioners, April 28, 1735, 2: 60a; Johnson Gaylord Cooper, "Oswego in the French-English Struggle in North America 1720–1760" (Ph.D. diss., Syracuse University, 1961), pp. 77–79.

13. Minutes of the Indian Commissioners, March 4, 1734, 2: 51; Philip Livingston to Storke and Gainsborough, November 1, 1736, in Miscellaneous Manuscripts, vol. 5, New York State Library, Albany.

When Cosby died in 1736 the chances for progress improved considerably under the conciliatory leadership of Lieutenant Governor George Clarke, who acted as the colony's chief executive until 1743. After a tumultuous beginning, Clarke succeeded in calming political strife, and he did everything in his power to improve the deplorable conditions on the frontier. During the first year of his administration, he asked the assembly to support a policy that would strengthen fortifications and lead to better relations with the Iroquois. These early measures were mainly defensive, but before long he began to view Canada as an enemy country that had to be conquered. In letter after letter to England, he warned of the French threat and outlined plans for Canada's eventual conquest.[14] Clarke's increased aggressiveness may have developed as a result of his friendlier relations with the New York imperialists after 1737 or because of his desire to enhance the value of a huge land grant that he acquired in the Mohawk Valley in 1738. In addition, he reacted angrily to French successes among the Iroquois and to reports about Canadian plans for a settlement to the southeast of Lake George.[15]

Apathy in both New York and Great Britain prevented Clarke from accomplishing very much, but he did have some success in his efforts to improve relations with the Iroquois and to protect the fur trade as well as to provide for its better regulation. After meeting with the Iroquois on several occasions, Clarke succeeded in strengthening the "Covenant Chain," and the Iroquois agreed to renew those treaties with the western tribes that had been made earlier in the century. He also persuaded them to sign treaties with several additional tribes.[16]

One of Clarke's objectives in dealing with the Iroquois was to prevent the French from establishing a trading post at Irondequoit on Lake Ontario. Such an event, he believed, would mean the "loss of all our fur Trade" and with it the Six Nations.[17] In a speech to the assembly,

14. *Journal of the Votes and Proceedings of the General Assembly of the Colony of New York [1691–1765]*, 2 vols. (New York, 1764–66), October 16, 1736, April 5, 1737, 1: 689, 696, hereafter cited as *Assembly Journal*; Colden, *History of Governor William Cosby's Administration*, in *Colden Papers*, 9: 347–55; Smith, *History*, 2: 27–33; George Clarke to the Board of Trade, February 17, 1738, December 15, 1741, August 24, November 29, 1742; Clark to Newcastle, April 22, 1741, in *NYCD*, 6: 112–14, 207, 215, 220–21, 183.

15. Katz, *Newcastle's New York*, pp. 147, 152–55; Irving Mark, *Agrarian Conflicts in Colonial New York, 1711–1775* (New York, 1940), pp. 31, 31n; Smith, *History*, 2: 33, 45–46; George Clarke to Beauharnois, October 26, 1736, in C.O. 5/1094; *Assembly Journal*, October 13, 1738, 1: 742.

16. Indian Conference, August 12, 1740, in *NYCD*, 6: 178; Minutes of the Indian Commissioners, July 30, August 2, 1743, 2: 253a–55a.

17. George Clarke to the Board of Trade, February 17, 1738, in *NYCD*, 6: 112.

he exclaimed, "The Preservation of Oswego, and of the Fidelity of the six Nations, is of more Consequence to the Province, than any other Thing whatsoever . . . I, for my Part, will spare no Pains to retain them in their Fidelity to his Majesty."[18] For many years the Iroquois had succeeded in turning down the demands of the French for the purchase of Irondequoit. They also rejected Clarke's request for this territory, but promised that they would never sell it to the French. In one of their meetings with Clarke, they demonstrated the wisdom of their diplomacy when they noted that "the trading house at Oswego and that at Niagara are near enough to each other" and that the French and English would "quarrel about the trade" if the Iroquois allowed the construction of trading posts in close proximity to one another.[19] Peter Wraxall seems to have been correct in his assessment that "to preserve the Ballance between us and the French is the great ruling Principle of the Modern Indian Politics."[20]

In addition to his personal negotiations with the Iroquois, Clarke improved Indian relations by getting the assembly to pass a comprehensive act regulating the fur trade. This law of 1740 not only renewed and augmented previous regulations, but also added several new ones to protect the Indians. Over the years, the most frequent complaint from the tribesmen had been that traders sold them rum that was either adulterated or unfit to drink. To remedy this problem, the law required every trader to take an oath promising not to sell such "unmerchantable Rum." Violators were to be punished by a fine of £25, a mandatory sentence of three months in the Albany County jail, and banishment from the fur trade for two years. To provide for effective enforcement, the regulations required the commissary to frequently test the quality of rum at Oswego. The new law also alleviated an old and bitter complaint of the Iroquois sachems by prohibiting traders from selling rum in the villages between Schenectady and Oswego.[21]

Since the regulatory act did not cost anything, the assembly passed it without hesitation, but Clarke had little success in getting the legislators to appropriate any funds for improvements at Oswego. Both Clarke and his successor, George Clinton, found themselves faced with an assembly that had learned how its control of the purse strings could

18. *Assembly Journal*, April 27, 1741, 1: 800.

19. Indian Conference, August 12, 1740, in *NYCD*, 6: 177.

20. Wraxall, *Abridgment*, ed. McIlwain, p. 219n.

21. Katz, *Newcastle's New York*, p. 153; *Colonial Laws of New York from the Year 1664 to the Revolution*, 5 vols. (Albany, 1894–96), November 3, 1740, 3: 110–20.

lead to increased independence from the royal governors.[22] Thus, the assembly was often motivated as much by politics as it was by a desire to save money. In the case of needed improvements at Oswego, many representatives could see no reason to concern themselves with imperial problems. Clarke complained to the Board of Trade that the French would soon make themselves "masters of all the Indians and Indian Trade" and would be able "to annoy the Colonys upon every occasion And yet my Lords the Assembly think that things are not come to that pass . . . ."[23]

One reason for the assembly's attitude was the lack of interest in the fur trade among the Philipse and DeLancey families, who usually dominated the lower house during the 1730s and 1740s. Except for George Clarke, a few imperialists, and the representatives from the Albany area, no one reacted with alarm when the assembly heard reports that the French were planning a settlement near the strategic portage between the Hudson River and a stream flowing into Lake Champlain. Once established at this location, Canadian officials would have been able to eliminate all commerce between Montreal and New York.[24] In the 1720s the DeLanceys and the Philipses would have rushed to the aid of their commercial associates in Albany. But now that the Albany merchants conducted all of their business directly with factors in England or in Amsterdam, the New York City merchants had simply lost interest in the problems of the upper counties.

Of all the unconcerned assemblymen, the worse offenders seem to have come from the middle counties of the province. In utter disgust Philip Livingston told a family friend in another colony, "Some Narrow lac[e]d fools that have their Estates in the Center of Country care not what becomes of our fronteers Imagei[ni]ng to be Safe and Secure, but that is a gross Error for the French aim at nothing less than to have the whole Continent."[25]

Even when war clouds became clearly visible in the years after 1740, the assembly demonstrated great reluctance to take the necessary precautions. Nothing had been done to improve Oswego since the original blockhouse was completed in 1727, and the entire annual support for the establishment came from the duties on trading goods, amounting to

22. Varga, "New York Government and Politics," pp. 48–51; Smith, *History*, 2: 42–45.

23. George Clark to the Board of Trade, February 17, 1738, in *NYCD*, 6: 113–14.

24. *Assembly Journal*, September 21, 1739, 1: 761; Smith, *History*, 2: 49, 50–51.

25. Philip Livingston to Jacob Wendell, January 14, 1746, in Livingston Papers. Also see George Clarke to the Board of Trade, June 19, 1743, in *NYCD*, 6: 225.

£500. With the morale of the poorly supplied garrison at an extremely low level, no one in the colony believed that the fort would hold out against even the slightest French assault. In 1738 Clarke increased the size of the garrison from twenty-five to forty, but in the following year the extra soldiers had to be withdrawn when the legislature refused to provide the money needed to supply them. Finally in 1741, after an impassioned speech from Clarke, the assembly appropriated £600 for the construction of a stone wall around the blockhouse. After this, the assemblymen refused to appropriate any additional money for Oswego, even on occasions when the soldiers had no ammunition for their muskets.[26]

When Governor George Clinton arrived in the late summer of 1743, the Commissioners of Indian Affairs immediately began sending him warnings and recommendations in the hope that he would be able to awaken the assembly to the dangers of the approaching war. For the most part, they stressed the need for rebuilding forts on the frontier and for providing the garrisons with adequate supplies. The problem had now become acute; Albany merchants, knowing that they would have to wait two or three years for payment, were refusing to advance credit to the Indian Commissioners. If Oswego fell to enemy forces, the Albany officials warned, the Iroquois were likely to go over to the French. Without more than their annual allotment of £170 for Indian presents, the commissioners doubted that they could keep the Iroquois loyal even if Oswego did not fall into French hands.[27]

Clinton soon proved to be a disappointment to the Indian Commissioners. As an admiral in the British Navy, his instincts favored aggressive action to meet the French threat, but his political ineptitude forced him at the beginning of his administration to follow the path of least resistance. Thus, instead of reuniting the disorganized imperialists, he put himself in the hands of Chief Justice James DeLancey, whose party dominated the parsimonious assembly. The reaction of the assembly to the urgent pleas from Albany in 1743 almost seems to have been intended as a gratuitous insult. The legislators voted to appropriate the regular £170 to be used for Indian presents, and because the colony was

26. *Assembly Journal*, April 15, 1741, 1: 793; Minutes of the Indian Commissioners, March 25, 1740, September 14, 1742, 2: 182, 234a; Clarke to the Board of Trade, December 15, 1741, August 24, 1742, in *NYCD*, 6: 207, 215; Clarke to the Board of Trade, August 20, 1742, in *New York Documentary History*, 1: 301; John Rutherfurd to Cadwallader Colden, January 10, 1743, in *Colden Papers*, 3: 2; Cooper, "Oswego in the French-English Struggle," pp. 80–82.

27. Smith, *History*, 2: 68–69; Minutes of the Indian Commissioners, October 24, 1743, 2: 260a; Indian Commissioners to George Clinton, October 29, 1743, in C.O. 5/1094.

at a "critical junction," they authorized the commissioners to spend an additional £30, but only if it was needed![28]

When King George's War broke out in the spring of 1744, Clinton immediately began to see evidence that New Yorkers were in no mood to fight. As soon as the fur traders at Oswego heard the first news of war, they sold their goods for whatever prices they could get and retreated to their homes in Schenectady or Albany, leaving the soldiers to fend for themselves. "How mean an Opinion," the outraged governor told the assembly, "must the Savages entertain of us, when they find our People so easily frightened ... that the Great Gains, which are constantly reaped by this advantageous Traffick, are not sufficient to excite a Resolution in our Traders, to stand to the Defense of this Fortress . . . ." To prevent the "pernicious Consequences" of "this sort of Demeanour," he recommended that the assembly consider reforms in the fur trade and establish such "reasonable Rates" for merchandise that even the most remote nations would bring their furs to Oswego.[29]

While considering Clinton's speech, the assembly also had before it a plan recently sent to the governor by the Indian Commissioners. They requested a ten-point program that included the construction of a fort in Seneca country and another one at the portage between the Hudson River and the route to Canada. In answer to these requests, the assembly once again proved reluctant to spend any substantial amounts of money. As for the fur trade, the assemblymen made no response to the governor's recommendations.[30]

Despite the frequent rebuffs from the assembly, the Indian Commissioners worked diligently throughout the next three years to maintain the loyalty of the Iroquois and to keep the frontier defenses in as good a condition as possible. One of their most serious problems occurred in the early months of 1745, when the Mohawks and other Iroquois tribes became almost hysterical after hearing a rumor that the British and French were arming not to fight one another, but rather to destroy the Six Nations. Overcoming the scarcity of presents, the commissioners managed to calm the hysteria, which had been partly brought on by the realization of the Mohawks that New Yorkers would eventually seize all their lands. Delighted by this diplomatic success, Clinton told the Board of Trade that if the Indian Commissioners had not "been very alert

28. Katz, *Newcastle's New York*, pp. 165–68; *Assembly Journal*, December 1, 1743, 2: 9.

29. *Assembly Journal*, August 20, 1744, 2: 31–32.

30. Wraxall, *Abridgment*, ed. McIlwain, July 6, 1744, pp. 236–37; *Assembly Journal*, August 24, 1744, 2: 33–34; Minutes of the Indian Commissioners, October 8, 1744, 2: 307.

and diligent to quell this report and remove their fear, in all likelyhood, we should have lost our Indians."[31] At this point in March 1745 the governor still maintained good relations with the Indian Commissioners, but conditions were about to change both in the military situation and in the colony's political alignments.

In November a large force of about six hundred French and Indians descended upon the village of Saratoga, burning the fort and the farm houses to the ground. With the exception of one family, all the residents were killed or marched off to Canada, where some of them were given to the Indians as slaves. Terrified farmers in the region between Saratoga and Albany immediately abandoned their homes, and for the rest of the war the northern Hudson Valley remained deserted. As Albany became crowded with refugees, some of the inhabitants retreated to the protection of New York City.[32]

With the frontier in an almost defenseless condition, Albany officials could only hope that the numerous French Indians having treaties with the Iroquois would respect their agreements to remain neutral. After the destruction of Saratoga, most of the city's residents probably united with the element in Albany politics that had always favored a policy of neutrality.[33] Thus, the city leaders found themselves on the way to an alliance with the neutralist party in the assembly.

In the meantime, Governor Clinton had been moving in a direction that would lead to the end of his friendship with James DeLancey. By the spring of 1745 Clinton had become extremely annoyed with the assembly's refusal to appropriate adequate defense funds. In May he told the legislators, "through your Carelessness and Improvidence, we must hazard the Seduction of the Six Nations, and our Northern Fron-

---

31. Clinton to the Board of Trade, March 27, 1745, in *NYCD*, 6: 275. For a full discussion concerning the successes of the Indian Commissioners from 1743 to 1746, see Armour, "Merchants of Albany," pp. 239–53.

32. Leach, *Northern Colonial Frontier*, p. 193; Kingsford, *History of Canada*, 3: 330–31. In his *History*, 2: 76, Smith noted, "The country being uncovered down to the very city of Albany, this event not only spread a general consternation among the northern settlers, who all fled from their habitations, but raised a general dissatisfaction."

33. In 1734 Jeremiah Van Rensselaer and "another influential gentleman" of the Albany area visited with Governor Beauharnois in Montreal. They told him that during the last war the father of one of them had kept up a secret correspondence with Governor Vaudreuil, who had agreed to spare New York from either French or Indian attack. The two New Yorkers expressed their desire to work out a similar agreement in case of a future war. In return, they would use their influence to keep the Iroquois from declaring war on Canada. Although Beauharnois made no commitments, he told them that he would give careful consideration to such an arrangement. Beauharnois to Maurepas, October 10, 1734, in *NYCD*, 9: 1039–40.

tiers . . . remain naked and open to the Incursions and Insults of our declared Enemies . . . ." Accusing them of having no concern for the lives of the people on the frontier, he then dissolved the assembly.[34] Although the Indian Commissioners hoped that members of the next assembly would have "a Hearty and sincere Desire to serve their Country," the new legislative body remained uncooperative. Then in early 1746 the personal and political friendship between Clinton and De-Lancey came to an abrupt end when they quarrelled over an issue indirectly related to the war effort. Needing an advisor, the governor quickly turned to Cadwallader Colden, who had long been an imperialist with a deep contempt for the Dutch merchants of Albany.[35]

Clinton's break with DeLancey did not necessarily mean an end to his friendly relations with the Indian Commissioners; but, as he was becoming disenchanted with the assembly in 1745, he was also developing a friendship with William Johnson. In the seven years that Johnson had spent as a fur trader in the Mohawk Valley, his influence among the Iroquois had gradually increased while the prestige of the Indian Commissioners declined. To explain this change, the imperialists claimed that the Indians had become tired of being cheated in business transactions with the Albany officials, who allegedly used their high positions to gain unfair advantages.[36] Actually, the influence of the commissioners had declined not because of dishonesty in the fur trade, but because they had no commercial relations with the Iroquois at all. After the establishment of Oswego in the 1720s, only a few Indians from the west bothered going clear to Albany. Once Johnson had built his trading post on the Mohawk, the number of Iroquois arriving in Albany for trading

34. *Assembly Journal*, May 14, 1745, 2: 61.

35. Wraxall, *Abridgment*, ed. McIlwain, May 17, 1745, p. 238; Smith, *History*, 2: 83, 84; Milton M. Klein, "William Livingston's *A Review of the Military Operations in North-America*," in *The Colonial Legacy*, ed. Lawrence H. Leder, vol. 2, *Some Eighteenth-Century Commentators* (New York, 1971), pp. 110–12; Katz, *Newcastle's New York*, pp. 169–73, 176–77.

36. Cadwallader Colden to William Shirley, July 25, 1749, in *Colden Papers*, 4: 125–26; George Clinton and William Shirley to the Board of Trade, August 8, 1748, in *NYCD*, 6: 349. The imperialists failed to point out that the Mohawks bitterly resented the efforts of Philip Livingston, the most prominent Indian Commissioner, to acquire lands belonging to them. Indian Conference, October 9, 1745, ibid., pp. 294–95. Colden and others of his party may have been reluctant to raise this question since they were also deeply involved in land speculation. On New York land speculation and frauds against the Iroquois, see Edith M. Fox, *Land Speculation in the Mohawk Country* (Ithaca, N.Y., 1949); Georgiana C. Nammack, *Fraud, Politics, and the Dispossession of the Indians: The Iroquois Land Frontier in the Colonial Period* (Norman, Okla., 1969); and Leach, *Northern Colonial Frontier*, pp. 164–71.

purposes dwindled to almost nothing.[37] The few Indian Commissioners still involved in the fur trade were wholesalers and had no direct business connections with any Indians except the Caughnawagas, who acted as porters in the trade between Albany and Montreal.[38]

When Clinton met with the Iroquois sachems and representatives from other colonies in October 1745, Johnson's great influence among the Indians soon became apparent. Frustrated by the inability of the Indian Commissioners to convince the Iroquois to take up the hatchet against the French, Clinton began in late 1745 or early 1746 to rely heavily on the services of Johnson and other fur traders. The commissioners naturally resented this infringement on their authority, and relations between them and Clinton had deteriorated considerably by the time the governor broke with DeLancey in 1746. In April the commissioners offered to resign, but since Clinton did not respond to their offer, they continued to perform their duties until near the end of the year.[39]

At this point in the spring of 1746, the Indian Commissioners had probably accepted neutrality as the best policy, but they still remained apart from the DeLancey party, which refused to provide funds for even defensive purposes. Only four days before offering their resignations in early April, they sent a letter to the governor bitterly denouncing the failure of the assembly to protect the frontier.[40] Two months later, Philip Livingston declared in a letter to Jacob Wendell, the Boston merchant, "I shall do all in my power to bring our grandees to prevent more mischief, but most of the Gentry here are no more Concerned with the murders Committed above Albany than I am to killed [sic] a fatt pigg / they Seem to have no Charity nor Compassion."[41] Clinton and Colden should have used the resentment of Livingston and his Albany neighbors to keep them from aligning with the DeLancey party. Instead, the governor and his confidant almost seem to have deliberately forced the Indian Commissioners into DeLancey's hands by denouncing them and other Albany residents at every opportunity.

In the fall Clinton opened the propaganda campaign by telling the assembly that Indian affairs had always been poorly managed, because as it was "so notoriously known . . . most of those usually employed in

37. Colden, "The present state of the Indian Affairs . . . ," August 8, 1751, in *Colden Papers*, 4: 273; Armour, "Merchants of Albany," p. 253.

38. Minutes of the Indian Commissioners, November 27, 1746, 2: 405–6; chapters 6 and 8.

39. Indian Conferences, October 5–10, 12, 14, 1745, in *NYCD*, 6: 289–305; Minutes of the Indian Commissioners, April 12, 1746, 2: 358; Smith, *History*, 2: 83–84.

40. Minutes of the Indian Commissioners, April 8, 1746, 2: 345a.

41. Philip Livingston to Jacob Wendell, June 2, 1746, in Livingston Papers.

the Conduct of *Indian* Affairs" were "Traders and Dealers with the *Indians*."[42] In this statement, he set the tone for the polemics that the imperialists were to use for the rest of his administration and for years afterwards. Earlier in the summer, Clinton had already antagonized the Indian Commissioners by appointing William Johnson as colonel in charge of Iroquois military operations.[43]

Having publicly attacked the Indian Commissioners in general, the governor then turned the full force of his anger against Philip Livingston. Declaring that Livingston, the leading member of a "vile Family," favored a neutrality areement with Canada, he asked the British ministry to remove him from his position as Indian Secretary. Until Livingston's death in 1749, Clinton never wavered from his conviction that this Albany leader had attempted to maintain "a State of Neutrality" in order to "carry on a private Commerce with the French in Canada."[44] This accusation was unfounded, because Livingston never favored a policy of neutrality. He had long deplored the timidity of colonial assemblies and hoped that King George's War would mark an end to French rule in Canada.[45]

The reasons for Clinton's attack on Livingston remain unclear, but it seems unlikely that he would have made such a move without the approval of Cadwallader Colden. In referring to Clinton, Livingston himself explained, "I find nobody can be his friend but those who will do, say, and think as he doth, which I would not do for His Government and all he has ... as long as men who can't manage their own affairs are appointed to Reign over us, we must be Governed as we are . . . ."[46] For at least a year, Colden had favored the dissolution of the Commissioners of Indian Affairs, and by now he undoubtedly knew that such an occurrence would strengthen the hand of his political ally, William Johnson.

42. *Assembly Journal*, November 10, 1746, 2: 134; also see Smith, *History*, 2: 88–92.

43. Arthur Pound, *Johnson of the Mohawks* (New York, 1930), p. 113; David S. McKeith, "The Inadequacy of Men and Measures in English Imperial History: Sir William Johnson and the New York Politicians, A Case Study" (Ph.D. diss., Syracuse University, 1971), p. 63.

44. George Clinton to Newcastle, November 18, 1745, December 9, 1746, in *NYCD*, 6: 286, 314; Memorial of George Clinton to the Duke of Bedford, April 20, 1749, in C.O. 5/1096.

45. Philip Livingston to Robert Livingston, September 6, 1725, in Livingston Family Papers (microfilm), Franklin D. Roosevelt Library, Hyde Park, N.Y.; Philip Livingston to Storke and Gainsborough, November 1, 1736, in Miscellaneous Manuscripts, vol. 5; Philip Livingston to Jacob Wendell, January 14, December 16, 1746, in Livingston Papers; Klein, "William Livingston's *A Review*," pp. 116–17.

46. Philip Livingston to Jacob Wendell, February 13, 1747, in Livingston Papers.

If Colden planned to force the Albany Indian officials out of their traditional role, he did not have long to wait.[47]

Having been "treated with Contempt," the Indian Commissioners resigned in November 1746. In their letter of resignation, they correctly pointed out that the men who now had a "Considerable Share in transacting public Affairs with the Indians" were the "Chief Indian Traders." As for themselves, they admitted to trading with the Indians in the past, but denied that such economic relations had existed in recent years.[48] This letter was a fairly honest assessment of their role in Indian affairs. None of them maintained direct business relations with the Iroquois, and out of the dozen or more commissioners only Cornelius Cuyler and Hendrick Ten Eyck are clearly identifiable as Canada traders in the 1740s. Except for the accusations of the imperialists, there is no evidence to suggest that the commissioners were trying to protect the Canada trade. On one occasion in the early fall of 1745, they refused to allow some Caughnawaga Indians to trade in Albany unless the tribe agreed to stop their attacks on the New England border. Canada traders would hardly have done anything to antagonize the Caughnawagas.[49]

Now that the former Indian Commissioners and their political friends could expect no help from the governor, they had no choice but to hope that the assembly would prove to be friendlier than it had been during the first two years of the war. James DeLancey wanted to consolidate his power to such an extent that he would receive an appointment as lieutenant governor, and once Clinton left the colony, DeLancey hoped that he would be left in control. With such ambitions, he was not likely to turn away any additional supporters. Probably, then, it was not a coincidence that in 1747 the assembly took far more interest in frontier security than it had in the past.[50] In the late spring of 1747 the legislators displayed their new friendship with the Albany Dutch when they vigorously protested that they could not understand how Clinton had "conceived such inveterate Prejudices against the People of *Albany*."[51]

In an effort to attribute the basest economic motives to their opponents, the imperialists continued throughout the war and afterwards to direct their polemical attacks against the residents of Albany. Contradicting their contention that the Indians no longer listened to the Dutch,

47. Colden to ———, August 7, 1745, in *Colden Papers*, 3: 137–38.

48. Minutes of the Indian Commissioners, November 27, 1746, 2: 405–6.

49. Ibid., September 18, 1745, 3: 97.

50. Katz, *Newcastle's New York*, p. 171; Smith, *History*, 2: 104, 115; Cooper, "Oswego in the French-English Struggle," p. 120.

51. *Assembly Journal*, May 19, 1747, 2: 154; also see Smith, *History*, 2: 100.

the imperialists claimed that the "principal Traders" and "richest Men" in Albany had persuaded the Six Nations to remain neutral in order to protect "their private Advantage, gained by a Trade with *Canada*."[52] Actually, the Iroquois, like many of the colonists, could see that the British were in no position to launch a successful attack against the French. In describing Iroquois policy, Reverend Henry Barclay, a minister to the Mohawks, explained, "They plainly see that we Intend to do nothing Ourselves to Anoy the Enemy, But endeavour only to Set them on, and Use them like a Pack of Hounds to Hunt them for us."[53] During wars, the Iroquois were invaluable for scouting and for raiding unfortified enemy positions, but they were vulnerable to attacks on their villages while the warriors were engaged in military expeditions. In King George's War, their refusal to fight resulted mainly from the obvious inability of New York to protect their villages and their families. Furthermore, the Six Nations knew that upon entering a war with Canada they would have to fight their friends and relatives among the Caughnawagas. Although the imperialists, including Clinton, fully understood why the Iroquois refused to fight, they continued to blame Albany for this problem.[54]

Even with more influence and far greater resources than the Indian Commissioners, William Johnson had little success in recruiting Iroquois warriors for the war. At an emotional conference in the summer of 1746, he convinced all the Six Nations to join the British against the French, but only the Mohawks contributed any significant military service. By appointing Johnson as colonel and commissary of the Indian forces, the imperialists assured themselves that they would administer all the funds appropriated for Indian affairs by either New York or Great Britain. The latter proved to be generous, and in his first year as Indian Commissary Johnson spent over £3000 sterling on the Iroquois. The former Indian Commissioners could hardly have been blamed for displaying

52. *Assembly Journal*, April 24, 1747, 2: 147. Also see George Clinton to William Johnson, April 25, 1747, in *Johnson Papers*, 1: 87; George Clinton to the Board of Trade, November 30, 1747, in *NYCD*, 6: 413; and Archibald Kennedy, *The Importance of Gaining and Preserving the Friendship of the Indians to the British Interests, Considered* (New York, 1751), p. 12.

53. Henry Barclay to Daniel Horsmanden, April 10, 1746, in Selections from the Daniel Horsmanden Papers (microfilm), New-York Historical Society, New York City.

54. George Clinton to Jacob Glen, March 10, 1745, in George Clinton Miscellaneous Manuscripts, New-York Historical Society, New York City; Philip Livingston to Jacob Wendell, January 14, 1746, in Livingston Papers; Kennedy, *Importance of Gaining and Preserving the Friendship of the Indians*, p. 11.

envy after learning that Johnson had received a sum many times greater than their financial allowances in the early years of the war.[55]

Despite their vituperative attacks on those Albany citizens who traded with Montreal, the imperialists did not mind in the least if their own supporters benefited from this trade. A generation earlier, Governor Burnet had apparently looked the other way when his supporters in Albany traded with the French. In Clinton's administration, a man's allegiance to a political party actually had nothing to do with whether or not he participated in the Canada trade. In fact, Robert Sanders and John Henry Lydius, both notorious Canada traders, were two of William Johnson's closest business and political associates. As Johnson's most important ally in Albany, Sanders often entered into business ventures with him, and in 1750 Clinton appointed Sanders as mayor of the city.[56]

Originally from Massachusetts, the disreputable John Henry Lydius earned the dubious distinction of eventually incurring the enmity of nearly everyone who came to know him. In 1725 he moved to Montreal, where he married a French woman and acted as an agent for New Englanders who participated in the clandestine fur trade. After being expelled from Canada, he settled on New York's northern frontier, where he eventually built a blockhouse on the route between the Hudson River and Lake Champlain. Traveling back and forth between Albany and this fort, he carried on a profitable trade with Canada, probably through his oldest son, who lived there. When in Albany, he acted as a shipping agent for Johnson.[57] Although Clinton had once described Lydius as "either Mad or a Knave," the governor and Johnson unsuccessfully attempted to have the British government appoint him as Indian Secretary when Philip Livingston died in 1749.[58] The governor and his

55. Charles Roscoe Canedy, III, "An Entrepreneurial History of the New York Frontier, 1739–1776" (Ph.D. diss., Case Western Reserve University, 1967), p. 107; W. J. Eccles, *The Canadian Frontier, 1534–1760* (New York, 1969), p. 150; Leach, *Northern Colonial Frontier*, p. 194; Smith, *History*, 2: 111–12.

56. Robert Sanders to William Johnson, June 19, November 28, 1745, [May 8, 1751], July 27, October 23, 1758, in *Johnson Papers*, 1: 36, 43, 329, 2: 881, 3: 9.

57. Beauharnois and Hocquart to Maurepas, October 15, 1730, in *NYCD*, 9: 1019–20; Minutes of the Indian Commissioners, November 13, 1738, April 7, July 4, 1745, 2: 155a, 3: 47, 71–72; Philip Livingston to Jacob Wendell, March 9, 1745, in Livingston Papers; Daniel Horsmanden to Edward Collins, November 12, 1746; Henry Barclay to Daniel Horsmanden, April 10, 1746, in Selections from the Daniel Horsmanden Papers; John Henry Lydius to William Johnson, September 17, 1746, October 25, 1748, in *Johnson Papers*, 1: 66, 193; Peter Kalm, *Peter Kalm's Travels in North America*, ed. Adolph B. Benson, 2 vols. (New York, 1937), 1: 360; Kingsford, *History of Canada*, 3: 287–88.

58. George Clinton to Daniel Horsmanden [1745], in Selections from the Daniel Horsmanden Papers; Cadwallader Colden to William Shirley, July 25, 1749, in

associates valued Lydius for his influence among the Indians, but eventually the Iroquois discovered that the old rogue had been trying to cheat them out of their lands, and at a conference an Oneida sachem told Johnson, "You promised us that you would keep this fire place clean from all filth and that no snake should come into this Council Room. That Man sitting there (pointing to Coll: Lyddius) is a Devil . . . ." Johnson, who had recently broken with Lydius, had to admit that the Indian charges were in "a great measure true."[59]

Another Johnson associate trading with the French was Benjamin Stoddert, who conducted most of his business on Lake Ontario. Purchasing his goods on credit from Johnson, he did not bother to sell them piecemeal to the Indians. Instead, he sold them to French traders located at Fort Frontenac and elsewhere on Lake Ontario. Johnson knew about these transactions, and after his associate's death he attempted to collect debts owed to Stoddert by Frenchmen.[60]

After King George's War had drawn to an indecisive conclusion in 1748, Johnson found that the profits from his contracts to supply the Iroquois and the Oswego garrison had made him a creditor of both the New York and British governments. Although he had some difficulty in immediately raising cash, Johnson, as the largest wholesaler to Oswego, must have profited greatly from the banner trading year of 1749. As a large merchant and land owner, his economic future seemed secure. Politically, however, he was firmly attached to a party that had been unable to use the neutrality issue to gain any ground against the DeLanceys. Compounding this problem, Johnson found himself in the opposite political camp from his uncle and benefactor Admiral Peter Warren, who as an absentee New York councilor vigorously supported James DeLancey in England.[61]

An additional problem developed for Johnson when he discovered that control of Indian affairs in peacetime could be an economic liability, rather than an asset. Now the only source of revenue came from the New York legislators, and they already owed him a large sum of money that remained unpaid for several years. Within a year after the

Colden Papers, 4: 126–27; Memorial of George Clinton to the Duke of Bedford, April 20, 1749, in C.O. 5/1096.

59. Indian Conferences, July 3, 4, 1755, in _NYCD_, 6: 984, 986–87.

60. Canedy, "An Entrepreneurial History," pp. 111–12; Benjamin Stoddert to Johnson, July 2, 1749, May 20, 1751, in _Johnson Papers_, 9: 40, 1: 336.

61. Johnson to John B. Van Eps, September 6, 1748, in _Johnson Papers_, 1: 183; Smith, _History_, 2: 83; Katz, _Newcastle's New York_, pp. 210–12. For a full discussion of Johnson's business affairs from 1738 to 1755, see Canedy, "An Entrepreneurial History," pp. 55–139.

war, he wanted to relinquish his position, but such a move was likely to cause confusion among the Indians. Nevertheless, the shrewd Indian agent may have foreseen that a resignation would work to his political advantage; and in 1751, despite protests from the Mohawks, he gave up his role as colonel and commissary of the Six Nations. Although he had no intentions of withdrawing from either provincial or Indian politics, Johnson could now concentrate on increasing his estates, while the other members of his party incurred the wrath of a defiant assembly.[62]

At first glance it would appear that Johnson, for purely personal reasons, had deserted his allies in a time of crisis. Actually, he and the the other imperialists knew that no one could effectively administer Indian affairs as long as he had to depend on the resources of even a cooperative provincial assembly. Nothing of significance could be accomplished with the Indians unless the British government created some kind of central authority, financed by either the mother country or by all the colonies. It seems to have been more than a coincidence, then, that in the year of Johnson's resignation the imperialists began to promote the creation of a single office of Indian affairs for the northern colonies.

The most significant contribution to the promotion of this effort was a pamphlet, *The Importance of Gaining and Preserving the Friendship of the Indians to the British Interest, Considered,* written in 1751 by Archibald Kennedy, who was a Clinton supporter on the New York Council and the colony's receiver general. Declaring "that the Preservation of the whole Continent" depended on the "proper Regulation of the *Six* Nations," he recommended that Indian affairs and the fur trade should be controlled by "one single Person of Capacity and Integrity" to be called the Superintendent of Indian Affairs. Even while denouncing the former Indian Commissioners, Kennedy called for a series of defensive measures that did not differ greatly from the ones proposed by Albany officials at the beginning of King George's War. If the British built a line of blockhouses and forts along the frontier, Iroquois, he declared, would no longer fear French attack on their villages. Within a year, his pamphlet was republished in England.[63]

After reading Kennedy's essay, Cadwallader Colden prepared a re-

---

62. George Clinton to Johnson, March 20, 1750; John Ayscough to Johnson, January 3, February 21, 1752, in *Johnson Papers,* 1: 322, 9: 86–87, 89; Pound, *Johnson of the Mohawks,* pp. 125–26.

63. Kennedy, *Importance of Gaining and Preserving the Friendship of the Indians,* pp. 7, 10–13; Milton M. Klein, "Archibald Kennedy: Imperial Pamphleteer," in *The Colonial Legacy,* ed. Leder, p. 100.

port for Clinton, in which he outlined a plan very similar to the one proposed by his fellow councilor. Stressing the importance of the fur trade in gaining the allegiance of Indian tribes, he argued that the British should take advantage of their ability to produce inexpensive merchandise by removing all duties from trading goods. Since low prices would do no good if the Indians were cheated, he suggested the development of a better legal system for handling Indian complaints against traders. Much could be done to prevent the "Frauds and abuses in Trade" by simply allowing Indians to give testimony in court. To administer his proposed system, Colden called for the appointment of a superintendent whose salary would be high enough to interest "a gentlemen fitly qualified for these purposes."[64]

An obstacle to the success of this plan developed when the assembly insisted that Governor Clinton do something about the state of confusion concerning Indian affairs. After Johnson's resignation, Clinton made no move to replace him even though DeLancey's partisans in the lower house wasted no time in putting pressure on him to appoint Indian Commissioners. In the fall of 1751 the legislators approved a bill to supply the governor with his regular biennial £1000 for Indian presents but warned that additional funds, requested by him for Indian affairs, would not be appropriated until he responded to their demands. After stalling for more than a year, Clinton informed Johnson in November 1752 that the assembly was determined to force the appointment of Indian Commissioners. Lamenting that he could no longer procrastinate on this issue, he sent Johnson the names "of almost all your inveterate Opposers," who had been suggested by the assembly as new commissioners.[65]

Within two weeks after Clinton's letter to Johnson, the Council approved of the assembly's recommendations, but the new appointees refused to serve until they were provided with enough money to cover their expenses. Even after the granting of this demand, the commissioners made little effort to assert themselves. Their lack of enthusiasm is not difficult to understand. Knowing that the allegiance of the Six Nations now firmly belonged to Johnson, they did not relish the role of pawns in the political games being played by DeLancey and Clinton,

---

64. Colden, "The present state of the Indian affairs . . . ," August 8, 1751, in *Colden Papers*, 4: 281–84; Klein, "Archibald Kennedy," p. 100.

65. *Assembly Journal*, October 14, November 20, 1751, 2: 313, 327; New York Executive Council Minutes [November 7, 1751], vol. 23, New York State Library, Albany, hereafter cited as Council Minutes; George Clinton to Johnson, November 5, 1752, in *Johnson Papers*, 1: 383.

while the French did everything in their power to win allies among the Indians.[66]

At the end of King George's War, French officials in Canada began to make preparation for a new outbreak of hostilities. In addition to their well-known efforts to stem the tide of English expansion into the Ohio Valley, they vigorously renewed their efforts to prevent the fur trade at Oswego from luring away their Indian allies. To attract the Indians away from Oswego, they made an effort to artificially lower the prices of merchandise at Niagara. Governor La Jonquière and Intendant Bigot noted that "it would be incomparably more advantageous to advance the price of Beaver hats twenty *sous* each, than . . . to risk the loss of the entire Beaver trade, and perhaps of the Colony."[67] Indians living to the north of Lake Erie had often avoided the aggressive traders at Niagara by following a route to Lake Ontario that came out near Toronto, but in 1750 the French built a fortified trading post at this location. Both Governor La Jonquière and his predecessor, La Galissonnière, attempted to increase French influence among the Iroquois, and they bluntly told Clinton that the Treaty of Utrecht had not recognized the Iroquois as subjects of Great Britain. Besides, added La Jonquière, if the independent Iroquois desired to subject themselves to a European nation, it would be "their natural Inclination" to accept the rule of the French king.[68]

During the first three years of French activities after King George's War, the reaction of New York did not differ greatly from what it had been before and during the conflict. While the imperialists continued to complain, the DeLancey party remained reluctant to pass legislation that would be of assistance to Clinton. Although DeLancey had won an appointment as lieutenant governor in 1747, Clinton refused to present him with the commission and did everything in his power to secure it for Colden or someone else. Knowing by 1751 that Clinton would soon be leaving the colony, DeLancey realized that further resistance might be a source of difficulty for him in England. As his later actions were to

66. Council Minutes [November 16, 1752], vol. 23; Robert Sanders to George Clinton, December 28, 1752, July 4, 1753, in Robert Sanders Letter Book, 1752–1758, New-York Historical Society, New York City; *Assembly Journal*, June 6, 1753, 2: 339.

67. La Jonquière and Bigot, Abstract of their dispatch from Canada, October 1, 1749, in *NYCD*, 10: 201; Colden, "The present state of the Indian affairs . . . ," August 8, 1751, in *Colden Papers*, 4: 280; Council Minutes [October 18, 1751], vol. 23.

68. La Jonquière and Bigot, Abstract of their dispatch from Canada, October 1, 1749; La Galissonnière to George Clinton, August 25, 1748; La Jonquière to Clinton, August 10, 1751, in *NYCD*, 10: 201, 6: 489, 731–32.

demonstrate, he was also concerned about the threat from Canada. He therefore softened his attacks on Clinton, but the embittered governor demonstrated no desire for reconciliation and waited impatiently for the day of his departure. In October 1753 Clinton turned over the reins of government to his successor, Sir Danvers Osborne, but within days the new governor committed suicide. DeLancey was now New York's chief executive.[69]

Several months before reaching this goal, DeLancey and his party had taken a significant step toward reconciling their differences with William Johnson. At a meeting in June 1753 among Clinton, the members of the Council, and the Mohawks, the Indian spokesman, Hendrick, denounced New Yorkers for their failure to provide Indian villages with protection and for their attempts to swindle the Iroquois out of their lands. Storming out of the meeting in a rage, Hendrick declared that the covenant chain was broken. Although Hendrick, who was Johnson's closest ally among the Iroquois, did not speak for all of the Six Nations, his outburst caused a wave of apprehension that swept over much of the British Empire and helped to bring the colonists together for the Albany Congress in the following year. In an immediate reaction, the New York assembly and Council, with the full approval of James DeLancey, appointed Johnson to go to Onondaga, where he succeeded in calming the anger of the Iroquois.[70]

When DeLancey began his administration a few months later, he lost no time in acquiring Johnson's services. Having ended their feud, Johnson and DeLancey began preparations for the Albany Congress. The assembly, so often condemned for advocating a neutrality with Canada, now appropriated £1000 for the lieutenant governor's expenses at the conference. When he requested additional funds, the legislators replied that the colony simply could not afford it and pleaded for financial assistance from Great Britain. Instead of being abusive as previous governors had been, DeLancey admitted his awareness of "the heavy Expence the People were put to for the publick Services" and promised to present the assembly's case to the king. As he prepared to preside over the great conference, DeLancey received strong support from the assembly, and his political opponents at least temporarily refrained from criticism. Significantly, William Johnson and William Smith, Sr., both imperialists, were two of the New York delegates who went with De-

69. Katz, *Newcastle's New York*, pp. 230–36; Smith, *History*, 2: 146–47, 151–58.
70. Indian Conferences, June 12, 15, 16, 1753; Board of Trade to Sir Danvers Osborne, September 12, 1753; Johnson to the Board of Trade, May 24, 1765, in *NYCD*, 6: 783–88, 801, 7: 715. For a detailed account of this affair, see Osgood, *American Colonies in the Eighteenth Century*, 4: 306–9.

Lancey to Albany. Later, DeLancey became involved in a series of disputes between his supporters, including William Johnson, and the more vehement imperialists, but the political controversies then centered on questions of how the war should be fought and who should take the credit for victories or the blame for defeats.[71]

At the Albany Congress in the summer of 1754, the Iroquois made no secret of their grievances against the British. While expressing the usual complaints over frauds committed by fur traders, they now directed their major attack against land speculators. To remedy their problem, they strongly advocated the appointment of Johnson as Superintendent of Indian Affairs and asked DeLancey to take this step immediately. Instead, the lieutenant governor told them that he would give the commissioners another year to prove themselves. DeLancey expected the British government to act favorably upon the recommendation of the Albany Congress to appoint Indian superintendents in the north and south. Thus, he would not have to offend his friends in Albany by immediately acting upon the Iroquois demands. His calculations proved correct, and in the following spring the ill-fated General Edward Braddock delivered a commission to Johnson that gave him control of all relations with the Iroquois and their allies.[72]

The general swirl of events surrounding the Albany Congress and the first battles of the great war almost entirely obscured the feelings of the Albany Dutch toward the inevitability of military conflict. The only specific complaints against them resulted from the presence of Caughnawaga Indians trading in Albany during the summer of 1755. Most of this commerce, however, occurred before news of Braddock's defeat reached New York, and even Johnson advocated a policy of remaining friendly with these Indians in case the opportunity arose to lure them away from Canada.[73] Unlike previous wars, there were no serious

71. *Assembly Journal*, April 12, 1754, 2: 375; Board of Trade to the Earl of Holdernesse, September 18, 1753; James DeLancey to the Board of Trade, December 24, 1753, in *NYCD*, 6: 799, 817–18; Smith, *History*, 2: 180; Klein, "William Livingston's *A Review*," pp. 119–34; Osgood, *American Colonies in the Eighteenth Century*, 4: 310, 312.

72. Proceedings of the Albany Congress, June 19–July 11, 1754; Board of Trade to George II, October 29, 1754, in *NYCD*, 6: 865–66, 870–71, 878–79, 917–19; Edward Braddock to William Johnson, April 15, 1755, in *Johnson Papers*, 1: 465. On the connection between the Albany Congress and the development of imperial Indian policy, see John R. Alden, "The Albany Congress and the Creation of the Indian Superintendencies," *Mississippi Valley Historical Review* 27 (1940): 193–210. For a general account of the great conference, see Robert C. Newbold, *The Albany Congress and the Plan of Union of 1754* (New York, 1955).

73. Indian Conferences, June 29, July 1, 1755, in *NYCD*, 6: 979–80; William

accusations that Albany wanted to negotiate a neutrality agreement with the French. Because of the close relations maintained by Robert Sanders with Montreal, there were rumors early in 1755 of diplomatic contacts between him and the governor of Canada, but Sanders claimed to be "as Innocent as a Dove."[74] Once hostilities officially commenced in 1756, the fur trade nearly came to a complete standstill. Without a hint of regret over the loss of fur-trading revenues, merchants turned to the lucrative business of supplying the troops who congregated on the frontier.[75]

Now that the people of Albany could see a realistic chance of defeating the French, they did not hesitate to support an all-out offensive. During those years when their nearly defenseless homes sat on the edge of a hostile wilderness, the 2,200 residents of Albany County in 1703 and the 10,000 in 1744 had opposed war with France mainly in order to protect themselves from violent destruction. In their opposition to war, they had followed the lead of the Iroquois Confederacy and had maintained a policy of neutrality that saved them from bearing the full force of French and Indian raiders, who had so often demonstrated their ability to sweep down from Lake Champlain with terrifying speed and ferocity.[76]

Shirley to James DeLancey, May 25, 1755; Johnson to DeLancey, June 15, 1755, in *Johnson Papers*, 1: 543, 595.

74. Sanders to Jacob Wendell, March 26, 1755, in Robert Sanders Letter Book, 1752–1758.

75. Cornelius Cuyler to Peter Van Brugh Livingston, February 4, February 20, 1756; Cuyler to John Ledyard, April 11, May 13, 1758, in Cornelius Cuyler Letter Book, 1752–1764 (microfilm), American Antiquarian Society, Worcester, Mass.; Philip Cuyler to John Hamensly, October 15, 1755, in Philip Cuyler Letter Book, 1755–1760, New York Public Library, New York City; Robert Sanders Account Book, 1754–1758, New York State Library, Albany; Edna L. Jacobsen, "Eighteenth-Century Merchants in Colonial Albany," *Yearbook of the Dutch Settlers Society of Albany* 20 (1944–45): 5–15, esp. 10–13.

76. Population statistics of New York, in *New York Documentary History*, 1: 465–74.

11

REVOLUTIONARY POLITICS AND

THE DISRUPTION OF TRADE

IN STUDYING the aftermath of the Seven Years' War, historians have given careful attention to questions involving the fur trade and land speculation in the west. Much of their scholarship has centered on the policies of officials in America and in Great Britain, and it is not necessary to retrace their steps. Nor is it the purpose here to undertake extensive research into New York's political and economic life in the revolutionary era. From previous studies, however, and with some additional research, it is possible to determine why the fur trade declined in New York during the years between 1763 and the outbreak of the Revolution. Political turmoil, which forced economic changes, seems to have been the most decisive factor.[1]

In New York, businessmen looked upon the situation after the Seven Years' War with a mixture of anticipation and anxiety. Fearing the effects of competition from Montreal merchants, the New Yorkers hoped that the advantages of the Hudson River over the St. Lawrence would help them to become the major fur exporters of North America. "The Fur Trade," noted John Watts, a merchant of New York City, "should have its natural course, either thro' the St. Lawrence or Hudsons River . . . each no doubt will possess some Share . . . and where the largest Capital in Commerce circulates, and the best Supplys of proper Goods

1. For discussions of British policy in the American West during this period, see Clarence W. Alvord, *The Mississippi Valley in British Politics: A Study of the Trade, Land Speculation, and Experiments in Imperialism Culminating in the American Revolution,* 2 vols. (Cleveland, 1917); Bernhard Knollenberg, *Origin of the American Revolution: 1759–1766* (New York, 1960); John Shy, *Toward Lexington: The Role of the British Army in the Coming of the American Revolution* (Princeton, 1965); Jack M. Sosin, *The Revolutionary Frontier, 1763–1783* (New York, 1967); and Sosin, *Whitehall and the Wilderness: The Middle West in British Colonial Policy, 1760–1775* (Lincoln, Nebr., 1961).

are found most probably the largest Share will center." In making this observation in 1762, Watts saw no need to place any legal restrictions on the Canadian merchants. "The endless Winters and tedious Navigation are Limitations enough."[2] No one, of course, could have anticipated the political developments that would handicap the New York traders for more than a decade and finally put the trade entirely into the hands of the Canadians.[3]

Well before New Yorkers began to face the problems of revolutionary politics, they encountered tremendous changes in the nature of their business. In the first half of the century, Albany had occupied a distinctive position as a Dutch-controlled British outpost, serving as Great Britain's major source of furs from the Great Lakes region. Now, the Albany-Schenectady area became only one element of a complex trading operation that encompassed more than half a continent. With a population increase from 10,000 before the war to more than 42,000 in 1771, Albany County was rapidly expanding, and the frontier was advancing westward.[4] The most important New York traders were now Scotsmen, and they sold far more rum than textiles. Probably the greatest change in the trade was that by the late 1760s the Indians no longer came to the traders. Instead, the British now carried their goods directly into the Indian villages at locations far removed from the port cities where furs were exported or made into hats.

Before the Seven Years' War, New York had been producing about 25 percent of England's total fur imports. With the addition of Canada to the Empire, New York's share in the English market fell to only a little more than 5 percent. In relation to total New York exports to England after the war, furs seldom amounted to as much as 5 percent. Despite this decline in relative importance, New Yorkers continued to handle a large volume of furs, especially when they were unimpeded by political difficulties or other noneconomic factors. In 1765, for instance, New York

2. John Watts to Isaac Barré, February 28, 1762, in *Letter Book of John Watts: Merchant and Councillor of New York*, New-York Historical Society *Collections* 61 (1928): 26–27. For more on Watts, see Virginia D. Harrington, *The New York Merchant on the Eve of the Revolution* (New York, 1935), pp. 309–11.

3. For accounts of Canada's fur trade in this era, see Harold A. Innis, *The Fur Trade in Canada*, rev. ed. (New Haven, 1962), pp. 149–262; Wayne Edson Stevens, *The Northwest Fur Trade, 1762–1800* (Urbana, Ill., 1928); Marjorie G. Jackson, "The Beginning of British Trade at Michilimackinac," *Minnesota History* 11 (1930): 231–70; and Marjorie G. Reid, "The Quebec Fur-Traders and Western Policy, 1763–1774," *Canadian Historical Review* 6 (1925): 15–32.

4. Population statistics of New York, in *Documentary History of the State of New-York*, ed. Edmund B. O'Callaghan, 4 vols. (Albany, 1850–51), 1: 465–74.

fur exports to England had a value of £5,565, which was more than most previous years in the first half of the century.[5] New York, moreover, continued to supply the numerous colonial hatters with a large percentage of their raw materials. Usually, the craftsmen made their purchases from merchants in their own cities, who sometimes traveled to Albany or Schenectady for the purpose of acquiring peltry. John Backhouse of Philadelphia often purchased amounts worth thousands of pounds directly from the traders, and he became a significant competitor of fur merchants residing in Albany County.[6]

As in earlier years, New Yorkers received their furs from both the Great Lakes region and from Canada. At the end of the Seven Years' War, some merchants hoped that Albany, not Montreal or Quebec, would become the main shipping center for Canadian furs. The Hudson River was shorter than the St. Lawrence, less treacherous, and frozen for fewer months in winter. Even after deducting expenses for transportation over the Lake Champlain route, residents of Albany foresaw an advantage in competition with the Canadians.[7]

Not surprisingly, the leaders of the effort to establish Albany as the link between Canada and England were Dutch merchants, who had previously established relations with London factors specializing in the fur trade. Having traded directly with both Europe and Montreal since the 1720s, Cornelius Cuyler viewed the conquest of Canada as a golden opportunity. In 1758 he had demonstrated considerable foresight by sending his young son, Abraham, to New Rochelle for the purpose of learning French. Three years later Abraham went to Montreal, where he established a branch of his father's business and soon began sending a significant amount of peltry to Albany. Apparently, Abraham spent the winters at home but journeyed early each spring to Canada with a large supply of woolens and other goods. By using his son as an agent in Montreal, Cuyler conducted a business that was similar to his trading operations in the first half of the century. In good years, Abraham

5. Murray G. Lawson, *Fur: A Study in English Mercantilism, 1700–1775* (Toronto, 1943), pp. 33–34, 109, 135; Harrington, *New York Merchant*, p. 167.

6. Governor Henry Moore to the Board of Trade, January 12, 1767, in *Documents Relative to the Colonial History of the State of New York*, ed. Edmund B. O'Callaghan and Berthold Fernow, 15 vols. (Albany, 1856–87), 7: 888–89; hereafter cited as *NYCD*; Phyn and Ellice to Hayman Levy, July 21, 1769, June 23, 1772; Phyn and Ellice to George Meade and Company, June 14, July 10, 1773, in Phyn and Ellice Letter Book (microfilm), 1: 197, 2: 157, 328, 347, Buffalo and Erie County Historical Society, Buffalo, N.Y.

7. For a discussion of why colonists considered the Hudson River to be superior to the St. Lawrence, see Cadwallader Colden, Memoir on the Fur Trade, November 10, 1724, in *NYCD*, 5: 728.

shipped as many or more skins to Albany than his father had received before the war, but furs now represented only a small part of the family's business interests. When profits declined, they did not hesitate to turn away from the Canadian trade in favor of their other interests; and in 1765 Abraham closed down the operations in Montreal.[8]

Another Albany merchant, David Vander Heyden, also entered the new Canadian trade with considerable enthusiasm. Probably no one else so completely reflected the traditional colonial practice of keeping business affairs within the family. His son, Dirk, had become a merchant in London during the early 1750s and acted as a factor for his father. Dirk's brother, David, Jr., was a Manhattan merchant, who served as the family's shipping agent. A third son, Jacob, handled Vander Heyden's operations in Montreal with the assistance of John Mynderse. In later years Vander Heyden imported goods directly to Canada from London, but in the early 1760s he usually employed the Caughnawaga Indians to act as porters between Albany and Montreal. He also hired a man to run a trading house for him among the Indians of Quebec.[9] Although the business prospered for several years, Vander Heyden suffered a severe setback in 1765, when a warehouse fire destroyed amost all of his merchandise, valued at "£6000 Currency." He also lost, at least temporarily, the services of his son, Jacob, who had become completely distracted by "an amourous Fit with one of the most fickle Ladies" in Montreal, "the famous Miss La Rat De Couagne."[10] Despite these difficulties, Vander Heyden continued to trade in Canada, but his business never prospered as it had done before the fire.[11]

Although a few other merchants participated in the Canadian trade on a smaller scale than Cuyler and Vander Heyden, the major part of New York's fur supply came from the west. Due to the utilization of

8. Cornelius Cuyler to Philip Cuyler, October 18, 1758; Cuyler to Abraham Cuyler, June 15, 1758, June 14, 1762; Cuyler to Isaac Low, May 14, July 10, 1761, April 11, 1764; Cuyler to Henry Bonnin, May 18, 1761; Cuyler to Henry Cuyler, January 25, 1761; Cuyler to Champion and Hayley, May 5, 1764, in Cornelius Cuyler Letter Book, 1752–1764 (microfilm), American Antiquarian Society, Worcester, Mass.; Charles Roscoe Canedy, III, "An Entrepreneurial History of the New York Frontier, 1739–1776" (Ph.D. diss., Case Western Reserve University, 1967), pp. 201–11.

9. Dirk Vander Heyden to John Sanders, June 14, 1762, in Sanders Papers, New-York Historical Society, New York City; David Vander Heyden, Invoice Book, 1763–1769, passim, New York State Library, Albany. Also see chapter 7, and Harrington, *New York Merchant*, pp. 186, 238.

10. Daniel Claus to William Johnson, July 11, 1765, in *The Papers of Sir William Johnson*, ed. James Sullivan et al., 14 vols. (Albany, 1921–65), 4: 790, hereafter cited as *Johnson Papers*.

11. David Vander Heyden, Invoice Book, 1763–1769, passim.

former French forts in the interior, Oswego no longer served as a convenient trading center, where numerous independent traders could congregate each spring with small lots of merchandise. Several New Yorkers, therefore, developed firms for the purpose of supplying the traders who operated out of Niagara and Detroit. These large firms often avoided the more distant northern posts, such as Michilimackinac, because their Canadian competitors in these locations had the advantage in both the shorter route over the Ottawa River and in their ability to hire former *voyageurs* or *coureurs de bois*. A great variety of business arrangements existed on the frontier, but usually a member of each New York firm or a trusted factor sold goods at the trading posts to the multitude of small traders. Only in the early years when trade was legally restricted to the forts did the large firms participate in the retail market.[12]

Generally, the New York firms became based at Schenectady, but a few preferred Albany. In a reversal of the commercial pattern in existence for thirty years, some New York City merchants now began to take a direct interest in the trade. Peter Van Brugh Livingston invested heavily in a firm that attempted to monopolize the trade around Niagara, and Hayman Levy frequently purchased furs from up-river merchants, who also employed him as a factor or simply as a shipping agent. By employing Schenectady merchants to act in his behalf, John Wetherhead of New York City actually became a direct supplier of Indian traders at Detroit.[13]

In this era, Scotsmen operated almost all major New York firms trading to the west. Names like Macomb, Campbell, McTavish, and Duncan were the ones most frequently mentioned in discussions of the colony's fur trade. Among the Dutch, only Henry Van Schaick matched the efforts of the Scottish to exploit the trade at Niagara and Detroit. A few Dutchmen, such as Jacob Van Schaick, continued to follow the traditional procedure of importing their own goods and trading directly with the

---

12. For a contemporary discussion of New York trading procedures in this period, see William Johnson, "a Review of the progressive State of the Trade . . ." [September 22, 1767], in *NYCD*, 7: 953-78. For historical accounts, see Stevens, *Northwest Fur Trade*, pp. 13-41; Canedy, "An Entrepreneurial History," pp. 207-381; and R. H. Fleming, "Phyn, Ellice and Company of Schenectady," *Contributions to Canadian Economics* 4 (1932): 7-41.

13. Jacob Van Schaick to William Bayard, March 8, 1762, in Van Schaick Papers, New York State Library, Albany; John Duncan to Peter Van Brugh Livingston, August 13, 1762, in Peter Van Brugh Livingston Papers, New-York Historical Society, New York City; Phyn and Ellice to John Wetherhead, May 20, 1768, January 12, 1770; Phyn and Ellice Letter Book, 1: 66-67, 266, 2: 217; Harrington, *New York Merchant*, p. 237.

Indians, but they confined most of their activities to Niagara and other locations along the western shores of Lake Ontario. Even among the swarm of small retail traders, the Scottish and Scotch-Irish nearly equaled the number of Dutch. Many of these new Indian traders were British army veterans who had fought against the French in Canada and chose to remain in America after receiving their discharges. Some of the large merchants came directly from Scotland, and others were the sons of Scottish immigrants who had been encouraged by Governor Cosby to settle on the frontier in the 1730s.[14]

Among the Scottish entrepreneurs after the war, John Duncan, who had left his position as a lieutenant in the British army, quickly became one of the most aggressive merchants in the western trade. Along with several partners, including Walter Rutherfurd and Peter Van Brugh Livingston, Duncan attempted to establish a monopoly over the western trade by gaining control of the Niagara portage. Early in 1761, these partners asked General Jeffrey Amherst to give them a ten-thousand-acre grant of land surrounding Niagara. Not possessing the legal authority to make such a grant, Amherst gave them permission to begin a settlement in the area with the understanding that approval would eventually have to be given by the British government. By the end of July they had constructed a trading house on the portage, and James Sterling, one of the partners, began selling goods to the Indians. Sterling was virtually without competition along the portage because Amherst and Sir William Johnson, the Indian Superintendent, had decreed that the fur traders could not venture outside of certain military posts. Naturally, the other New York traders were outraged by the special privileges granted to Sterling, who was receiving his merchandise through Duncan in Schenectady. An even more disturbing possibility, they realized, was that if the partners obtained the area as a land grant, they would completely control the trade between New York and the Great Lakes.[15]

Probably following the lead of Henry Van Schaick, who was politically associated with Sir William Johnson, the Niagara traders petitioned

14. Ian Charles Cargill Graham, *Colonists from Scotland: Emigration to North America, 1707–1783* (Ithaca, N.Y., 1956), pp. 47–49, 77–81; Jacob Van Schaick to William Bayard, March 8, 1762, in Van Schaick Papers; Thomas Gage to Jeffrey Amherst, 1762, in *Johnson Papers*, 2: 943; Frederick W. Barnes, "The Fur Traders of Early Oswego," New York State Historical Association *Proceedings* 13 (1914): 134.

15. William Johnson to Amherst, July 29, 1769; Johnson, Journal of a trip to Detroit, October 6, 1761, in *Johnson Papers*, 10: 321–22, 13: 266; Petition of the Albany merchants to the Board of Trade, January 28, 1762; Amherst to William Sharpe, October 20, 1762, in *NYCD*, 7: 488–89, 508–9; John Duncan to Peter Van Brugh Livingston, August 13, 1762, in Peter Van Brugh Livingston Papers.

the Indian Superintendent early in 1762 for a redress of their grievances against Sterling. Johnson strongly opposed monopolies in the fur trade and feared that a plan to settle around Niagara would anger the Senecas, who greatly valued their control over this portage. He therefore suggested to Amherst that steps should be taken to limit Sterling's activities. At the same time, a large number of Albany merchants petitioned the Board of Trade with a similar request. Most of them had little interest in the western trade, but they were opposed to restrictions on commerce, and they soon discovered that the British ministry agreed with them. Seemingly embarrassed by the opposition and by the disapproval of his superiors in London, Amherst immediately ended all special privileges and denied that he had even intended to encourage a land grant at Niagara.[16]

Having been defeated in this effort to establish a monopoly, the company soon dissolved, but Duncan and Sterling continued their partnership, which led to the development of the most important firm involved in the New York trade during this period. Sterling moved to Detroit, and Duncan continued shipping merchandise to him. During the middle years of the decade, John Porteous, James Phyn, and Alexander Ellice joined the firm as partners. The latter two had arrived in Schenectady directly from Scotland. After a reorganization necessitated by Duncan's retirement in 1767, the firm became known as Phyn and Ellice, and was soon expanded by the addition of Ellice's two brothers, Robert and James. Sterling and Porteous, who formed their own trading company in Detroit, maintained a close association with the Schenectady firm.[17]

For the next several years the firm of Phyn and Ellice increased the volume of its business and established close connections with "at least Eight or Ten" merchants, who were the "most principal dealers" at the frontier posts.[18] In addition, the firm operated its own warehouse at Detroit, where a partner spent each summer, selling merchandise to the traders. For a while, John Porteous again participated as a partner in the firm; and through him, Phyn and Ellice attempted to compete with the

16. William Johnson to Amherst, July 29, 1761, February 6, 1762; Amherst to Johnson, February 14, 1762; Johnson to William Walters, April 29, 1762, in *Johnson Papers*, 10: 321–22, 3: 623, 10: 382, 3: 727–28; Petition of the Albany merchants to the Board of Trade, January 28, 1762; Board of Trade to George III, June 3, 1762; Amherst to William Sharpe, October 20, 1762, in *NYCD*, 7: 488–89, 502–3, 508–10.

17. Fleming, "Phyn, Ellice and Company," pp. 8–10; John Duncan to William Johnson, March 12, 1766, in *Johnson Papers*, 5: 70.

18. Robert Ellice to Nathaniel Marston, March 1, 1776, in Phyn and Ellice Letter Book, 3: 254.

Montreal merchants at Michilimackinac. Like other New Yorkers, they discovered that the shorter route between Montreal and Michilimackinac over the Ottawa River often allowed their competitors to undersell them.[19]

Even when transporting goods no farther than Detroit, the firm faced numerous expenses and other difficulties. Because of high wages, the cost of sending battoes from Schenectady to Oswego was nearly prohibitive. To lessen this expense, Phyn and Ellice, as well as their competitors, did not hesitate to use Negro slaves.[20] Although battoes in the 1760s were often taken clear to Detroit, most merchants preferred to load their merchandise on sailing vessels at Oswego. After the goods reached Niagara, a firm's agent arranged for transportation over the portage, which was controlled by a monopoly that charged a high fee for its services. Then another sloop transported the goods to Detroit. On these vessels, military shipments received priority, and the traders were often at the mercy of Alexander Grant, who had gained control of shipping on the Lakes in the 1760s and often gave preference for the limited cargo space to favored companies. To solve this problem, Phyn and Ellice and some of their associates built a sloop of about forty-five tons on Lake Erie in 1769. Soon after launching the vessel, the owners sold it to Grant for a profit and the promise of certain concessions in the transportation of their goods. When Grant again proved unreliable, Phyn and Ellice entered into an agreement with several other merchants to build the *Angelica*, a sloop of sixty-six tons, which served them for several trading seasons.[21]

While attempting to refine their transportation system, Phyn and Ellice also improved the method of marketing their peltry. After the Seven Years' War, the low-quality New York beaver, obtained mostly from south of the Great Lakes, had to compete with a great quantity of prime northern pelts from both Hudson's Bay and Canada. Consequently, it was sometimes useless to export "Detroit" or "Five Nations" beaver

19. Phyn and Ellice to John Stedman, March 8, 1773; Phyn and Ellice to Hayman Levy, June 16, 1774, ibid., 2: 288, 3: 87; Fleming, "Phyn, Ellice and Company," pp. 14, 21.

20. Phyn and Ellice to James Sterling, August 23, 1769; Phyn and Ellice to John Porteous, June 6, 1771, in Phyn and Ellice Letter Book, 1: 201, 434; Cornelius Cuyler to Henry Cuyler, July 3, 1762, in Cornelius Cuyler Letter Book, 1752–1764. The merchants at Detroit also used slave labor; see John Campbell to Thomas Gage, May 10, 1766, in *Johnson Papers*, 5: 161–62.

21. Canedy, "An Entrepreneurial History," pp. 337–41; Phyn and Ellice to John Porteous, August 23, 1769, January 13, 1771; Phyn and Ellice to Alexander Grant, March 15, 1771, in Phyn and Ellice Letter Book, 1: 202–4, 392–93, 426.

from New York, because it would not bring a decent price in England. Many fur traders were therefore satisfied with selling their peltry on the colonial market to such merchants as Hayman Levy, who either sold it to local hatters or waited for prices to rise in London. Such a marketing system meant that the Schenectady firms could seldom obtain sterling bills of exchange. Although John Duncan apparently had dealt only with Haymen Levy or other colonial merchants, the partners of the reorganized firm were not satisfied with a system that prevented them from enjoying the main benefit of the fur trade. Shortly after the firm's reorganization, they began looking for a factor in England to handle the better quality beaver that they soon began to acquire from their operations at Michilimackinac. For three years they experimented with factors in Scotland and England, but dealt mainly with Neale and Pigou, a London firm that maintained a branch in New York City under the direction of Benjamin Booth.[22] In 1770 the Schenectady firm dropped Neale and Pigou and settled on John Blackburn of London, who had become the most important British merchant dealing in the New York fur trade.[23]

Although Phyn and Ellice developed the largest New York trade with Detroit, they were not without significant competition from other merchants who maintained overseas connections. Henry Van Schaick, for example, was instrumental in reopening the trade at Niagara in 1760, and later he expanded his business to Detroit. In 1766 Van Schaick and his partner, Edward Cole, exported a shipment of furs to London that included beaver skins weighing 3,535 pounds.[24] Next to Phyn and Ellice, Daniel Campbell of Schenectady was probably New York's most important fur merchant in this period. As an importer of trade goods, he may have surpassed any of his competitors, because he was politically connected with Sir William Johnson and often received orders to supply the Indian department with merchandise for presents. At Detroit, his

22. Innis, *Fur Trade in Canada*, pp. 174–77; Lawson, *Fur*, pp. 66–67; Harrington, *New York Merchant*, pp. 309–10; Fleming, "Phyn, Ellice and Company," pp. 11–12, 16. Also see chapter 7. It appears that Duncan purchased his goods mainly from Hayman Levy but also from Daniel Campbell, a Schenectady merchant with connections in London. Daniel Campbell, Account Books, February 6, 7, 22, May 9, 1764, vol. 3, New York State Library, Albany.

23. Phyn and Ellice to John Porteous, September 20, 1770; Phyn and Ellice to John Blackburn, October 30, 1770, in Phyn and Ellice Letter Book, 2: 12, 32–33.

24. Peter Du Bois to Hayman Levy, September 25, 1760, in Peter Du Bois Letter Book, March-October 1760, New-York Historical Society, New York City; Edward Cole to Henry Van Schaick, November 19, 1763; Account of sales, June 30, 1766, in *Johnson Papers*, 4: 247, 5: 291–93. For biographical information about Edward Cole, see Johnson to Thomas Gage, March 15, 1766; and Edward Cole to Johnson, June 23, 1766, ibid., 5: 80, 278.

partner, Samuel Tyms, looked after the western end of the business.[25]

In addition to the well-established fur exporters, there were numerous small merchants, who did not always follow consistent business patterns. In the early 1760s, when trade was confined to the military posts, they acted as retailers and conducted all of their business through the large firms. Later, the more successful ones became small merchants and personally transported their merchandise to the western posts. By 1772 many of them, as Phyn and Ellice complained, had "fallen upon means to supply themselves with Goods from London."[26]

Although the majority of small merchants did not achieve great prosperity, some of the younger ones had very successful careers. Simon McTavish learned the trade as an aggressive merchant in New York; and, at the outbreak of the American Revolution, he transferred his operations to Canada, where he achieved fame as head of the Northwest Company. Peter Pond was another small New York trader, who later became well known for his role in the opening of the Canadian Northwest. Most of these merchants who went to Canada at the beginning of the Revolution achieved success due to their knowledge of shipping on the Great Lakes. Since the Montreal merchants had been concerned mainly with canoe transportation over the Ottawa River, the newcomers were able to monopolize the trade with Detroit, and later they took the lead in building sloops on Lakes Huron, Michigan, and Superior.[27]

All New Yorkers trading to the west in this period specialized in the merchandising of rum. Under French rule, the sale of alcohol to Indians had been limited by the influence of the Jesuits. Except for a brief period after the Seven Years' War, the British imposed no such restrictions, and the New Yorkers now found themselves with a vast, new market for their fiery, liquid merchandise. Even among their older customers such as the Iroquois, the demand increased due to the rapidly growing problem of alcoholism as more and more tribesmen became demoralized by the encroachment of Europeans upon their lands.[28] When the British

25. Phyn and Ellice to Hayman Levy, September 14, 1771; James Phyn to Alexander Ellice, March 12, 27, 1772, in Phyn and Ellice Letter Book, 2: 10, 94, 112; Daniel Campbell to Johnson, January 13, 1763, March 24, 1772, in *Johnson Papers*, 4: 14, 8: 432.

26. Phyn and Ellice to John Blackburn, November 26, 1772, in Phyn and Ellice Letter Book, 2: 231.

27. Innis, *Fur Trade in Canada*, pp. 177, 180, 219–22. In 1769 Peter Pond was apparently in partnership with Felix Graham of Albany; see Philip Cuyler, Ledger, 1763–1794, folio 67, August 17, 1769, New York Public Library, New York City.

28. Anthony F. C. Wallace, *The Death and Rebirth of the Seneca* (New York, 1970), p. 199. Also see Arthur Pound, *Johnson of the Mohawks* (New York, 1930), pp. 294–308.

began allowing traders in the late 1760s to leave the forts, Indians constantly had to face the temptations of alcohol. Avaricious rum traders even followed the tribesmen to their hunting grounds.[29]

From 1768 to 1773 the merchants of Quebec imported a yearly average of more than 250,000 gallons of rum, and tremendous quantities also reached the interior through the other colonies. Phyn and Ellice were constantly sending orders to distillers in New York, and occasionally they went as far as Philadelphia to get a sufficient supply. In 1769 they estimated that they would have to send about 450 barrels of rum to the western forts.[30] By specializing in rum, New Yorkers had an advantage over their competitors in Canada. After the American Revolution, a group of leading Canadian merchants recalled, "It is true, that . . . previous to the Late War . . . they had the principal part of the Detroit Trade because the Ports on the Atlantic, being open at all seasons, gave a decided superiority over us in the West India Trade, by which means they could always undersell us in Liquors." On the other hand, the Canadians under British rule had always been "equal, if not superior," to New Yorkers in the importation of European goods.[31]

The intercolonial trade in molasses and the distillation of rum had an economic significance in New York that extended to a much greater segment of the business community than simply the fur traders of Albany County. Although New York City merchants generally ignored the fur trade, they came to its defense in the one instance when it related to the colony's overall investment in commerce. After the passage of the Sugar Act in 1764, the Manhattan merchants protested in a memorial to Parliament that the new law would hurt the Indian trade by raising the price of rum and thus preventing the colony from obtaining the furs that constituted a "very considerable Remittance to our Mother Country." They

29. Daniel Claus to Johnson, July 8, 1772, in *Johnson Papers*, 12: 971. For the opposition of Indian leaders to the sale of rum, see chapter 3. After 1760 many sachems intensified their campaign against liquor. See for examples, Indian Conferences [September 16, 1760], April 24, 1764; Sachems of Oquaga to Johnson, January 22, 1770; Johnson to Thomas Gage, November 18, 1772, in *Johnson Papers*, 13: 164, 3: 700, 7: 348, 639.

30. Haldimand Collection, Calendar III, p. 6, in *Report on Canadian Archives, 1888*, ed. Douglas Brymner (Ottawa, 1889); Phyn and Ellice to Alexander Grant, December 23, 1769; Phyn and Ellice to George Meade and Company, September 9, 1773, in Phyn and Ellice Letter Book, 1: 255, 3: 9.

31. McTavish, Frobisher and Company; Forsyth, Richardson and Company; Todd, McGill and Company to John Graves Simcoe, April 23, 1792, in *The Correspondence of Lieut. Governor John Graves Simcoe, with Allied Documents relating to his Administration of the Government of Upper Canada*, ed. E. A. Cruikshank, 5 vols. (Toronto, 1923), 1: 135.

further declared, "sugar and Molasses have been shewn to be the very Sinews of our Commerce, and the Sources from which . . . we draw the most valuable Remittances, it would therefore seem necessary that they should be imported in Quantities sufficient to supply the various Demands of our several commercial Interchanges . . . ."[32] By this time, however, the fur trade was only a minor one of the "several commercial Interchanges." Several years earlier, the Manhattan merchants had made no great protest when Sir William Johnson and General Amherst had placed an absolute prohibition on the sale of rum to the Indians as part of their overall plan for the regulation of the fur trade.

Even before the conquest of Canada in 1760, Johnson had started to consider plans for the regulation of the fur trade. "An equitable, an open and a well Regulated Trade with the Indians," he wrote to the Board of Trade in 1759, "is and ever will be the most natural and the most efficacious means to improve and extend His Majesty's Indian Interest."[33] Appealing to Amherst shortly after the fall of Niagara in July, Johnson called for "a fair, free, and plentifull Trade with all the Nations of Indians."[34] During the war, Johnson had become well known to the British ministry as a military leader and as the Superintendent of Indian Affairs in the north.[35] For his success at the battle of Lake George in 1755 he received the title of baronet, and when Niagara fell to English forces, Johnson was in command due to the death of General John Prideaux.[36]

In the years from 1760 until his death in 1774, Johnson sent a steady flow of information about Indian affairs to the Board of Trade and other British officials. In the eyes of his superiors in London, the baronet became the best source of "information and intelligence of the true state of Indian affairs."[37] Even the imperious General Amherst once wrote to Johnson, "I must always submit to your better judgment with regard to the treatment of Indians . . . ."[38] In later years General Thomas Gage,

---

32. *Journal of the Votes and Proceedings of the General Assembly of the Colony of New York [1691–1765]*, 2 vols. (New York, 1764–66), April 20, 1764, 2: 741, 742.

33. Johnson to the Board of Trade, May 17, 1759, in *NYCD*, 7: 377.

34. Johnson to Amherst, December 8, 1759, in *Johnson Papers*, 3: 183–84.

35. For the activities of Johnson's southern counterpart, see John R. Alden, *John Stuart and the Southern Colonial Frontier: A Study of Indian Relations, War, Trade, and Land Problems in the Southern Wilderness, 1754–1774* (Ann Arbor, Mich., 1944).

36. Pound, *Johnson of the Mohawks*, pp. 225, 272–78; Johnson to John Stanwix, July 25, 1759, in *Johnson Papers*, p. 112.

37. Board of Trade to Johnson, August 5, 1763, in *NYCD*, 7: 535–36.

38. Amherst to Johnson, September 30, 1763, ibid., p. 568.

who succeeded Amherst as commander-in-chief of British forces in North America, displayed a similar deference to Johnson.[39] As a result of this almost universal recognition of his ability, the Indian Superintendent exerted considerable influence over trade regulations for almost a decade after the fall of Montreal in 1760. As might be expected, his political ally, Lieutenant Governor Cadwallader Colden, who served as New York's chief executive in many of these years, gave Johnson his cooperation. Surprisingly, Johnson also received support from the New York fur traders, who were locked in an economic struggle with their competitors in Montreal. Even with this support, however, forces beyond his control eventually succeeded in preventing an adequate regulation of the trade.[40]

In the summer and fall of 1761 Johnson made a trip to Niagara partly for the purpose of conferring with the commandants of the forts and establishing regulations for the trade. With the approval of General Amherst, he restricted commerce to the posts, established uniform prices for trading goods, and required the licensing of all traders. At first he simply attempted to limit the sale of rum, but in early 1762 he accepted advice from Amherst and completely prohibited the use of liquor in the Indian trade.[41]

On his own volition, Captain Donald Campbell, the commander at Detroit, had already outlawed the sale of rum; and before the trading season began in 1762, Major William Walters at Niagara locked up the entire liquor supply. In a petition to Johnson the New York traders at Niagara complained that they sold rum only in proportion to their other merchandise and that the Indians would not bother to collect many furs if they could not quench their thirsts. To no avail, they asked for permission to sell rum in small lots under the supervision of the commandant. This petition to Johnson was apparently the only protest against the prohibition of rum, and even these petitioners did not seem greatly upset. Rum, as the major weapon in economic competition with Canada,

39. Johnson to Thomas Gage, November 20, December 12, 1766, January 8, 1768; Gage to Johnson, December 1, December 29, 1766, January 16, 1768, in *Johnson Papers*, 12: 219, 227, 406, 225, 238, 414.

40. Although Johnson's knowledge of Indian affairs and his diplomatic abilities were unsurpassed, his motives and objectives were not always above criticism. See Sosin, *Whitehall and the Wilderness*, pp. 145–46, 173–80; and Albert T. Volwiler, *George Croghan and the Westward Movement, 1741–1782* (Cleveland, 1926), pp. 244–50.

41. Indian Conference, August 9, 1761; Amherst to Johnson, December 30, 1761; Johnson to Amherst, January 7, 1762, in *Johnson Papers*, 3: 463, 597–98, 601. For specific reference to trade regulations, see Stevens, *Northwest Fur Trade*, pp. 21–41; and Reid, "The Quebec Fur-Traders," pp. 18–27.

had not yet taken on the significance that it would within a few years.[42]

In the year following the rum prohibition, any plans for protests among the traders were quickly forgotten in their mad scramble to avoid the scalping knives wielded by warriors of the various tribes who joined in the Indian uprising led by Pontiac. Some of Pontiac's most ardent fighters were those Senecas who lived at Chenussio (or Geneseo), the closest Iroquois village to Niagara. Like the Shawnees, the Delawares, and other Indians who joined in the general uprising, the Chenussio Senecas had always distrusted the British and now feared that the defeat of the French would mean further encroachments on their lands. In addition, these Senecas had monopolized the transportation of goods over the Niagara portage during the French regime, and they now found themselves being shoved aside by British traders and other adventurers. As early as 1761 they began looking for allies among other tribes to join them in a war against the colonies. After the uprising began in 1763, Seneca warriors captured Fort Venango at the junction of French Creek and the Allegheny River. Before killing the commander of the garrison, Lieutenant Francis Gordon, they forced him to write down their two main grievances against the British: a resentment over mistreatment by the traders and a suspicion of a conspiracy to seize their lands.[43]

By the fall of 1763 British troops reversed the early successes of Pontiac's followers and put them on the defensive. Before arranging peace conferences, Amherst wanted to break the power of the enemy Indians, especially the Senecas. Johnson, however, opposed continuing the war any longer than necessary. Knowing that the Indians desired peace, he also realized that they still possessed the strength to inflict substantial damage. Furthermore, Johnson feared that many tribes would retreat west of the Mississippi, where they would assist French traders in their efforts to channel the western fur trade to New Orleans. As for the Senecas, he knew that vindictiveness toward them would weaken his influence among the rest of the Six Nations. Fortunately for the peacemakers on both sides, Amherst returned to England in November, and General Thomas Gage became commander-in-chief. Early in 1764 Johnson arranged a peace conference with the Senecas. Arguing that the war had been instigated by Shawnee and Delaware warriors, the Senecas

42. Donald Campbell to Johnson, July 8, 1761; William Walters to Johnson, April 27, 1762; Petition of Niagara traders to Johnson [April 27?], 1762, in *Johnson Papers*, 3: 550, 721–22, 720.

43. Johnson, Journal of a trip to Detroit, July 24, October 18, 1761; Johnson to Daniel Claus, November 14, 1761, ibid., 13: 227, 270, 3: 565; Johnson to Amherst, July 11, 1763, in *NYCD*, 7: 532; Howard H. Peckham, *Pontiac and the Indian Uprising* (Princeton, 1947), pp. 57–75, 167–68.

agreed to Johnson's mild demands and promised to force the other tribes to the conference table. Their only serious loss from the war was the surrender of their right to control the Niagara portage.[44]

Throughout the rest of 1764 Johnson continued to work for peace. By fall the fur trade had been entirely disrupted for two trading seasons, and even those tribes who had remained peaceful desperately needed European goods. At one conference, Johnson told the sachems, "You are not ignorant that we can reduce you to Beggary without fighting, by only Debarring you of Trade . . . ."[45] He seldom lost the opportunity to spread the word among the Indians that restoration of political stability would bring about the return of traders. Peaceful tribes, as well as Gage's troops, exerted increasing pressure on the warriors, and before the end of 1764 hostilities came to a close, although Pontiac remained defiant.[46]

The ferocity and early successes of the Indians demonstrated to British politicians that they could not delay in promulgating the trade regulations mentioned in the Proclamation of 1763. Although this famous document attempted to protect the Indians from land speculators, it only established the barest outline of commercial regulations.[47] Spurred by news of the Indian war, British officials during the first six months of 1764 worked to devise an imperial system for administering Indian affairs. During most of these months, George Croghan, Johnson's deputy, was in London, and on several occasions, he had the opportunity to offer suggestions to the policy-makers. In July the Board of Trade completed a "Plan for the Future Management of Indian Affairs," but the ministry did not present it to Parliament, because funds were not available to put the expensive project into operation. Instead, the Board of Trade sent copies to the Indian superintendents and other colonial officials to get their opinions on how to improve the plan and how to finance it.[48]

44. Amherst to Johnson, September 30, 1763; Johnson to the Board of Trade, January 20, August 30, 1764, in NYCD, 7: 568, 599–600, 649; Johnson to Amherst, October 13, 1763, in Johnson Papers, 10: 878–79; Sosin, Whitehall and the Wilderness, pp. 69–70.

45. Indian Conference, July 24, 1764, in Johnson Papers, 11: 293.

46. Johnson to Cadwallader Colden, June 9, August 23, 1764; Indian Conferences, July 9–14, 1764, ibid., 4: 443, 511–12, 464, 474, 480.

47. A Proclamation, October 7, 1763, ibid., 10: 983–84.

48. Alvord, Mississippi Valley in British Politics, pp. 211–28; Sosin, Whitehall and the Wilderness, pp. 73–78; Volwiler, George Croghan, pp. 169–72. For Johnson's detailed comments on the plan, see "Sentiments, Remarks, and additions . . ." [October 8, 1764], in NYCD, 7: 661–69. The opinion of John Stuart, the southern superintendent, can be found in "Observations of John Stuart and Governor James Grant on the Proposed Plan of 1764 for the Future Management of Indian Affairs,"

The forty-three articles of the plan established an Indian department with a northern and southern district to be controlled by superintendents, who would be assisted by deputies, commissaries, interpreters, missionaries, and blacksmiths. Every trader had to take out a license from a governor and post bond to guarantee his good behavior. In the south, traders could visit Indian villages. In the north, they could not venture away from approximately a dozen military posts, which would each have a commissary to enforce a variety of rules, designed to prevent "Frauds and Abuses." The sale of rum or other hard liquor was prohibited. This comprehensive plan covered nearly every aspect of the trade, but no one was able to devise a satisfactory scheme to finance the system. Consequently, the British ministry never presented the plan to Parliament.[49]

When the fur trade reopened in the spring of 1765, General Gage and the Indian superintendents, with approval from London, agreed to put the main principles of the plan into action and to finance it out of the military budget.[50] In the only major exception to the plan of 1764, they allowed the sale of rum. "It has been long my Opinion," wrote Gage, "That we must at length yield to the immoderate Thirst which the Indians have for Rum, and let them have it . . . ."[51] Johnson agreed, noting that "the Indians value it above any thing else."[52] In another departure from the original plan, Gage and Johnson reduced the number of trading posts from about twelve to five: Niagara, Detroit, Oswego, Michilimackinac, and Fort de Chartres on the Mississippi River.[53] By the summer of 1766 the system was in operation, but strong opposition soon came from both the highest and lowest classes of fur traders.

In their efforts to prevent frauds against the tribesmen the Indian superintendents and their subordinates had to contend with a disreputable horde of "Lawless Banditti," who lost no opportunity to violate the regulations.[54] One keen observer of the Indians noted, "their countries

ed. Clarence C. Carter, *American Historical Review* 20 (1915): 815–31. For the general reaction of the colonies to the efforts of Great Britain to deal with the Indians, see Peter Marshall, "Colonial Protest and Imperial Retrenchment: Indian Policy, 1764–1768," *Journal of American Studies* 5 (1971): 1–17.

49. "Plan for the Future Management of Indian Affairs," 1764, in *NYCD*, 7: 637–41; Alvord, *Mississippi Valley in British Politics*, pp. 224–25.

50. Sosin, *Whitehall and the Wilderness*, p. 77; Stevens, *Northwest Fur Trade*, pp. 24, 26–27.

51. Thomas Gage to Johnson, May 28, 1764, in *Johnson Papers*, 4: 432.

52. Johnson, "Sentiments, Remarks, and additions . . ." [October 8, 1764], in *NYCD*, 7: 665.

53. Stevens, *Northwest Fur Trade*, p. 26.

54. Thomas Gage to Johnson, May 5, 1766, in *Johnson Papers*, 5: 210.

swarm with white people, who are generally the dregs and off-scourings of our colonies . . . . the greater part of them could notably distinguish themselves, among the most profligate by land or sea . . . ."[55] In earlier years the Albany traders had annoyed the Indians with their sharp business practices, but this new breed of rootless wanderers bore little resemblance to the old-time traders, who had at least treated the Indians well enough to keep them coming back year after year to Oswego instead of going to the French. Even Johnson, who had so often maligned the Dutch, admitted that he was now dealing with a new type of trader. In complaining of these "very dregs of the people, such as discharged provincial Soldiers, Batteaumen ettc," Johnson noted that the change in the personnel of the fur trade had begun in the late 1740s, when many of the Dutch had not bothered to re-enter the trade after King George's War. From 1760 onwards, murders and assaults against the Indians were far more common than previously. The mood between colonists and Indians on the northern frontier had changed from one of economic disgruntlement to a more dangerous one of fear and hatred.[56]

As superintendent of the northern district, Johnson also had to contend with the merchants of Canada, who strongly opposed the confinement of trade to military posts. This restrictive policy prevented them from expanding to the north and west of Michilimackinac. In the strongest of several arguments against the restrictions, the Canadians pointed out that French traders from St. Louis were operating at will throughout the back country and were shipping peltry to New Orleans. Since Johnson frequently complained of this illicit competition from French traders, he had to agree that the Canadians had a point, but he refused to change his policy. As soon as the trade revived in 1765 after the Indian uprising, the merchants of Canada began a campaign to end the restrictions on freedom of travel for the traders. Without much difficulty, they won the support of Governor James Murray of Quebec, and in April they hired Fowler Walker, a London attorney, to lobby for them at a salary of £200 per year. When Sir Guy Carleton succeeded Murray, he became an even stronger supporter of the Canadian entrepreneurs. Like the merchants, Carleton knew that many interior tribes either were unfamiliar with canoe travel or had become accustomed to French

55. James Adair, *Adair's History of the American Indian* [1775], ed. Samuel Cole Williams (Johnson City, Tenn., 1930), p. 445.

56. Johnson to the Board of Trade, June 28, 1766; Johnson, "a Review of the progressive State of the Trade . . ." [September 22, 1767], in *NYCD*, 7: 837, 959–61, 963–65; Henry Van Schaick et al. to Johnson, November 26, 1767; Johnson to Thomas Gage, May 27, 1772, in *Johnson Papers*, 5: 826–30, 8: 495–97.

voyageurs and would not journey great distances to British forts. After receiving numerous reports on the subject from Carleton, the opinion of the British ministry began to swing in favor of the Canadians. Under pressure, Johnson agreed in 1766 to allow an unrestricted trade north of the Great Lakes. A year later, in an effort to hinder the French traders from St. Louis and to appease his critics, Johnson recommended the extension of the trade to several additional forts around the Lakes and in the Ohio Valley.[57]

In his struggle to keep traders restricted to the forts, Johnson received strong support from New Yorkers, who knew that they could be assured of profits from the trade only as long as Detroit remained a principal commercial center. On the other hand, if the Canadians expanded to the northwest, where the sale of rum would be less profitable due to transportation expenses, New York's role in the trade might decline. Consequently, New Yorkers vigorously supported Johnson's restrictive policies, and as early as March 1764 about seventy residents of Albany County sent a petition to the Board of Trade, requesting the approval of the policies suggested by the Indian Superintendent.[58]

New Yorkers generally remained unified in support of Johnson's policies until 1768, when the British government returned control of the fur trade to the individual colonies and eliminated the use of commissaries at the posts.[59] New York traders then divided over the best procedure to follow in competing with the Canadians, who could now roam wherever they pleased. In this competition for peltry, New York still had the advantage of being able to sell rum at rates considerably below those of the Canadians. The dispute between New Yorkers arose over how this advantage should be exploited. Following a policy that they had maintained consistently for a century and a half, the Albany Dutch wanted to keep the trade as close to home as possible. Thus, they advocated a New York law to prohibit the shipment of rum to any post except

57. Innis, *Fur Trade in Canada*, pp. 169–76; Reid, "The Quebec Fur-Traders," pp. 22–26; Stevens, *Northwest Fur Trade*, pp. 28–31; Johnson to the Earl of Shelburne, December 16, 1766; Johnson, "a Review of the progressive State of the Trade . . ." [September 22, 1767], in *NYCD*, 7: 882, 965, 973–75.

58. Petition of Albany merchants to the Board of Trade, March —, 1764, in *NYCD*, 7: 613–14.

59. The British claimed that they could no longer afford to finance the regulation of the trade, because the colonies refused to pay their share of the expenses. After 1768 the purpose of the Indian department was to protect the Indians from land frauds and to conduct negotiations with them. Board of Trade to George III, March 7, 1768, in *NYCD*, 8: 19–25; Thomas Gage to Johnson, August 7, 1768, in *Johnson Papers*, 6: 313.

Niagara, where western Indians would be attracted by the inexpensive liquor.[60] With Johnson's support, the expansionist merchants, mostly Scots in Schenectady, strongly opposed the Albany merchants. Believing that they would now have to challenge the Canadians in locations closer to peltry sources than Niagara or even Detroit, these optimistic entrepreneurs wanted to allow the transportation of liquor to Michilimackinac.[61]

Over this issue, the New York expansionists once again displayed an ethnic bias against the Dutch. One of the detractors was Richard Cartwright, an Albany merchant, whose Loyalist son later became a well-known Canadian politician. In describing petitions sent by the two sides to the assembly, Cartwright told Johnson that the Dutch plan was "calculated to take the trade Quite out of the hands of all Uropeans," but the "Senseable well wrote petition . . . Signed only by Uropean traders" was "just reverce of the Other."[62] Cartwright did not need to worry greatly about the outcome of this dispute in the assembly. If they were interested at all, most legislators favored competition with Canada, and they did nothing to prevent the transportation of rum to distant trading centers.[63]

Although Great Britain had given control of the fur trade to the colonies, the individual provinces displayed little desire to establish an intercolonial system. Despite appeals from General Gage and the Earl of Hillsborough, Secretary of State for Colonial Affairs, the colonies did almost nothing at all for more than a year. Wilderness commerce became chaotic, and the Indians grew dangerously dissatisfied. Finally,

60. "Petition of the Principal Merchants, Traders and others concerned in or affected by the Indian trade" (microfilm of copy), 1769, in Philip Schuyler Indian Papers, 1710–1796, New York Public Library, New York City. This copy does not include the signatures.

61. A petition to Philip Schuyler, Jacobus Mynderse, Abraham Ten Broeck, and Robert R. Livingston (copy), [1769], ibid. This copy of the petition did not list the signers, but they displayed their political sympathies by declaring, "This good work of Securing the Indians to our Interest has In a great measure been happily Effected by the unwearied labours and Influence of Sir William Johnson Baronet And we are happy to Embrace this Occasion of giving him our public thanks . . . ." The assembly received this petition, as well as the one from the Dutch merchants, on January 3, 1770. Neither the exact content nor the names of the petitioners were recorded. *Journal of the Votes and Proceedings of the General Assembly of the Colony of New York* (New York, 1766–76), January 3, 1770.

62. Richard Cartwright to Johnson, December 15, 1769, in *Johnson Papers*, 7: 301.

63. Cadwallader Colden to Johnson, January 28, 1770; Johnson to Thomas Penn, January 30, 1770; Daniel Campbell to Johnson, April 18, 1770, ibid., pp. 357, 363, 569.

in January 1770 the New York assembly took the initiative and appointed commissioners, who had authorization to sponsor a conference with representatives from other colonies. Only Virginia, Pennsylvania, and Quebec appointed commissioners to participate in the meeting, which was set for July. The Virginia delegates, Patrick Henry and Richard Bland, arrived on time; but due to a breakdown in communications, the Pennsylvanians failed to appear, and the Canadians backed out at the last moment. Further attempts to develop a unified system of trade regulations also failed due, in part, to a British policy of discouraging intercolonial conferences in this age of political turmoil. In addition, the Canadians, who were now free to develop the trade of the northwest, continued to display a reluctance to cooperate with the other colonies on matters related to the fur trade.[64]

Shortly after learning that they had lost the advantage of a trade restricted to the wilderness forts, the New York fur merchants ran afoul of the nonimportation agreement signed by businessmen in New York City on August 27, 1768. As they had done in the Stamp Act crisis, Albany merchants supported nonimportation, but the importers of Indian goods now complained that they would lose their customers to the Canadians, who were not participating in the protest against the Townshend Acts.[65] Daniel Campbell explained to the Sons of Liberty "that the Merchants in Canada will take the Advantage of us and import double the Quantity by which our Traders . . . will be Oblidg'd to go there to buy their Goods and we shall Lose the whole of the Indian trade which . . . is of no small Advantage to this province . . . ."[66] For the fur traders, the worst aspect of the agreement was the prohibition of the West Indies trade. Although the Sons of Liberty refused to make an exception for the fur trade, they did agree to allow commerce with the West Indies until the first day of November.[67]

Enough merchandise was on hand when nonimportation began so

64. Sosin, *Whitehall and the Wilderness*, pp. 211–17; Stevens, *Northwest Fur Trade*, pp. 26–32; Colden to Hillsborough, April 25, 1770; Colden to Richard Bland and Patrick Henry, July 11, 1770, in *The Colden Letter Books, 1760–1775*, 2 vols. New-York Historical Society *Collections*, vols. 9–10 (1876–77) (New York, 1877–78), 2: 218, 225; Thomas Gage to Johnson, April 3, 1769; Johnson to the Earl of Dunmore, March 16, 1771, in *Johnson Papers*, 12: 709, 8: 29; Hillsborough to Johnson, December 4, 1771, in *NYCD*, 8: 185, 287.

65. Arthur M. Schlesinger, *The Colonial Merchants and the American Revolution* (New York, 1918; reprinted, New York, 1957).

66. Daniel Campbell to the Sons of Liberty, November 14, 1769, in *Johnson Papers*, 7: 251–52.

67. Carl L. Becker, *The History of Political Parties in the Province of New York, 1760–1776* (Madison, Wis., 1909), p. 63.

that New Yorkers did not suffer greatly during the spring of 1769. By summer, however, the shortage of goods had become so acute that, according to Sir William Johnson, several fur merchants had "gone thro' all the stores and shops within 100 miles without being able to procure a dozen Blankets . . . ."[68] Merchants could see that they would not be able to supply their wilderness correspondents in the fall and in the following spring. "Its impossible," wrote Phyn and Ellice, "to conceive how scarce goods are at N: Y: not one article has been imported and no prospect before next spring."[69] Some importers simply threw up their hands in despair. John Wetherhead of New York City had developed such a large business that the traders of Niagara and Detroit owed him several thousand pounds, but he decided to suspend his operations in the interior for at least the 1770 season. On the other hand, a few merchants told their London factors to ship their goods to Quebec. Phyn and Ellice and Daniel Campbell ordered much larger quantities than usual. Campbell shipped part of his order directly from Montreal to Detroit and brought another part of it back to Schenectady. He told Johnson that, if Indian presents were needed, he could spare a thousand blankets, seventy pieces of woolen cloth, and many other items.[70]

Although there was some grumbling in New York over the importation of goods through Canada, no one made a serious effort to interrupt commerce over this route.[71] In a letter to their factor in Bristol Phyn and Ellice expressed a fear that other colonial merchants would not approve of this procedure even though the firm was helping New York's economy by preventing Canada from gaining control of the fur trade. "The Business we are engaged in," they pointed out, "can be carried on with equall if not superior advantages from Canada, should it be necessary to change our scene of action."[72] Such thoughts were put aside at least temporarily in the summer of 1770, when nonimportation came to an end. Business boomed as a result of a high demand from those Indians who had been deprived of English merchandise for a year. Despite the renewed prosperity, Alexander Ellice suggested that the firm move to Canada anyway, but his partners overruled him on the grounds

68. Johnson to Hillsborough, July 12, 1770, in *NYCD*, 8: 222.

69. Phyn and Ellice to John Porteous, August 23, 1769, in Phyn and Ellice Letter Book, 1: 202.

70. Phyn and Ellice to Pigou and Booth, May 19, 1770; Phyn and Ellice to Gregg, Cunningham and Company, May 19, July 16, 1770, ibid., 1: 303, 322; Campbell to Johnson, June 6, 1770, in *Johnson Papers*, 7: 1, 44-45, 714-15.

71. Henry Van Schaick to Johnson, August 16, 1770, in *Johnson Papers*, 12: 849.

72. Phyn and Ellice to Perry, Hays, and Sherbrook, May 14, 1770, in Phyn and Ellice Letter Book, 1: 291.

that the process would disrupt the structure of their existing system.[73]

If New York fur traders had not been discouraged enough by the difficulties of 1768 and 1770, they received another chance to display their fortitude when Parliament passed the Quebec Act. In order to establish stable government in the American wilderness, Great Britain changed the boundaries of Quebec so that the province now included all of the area between the Ohio and the Mississippi rivers. Although the fur trade was to remain open to all British subjects, anyone wanting to trade in the west now had to operate within the province of Quebec. Consequently, many people in England and America believed that the passage of the Quebec Act was the equivalent of turning the trade over to Canada. In addition to the Quebec Act, a revenue law of 1774 placed a high duty on all rum shipped into Quebec from the American colonies. Now that the boundaries of the former French province included Detroit, New Yorkers would be unable to make a profit from the sale of their most important commodity.[74]

Complaining about the new revenue law, Phyn and Ellice exclaimed, "this Cannada Law about Rum is so partial to the trading People of that Colony, as to take the Trade intirely from this, but it is so extremely unjust that we think a proper representation of our Situation would procure at least some Mitigation of it."[75] In the spring of 1775 Phyn and Ellice managed to get around the new revenue act by shipping their rum to Detroit before the law went into effect in May. Due to the rise in the price of rum in Quebec, the Canadian merchants also complained, and Parliament soon removed the new duty, which would have crippled the New York trade.[76]

With the removal of the harmful revenue act, New York traders might have survived the effects of extending Quebec's boundaries, but the First Continental Congress met in the fall of 1774 and decided to institute a policy of nonimportation to begin on December 1, 1774. Fur traders could not look forward to importing through Canada as they had done in 1770, because the Continental Congress had also called for

73. Johnson to Hillsborough, August 14, 1770, in *NYCD*, 8: 224–25; Phyn and Ellice to Alexander Ellice, August 28, 1772, in Phyn and Ellice Letter Book, 2: 189–90.

74. Sosin, *Whitehall and the Wilderness*, pp. 240–48; Alvord, *Mississippi Valley in British Politics*, 2: 241–44; Fleming, "Phyn, Ellice and Company," pp. 31–32.

75. Phyn and Ellice to James Phyn, January 5, 1775, in Phyn and Ellice Letter Book, 3: 174.

76. Phyn and Ellice to Isaac Todd, January 20, 1775; Phyn and Ellice to James Sterling, April 17, 1775, ibid., pp. 179–80, 193; Fleming, "Phyn, Ellice and Company," p. 32.

nonexportation to begin in September 1775.[77] Most New Yorkers, therefore, did not bother early in 1775 to order their London factors to ship their Indian goods to Quebec. Simon McTavish and Phyn and Ellice were apparently the only exceptions. Always ready to take advantage of indecisiveness on the part of their competitors, Phyn and Ellice seriously considered ordering twice the usual quantity of goods, but they were fortunate that they did not do so.[78]

Even before the agents of the Schenectady firms unloaded their merchandise at Quebec, the mood of the Sons of Liberty turned grim as news of the fighting at Lexington and Concord reached New York. The Albany Committee of Correspondence made it clear that commerce with Canada would not be allowed. By summer the firm of Phyn and Ellice had broken up, and other merchants were terminating the business associations that they had developed along the route to Detroit.[79]

With British troops occupying Oswego, Niagara, and Detroit, the colonial fur trade of New York came to an end. Anyone—colonist or Indian—wanting to remain involved in this commerce had to turn toward Canada. After a reorganization, the firm of Phyn and Ellice opened in Montreal, and many other New York traders transferred their operations to the north. During most of 1775 the Iroquois did their best to appear neutral, although they generally favored Great Britain because of their dislike of colonial land speculators and their loyalty to Guy Johnson, the son of the deceased baronet. The Continental Congress attempted to win the allegiance of the Iroquois by promising them inexpensive trading goods, but the Americans could not obtain enough merchandise. As the Indians had often said, commerce was the only link between them and Europeans. Knowing that fur traders were preferable to land-hungry colonists, most of the Iroquois abandoned their traditional neutrality policy and went to war against New York.[80]

77. Schlesinger, *Colonial Merchants and the American Revolution*, pp. 425–27.

78. Phyn and Ellice to James Phyn, January 25, 1775, in Phyn and Ellice Letter Book, 3: 182.

79. James Ellice to Hayman Levy, August 22, 1775, ibid., p. 216; Fleming, "Phyn, Ellice and Company," pp. 33–34; Innis, *Fur Trade in Canada*, p. 180.

80. Indian Conference with Guy Johnson, February 13, 1775; Indian Conferences with colonial commissioners, August 15–September 2, 1775, in *NYCD*, 8: 552–53, 605–27. For the effects of the American Revolution on the fur trade, see Stevens, *Northwest Fur Trade*, pp. 42–67. On the role of the Iroquois in the Revolution, see Barbara Graymont, *The Iroquois in the American Revolution* (Syracuse, N.Y., 1972); and William L. Stone, *Life of Joseph Brant—Thayendanegea*, 2 vols. (New York, 1838; reprinted, New York, 1970).

12

CONCLUSION

WITH THE END of the colony's fur trade, the old connections between New York and the Iroquois Confederacy rapidly disintegrated. In the first seventy-five years of colonization, both Indians and colonists had been interested in fur trading for mainly economic reasons, but in the eighteenth century New Yorkers had increasingly emphasized the trade's political and diplomatic significance. By the 1720s the fur trade had developed into a tool of imperial policy and had become a divisive political issue within the colony, even while declining in economic importance.

The volume of furs acquired by New Yorkers during the century remained fairly consistent, but the economy of the province was constantly expanding, with the result that the peltry business became proportionately less important as each year passed. In the early part of the century, New York City merchants were keenly interested in the trade. By 1730, however, they had turned to other business pursuits, and by 1740 most large merchants in Albany had also relinquished their interests in the wilderness commerce and had turned to exporting the products of the Hudson and Mohawk valleys to the West Indies. Thus, to a great extent, the peltry business fell into the hands of the small traders. After the French and Indian War, large firms once again played an important role in the fur trade, but now this commerce amounted to only a small part of the colony's overall economy.

Though constantly diminishing as an economic factor, the trade remained at the middle of the century nearly as important a political issue as it had ever been. This was due to increasing fear of a cataclysmic conflict with France and to the accusation made by New York imperialists that the Albany Dutch were disloyal to the British cause against the French. The disloyalty of the Dutch, according to the imperialists, was a result of their desire to protect the commerce between Albany and Montreal. New Englanders originated this accusation against New York during Queen Anne's War in the first decade of the

century, when the former Dutch colony managed to achieve an un-
written neutrality agreement with Canada. Later, the New York imperialists attempted to blame Albany for following this policy during
the war, even though almost everyone in the colony had supported
neutrality.

Despite the allegations of disloyalty, the Albany Dutch ranked among
the most vehement colonial critics of French expansion. Nevertheless,
for many years after Burnet's administration, the imperialists and the
Albany leaders frequently clashed over the best methods for meeting
the dangers presented by French Canada. The imperialists favored
aggressive economic and military policies, while the Dutch advocated
building a strong defensive network. Both sides found it nearly impossible to win any support among the assemblymen from Long Island
and the middle counties, who were not so concerned with frontier
affairs.

The most crucial issue involving the fur trade was the maintenance
of friendly relations with the Iroquois. In the decades after Queen
Anne's War, the French labored long and hard to win this powerful
confederacy away from the English; they achieved little success, however, because of economic factors and their previous years of warfare
with the Iroquois. Canada's most serious handicap was the inability of
French traders to sell goods, especially woolens and liquor, at low
enough prices to compete with New Yorkers, who had an abundance of
inexpensive English merchandise.

Due to its early position as a trading outpost, Albany became the
center for diplomatic negotiations between the Iroquois and the British
colonies. At first, Albany officials played only a small role in interna-
tional politics, but after the outbreak of the first intercolonial war with
France in 1689, the significance of Albany diplomacy greatly increased.
For the next sixty years, the Albany Dutch maintained the friendship
of the Iroquois for New York and the British, even though they received
little support from the rest of the colony.

Because the complicated development of New York colonial politics
has only begun to be clarified in the last few years, it has been easy for
historians to overlook the political connections among those politicians
who denounced the people of Albany. Consequently, historians have
been misled by the polemics left to posterity by such men as Cadwallader
Colden, Archibald Kennedy, and Peter Wraxall, and the role of the fur
trade in the conflict between Great Britain and France has been badly
misunderstood. For the most part, the British were fortunate to have
had the Dutch in Albany. If farmers and expansionists had originally
settled on the New York frontier, they would have almost assuredly

driven the Iroquois into the hands of the French, but the Dutch traders had little desire to seize Indian lands. Thus, the success of the New York colonial fur trade proved to be a valuable asset in Great Britain's efforts to gain control of North America.

BIBLIOGRAPHICAL
NOTE

INDEX

BIBLIOGRAPHICAL NOTE

READERS INTERESTED in the sources available for the study of the New York fur trade should consult the footnotes to this book and the bibliographical sections of Allen W. Trelease's *Indian Affairs in Colonial New York: The Seventeenth Century* (Ithaca, N.Y., 1960), and Stanley Nider Katz's *Newcastle's New York: Anglo-American Politics, 1732–1753* (Cambridge, Mass., 1968). In addition, a few of my own comments may be helpful.

Historians of the New York frontier are fortunate to have access to a number of valuable manuscript collections. The most important of these sources is the Minutes of the Commissioners of Indian Affairs, which can be obtained on microfilm from the Public Archives of Canada in Ottawa. The earlier years of these minutes were lost, but for the period from 1723 to about 1750 we are able to examine detailed records of Indian affairs as they were conducted by the Indian Commissioners at Albany. Some of the missing documents are summarized in Peter Wraxall's *An Abridgment of the Indian Affairs Contained in Four Folio Volumes, Transacted in the Colony of New York, from the Year 1678 to the Year 1751*, ed. Charles H. McIlwain (Cambridge, Mass., 1915). In addition to the minutes of the Indian Commissioners, other manuscript records are the New York Colonial Manuscripts and the New York Executive Council Minutes, both in the New York State Library, Albany. Fortunately calendars of these collections were prepared before they were damaged by fire; see the *Calendar of Historical Manuscripts in the Office of the Secretary of State*, ed. Edmund B. O'Callaghan, 2 vols. (Albany, 1865–66), and the *Calendar of Council Minutes, 1668–1783*, New York State Library Bulletin 58 (Albany, 1902).

Any letter written by Philip Livingston is likely to contain political commentary, and much of his correspondence can be found in three collections. In the Livingston Family Papers at the Franklin D. Roosevelt Library in Hyde Park, New York, there are several important letters written by Philip to his father in the 1720s, and this collection contains many other documents of importance to the study of colonial New York. At the Museum of the City of New York scholars can find some interesting political comments in Philip's letters to Jacob Wendell of Boston. For Livingston's participation in the fur trade, the most important documents are located in the Miscellaneous Manuscripts, volume 5, of the New York State Library.

The most extensive information about the business aspects of the New York fur trade is to be found in the Cornelius Cuyler Letter Books, 1724–1736, 1752–1764, located at the American Antiquarian Society, Worcester, Mass. Unfortunately, Cuyler usually confined his letters to business matters and had little to say about politics. Other important collections of correspondence dealing with the everyday affairs of the fur traders are the Johannes R. Bleecker Papers and the Hendrick Ten Eyck Papers (in the Harmanus Bleecker Papers) at the New York State Library; the Robert Sanders Letter Book, 1752–1758, located at the New-York Historical Society in New York City; and the Phyn and Ellice Letter Books in the possession of the Buffalo and Erie County Historical Society, Buffalo, New York.

Another source of information about the fur trade is the large number of account books and other financial records that are still in existence. From them we can learn a great deal about routine business operations, and by a careful examination we can also occasionally discover the various business associations that provide us with insight into political motivations. A good example of this type of source is the Account Book, 1732–1742, of Henry Van Rensselaer, Jr., in the New-York Historical Society. It gives us a fairly good idea of the business relationship that existed between Van Rensselaer and Philip Livingston.

Among the several significant printed sources, the most important is the *Documents Relative to the Colonial History of the State of New York*, ed. Edmund B. O'Callaghan and Berthold Fernow, 15 vols. (Albany, 1856–87). Mainly a collection of official correspondence, these massive volumes contain a wealth of information for the study of New York and for several of the other colonies as well. An entire volume is devoted to an index, but much of the material, especially the records of Indian conferences, must be gone over paragraph by paragraph. For another large collection, covering primarily the middle years of the eighteenth century, one should consult *The Papers of Sir William Johnson*, ed. James Sullivan et al., 14 vols. (Albany, 1921–65). The bulk of Cadwallader Colden's writings are found in various volumes of the *Collections* of the New-York Historical Society, but his voluminous correspondence does not contain much material about the fur trade. Even his famous *The History of the Five Indian Nations of Canada, Which are Dependent on the Province of New York in America, And Are a Barrier Between the English and French in That Part of the World*, 2 vols. (London, 1750) fails to provide much information that is not available in the minutes of the Indian Commissioners. An excellent contemporary account of New York politics is *The History of the Late Province of New-York from Its Discovery to the Appointment of Governor Colden in 1762*, 2 vols. (New York, 1829–30), by William Smith, Jr.

In addition to these general sources, there are several printed collections of a more specific nature. The *Annals of Albany*, ed. Joel Munsell, 10 vols. (Albany, 1850–59) has some editorial shortcomings, but these volumes contain many documents that were later lost or destroyed by fire. *The Livingston Indian Records*, ed. Lawrence H. Leder (Gettysburg, Pa., 1956) is particularly valuable when used in conjunction with Wraxall's *An Abridgment*, which has already been mentioned. Among the several sources for the study of the French role in New York's fur trade, one should not overlook *Royal Fort Frontenac*, ed. A. Richard Preston and Leopold Lamontagne (Toronto, 1958). *The Jesuit Relations and Allied Documents: Travels and Explorations of the Jesuit Missionaries in New France, 1619–1791*, ed. Reuben G. Thwaites, 73 vols. (Cleveland, 1896–1901) is not really of great value for a history dealing with the New York frontier, but a rather obscure source contains several significant documents; see the "Cadillac Papers," Michigan Historical Society *Collections*, vol. 33 (1904).

In the above sources, the reader should be able to find a significant amount of information previously hidden from view. To a great extent, however, any examination of the history of New York's colonial fur trade must be a synthesis of studies made by other scholars, because it would be impossible to master all the primary sources relating to such diverse topics as colonial economics, New York politics, and the Iroquois Confederacy. Fortunately in recent years historians have produced a number of excellent studies dealing with the major problems of New York's role in the colonial history of North America.

The most important achievement has been the unraveling of the mysteries involving New York's complex political history. For the late seventeenth and early eighteenth centuries, interested students should read Lawrence H. Leder's *Robert Livingston, 1654–1728, and the Politics of Colonial New York* (Chapel Hill, 1961), which is an outstanding example of meticulous scholarship. Patricia W. Bonomi's *A Factious People: Politics and Society in Colonial New York* (New York, 1971) is of a more general nature and is also of considerable value, as is Katz's *Newcastle's New York*. Beverley McAnear's "Politics in Provincial New York, 1689–1761" (Ph.D. diss., Stanford University, 1935) provides great detail, but the author often jumps to conclusions that are not warranted by the evidence. A concise summary of political activities is available in Milton M. Klein's "Democracy and Politics in Colonial New York," *New York History* 6 (1959): 221–46.

The footnotes in this book will provide the reader with an idea of the available literature on colonial economics, but a few items should be given special attention. Virginia Harrington's *The New York Merchant on the Eve of the Revolution* (New York, 1935) is the most important study for New York historians. Other works of particular value are Lawrence A. Harper's "The Effect of the Navigation Acts on the Thirteen Colonies," in *The Era of the American Revolution*, ed. Richard B. Morris (New York, 1965), and Murray G. Lawson's *Fur: A Study in English Mercantilism, 1700–1775* (Toronto, 1943). In addition, scholars should not overlook E. E. Rich's excellent "Russia and the Colonial Fur Trade," *Economic History Review* 7 (1955): 307–28, and William I. Roberts, III's, "Samuel Storke: An Eighteenth-Century London Merchant Trading to the American Colonies," *Business History Review* 39 (1965): 147–70.

Among those historians particularly interested in the New York fur trade, the most vehement dispute involves the role of the Albany Dutch. Until recently, historians generally accepted Cadwallader Colden's contention that the Albany merchants selfishly obstructed British imperial interests in order to protect their own interests in the fur trade. The severest damage to the historical reputation of the Albany Dutch resulted from a study done in 1915 by the highly respected scholar Charles H. McIlwain. In his introduction to Wraxall's *An Abridgment*, McIlwain vigorously took the side of Governor Burnet, who had attempted to make drastic changes in the trade patterns of northern New York. McIlwain insisted that the opposition of the Albany Dutch to Burnet's plans was an indication of their venality. Proceeding from the assumption that most fur traders were the "very scum of the earth," McIlwain found it easy to overlook the contributions of the Albany residents. He pointed out that the Iroquois frequently criticized the Commissioners of Indian Affairs, who were usually from Albany, but he failed to note that the great bulk of those complaints came in the late 1740s and early 1750s, when the allegiance of the main Iroquois spokesmen had been wrested away from the Albany officials by the ambitious William Johnson, an imperialist and a prominent fur trader. While stressing the crucial importance of the friendly relations between the British and the Five Nations, McIlwain overlooked the obvious presumption that the residents of Albany, because of their exposed position on the frontier, had the most to lose from a diplomatic break with the Iroquois and therefore would have done their best to maintain the friendship of these powerful neighbors.

McIlwain also inadvertently contributed to the condemnation of the Albany Dutch by publishing Peter Wraxall's abridgment of the four volumes containing the minutes of the Indian Commissioners. Wraxall, a close friend of William Johnson and Secretary of Indian Affairs from 1750 to 1759, was the most vitriolic critic of Albany. Supposedly as a public service, he condensed the collection of records kept by the Indian Commissioners into a single volume, which also included many footnotes containing his personal denunciations of the Dutch traders. Although it is difficult to say with certainty that Wraxall edited the records in a biased manner, the unabridged minutes give the historian a much fuller picture of the contributions made by the Albany officials than does the abridgment.

For decades after the publication of McIlwain's pioneer study of the New York trade, there were few serious challenges to his conclusions. The only professional historian who disagreed was Arthur H. Buffinton in his articles "The Policy of Albany and English Westward Expansion" *Mississippi Valley Historical Review* 8 (1922): 337–66, and "The Colonial Wars and Their Results," in *History of the State of New York*, ed. Alexander C. Flick, 10 vols. (New York, 1933–37). Although not directly seeking to refute McIlwain's contentions, Buffinton treated the Albany Dutch sympathetically in both of his studies. Judging them in the light of their own times, "when a sense of any community of interest had scarcely developed," Buffinton observed that the Albany fur traders "were not, perhaps, sinners above others." His strongest defense of Albany came in his account of the intercolonial wars, in which he pointed out that during King William's War the other colonies refused an order from the English government to send troops to the embattled New York frontier.

Recent historians have been inclined to agree with, and to expand upon, Buffinton's thesis. One of the best defenses of Albany is a dissertation, "The Merchants of Albany, New York, 1686–1760," written by David A. Armour (Northwestern University, 1965). Instead of concentrating on the fur trade and Indian relations, Armour examines all aspects of the Albany economy and discovers that the merchants were involved in a wide variety of interests. In his most significant conclusion, he demonstrates that Albany merchants by 1740 had either liquidated or greatly reduced their investments in the fur trade. Thus, in attempting to understand the policies of Albany in the middle decades of the century, historians cannot rest their interpretations on the importance of the fur trade as the only source of Albany's economic or political conduct. Surveying the problems of intercolonial defense in "New York's Role in Queen Anne's War, 1702–1713," *New York History* 33 (1952): 40–53, and in *Samuel Vetch, Colonial Enterpriser* (Chapel Hill, 1960), G. M. Waller strongly defends the Albany position as it related to New England. In her recent book, *A Factious People*, Patricia W. Bonomi notes that the accusations against the Albany Dutch were greatly exaggerated. She also seems to be the first historian to stress the force of ethnic hostility between the Dutch and French New Yorkers, on one side, and the English and Scottish on the other in creating political conflict and the unfavorable characterization of "the Albany spirit."

In any discussion of the New York frontier the role of the Iroquois Confederacy must be taken into consideration. For the development of Iroquois diplomacy as it related to the fur trade, three studies deserve particular attention. In his introduction to Wraxall's *An Abridgment*, McIlwain presented the theory that after exterminating all the beaver in their own territory the Five Nations maintained themselves economically by acting as middlemen between the western tribes and the traders in Albany. George T. Hunt's *The Wars of the Iroquois: A Study in Intertribal Trade Relations* (Madison, Wis., 1940) studies the problem in greater depth, emphasizing how economic considerations shaped Indian politics and diplomacy. Hunt modifies McIlwain's theory by concluding that the Iroquois acquired their furs through both trading and hunting. Rejecting the argument that they acted as middlemen, Allen W. Trelease in his article "The Iroquois and the Western Fur Trade: A Problem in Interpretation," *Mississippi Valley Historical Review* 49 (1962): 32–51, asserts that the Iroquois obtained their peltry by hunting and poaching on the lands of western or northern tribes. These historians have provided an understanding of how the Iroquois Confederacy originated economic and diplomatic policies in response to the competition between France and England, and my study of the fur trade should help to trace the further development of these policies during the eighteenth century. The culmination of the policies is fully explained in Barbara Graymont's *The Iroquois in the American Revolution* (Syracuse, N.Y., 1972).

INDEX

‹──────◄═╬═►──────›

TEXT DESIGNED BY IRVING PERKINS
JACKET DESIGNED BY KAREN FOGET
MANUFACTURED BY HERITAGE PRINTERS, INC.
CHARLOTTE, NORTH CAROLINA
TEXT LINES ARE SET IN CALEDONIA,
DISPLAY LINES IN CRAW MODERN AND CALEDONIA

Library of Congress Cataloging in Publication Data
Norton, Thomas Elliott, 1942–
The fur trade in colonial New York, 1686–1776.
Bibliographical note: p. 227–231.
1. Fur trade–New York (State)–History.
I.   Title.
HD9944.U46N45   380.1'45'675409747   73–2047
ISBN 0-299-06420-4